Exposition of

ZECHARIAH

By H. C. LEUPOLD, D. D.

Professor of Old Testament Exegesis
Capital University Seminary
Columbus, Ohio

BAKER BOOK HOUSE
Grand Rapids, Michigan

Reprinted 1971 by Baker Book House Company

ISBN: 0-8010-5512-1

TO THE REV. RUDOLPH W. GRABAU, D.D.

MY TEACHER AND FRIEND

Foreword

THE BOOK of the prophet Zechariah is not much studied nor adequately understood in our day. When it is used, the visions and the eschatological material are frequently given too much emphasis and attention so that somewhat fantastic results have been arrived at, which have caused men to wonder at the book rather than to seek to appropriate its wealth and comfort and instruction. A further reason that many by-pass the book is the fact that it presents an unusual number of difficulties. Besides, reliable helps in interpreting the book are not always readily accessible.

We should like to do a bit toward redeeming this rich book of prophecy from undeserved oblivion. It is not so difficult of interpretation as totally to baffle the student. Though the problems it offers are many, and we cannot presume to speak with authority on all of them, yet the book as a whole can be studied with great profit and to the strengthening of one's faith. The New Testament makes repeated use of the book. So should we.

I am particularly indebted to my son-in-law, the Rev. Russell C. Finkenbine, B.D., M.A., for painstaking care in the editorial work of preparing the manuscript for the press.

H. C. LEUPOLD

EXPOSITION OF ZECHARIAH

Introduction

I. Person of the Prophet

We have other records besides those found in our book concerning the prophetic activity of Zechariah. The book of Ezra, in 5:1 and 6:14, informs us that Zechariah was a contemporary of Haggai, and that he was working toward the same purpose as this prophet.

The first verse of the book informs us that Zechariah was "the son of Berechiah, the son of Iddo." Regarding this Berechiah, however, we have nothing beyond this notice. In fact, in Neh. 12:26 we are informed that in the days of Joiakim, who succeeded Joshua as high priest in the line of Iddo, Zechariah functioned as priest and head of a father's house. Now the term "son" is used interchangeably with "grandson," which is manifestly the case here. But why should the father be ignored in this record? It is commonly suggested that for some reason, not reported, the father never became prominent. As a result, Iddo's priestly line was carried on by Zechariah.

The familiarity of our prophet with priestly things is reflected in a number of references to the Temple, its rites and its equipment. See chapter 3; also 6:9–15; 9:8, 15; 14:16, 20, 21. In this respect he bears a resemblance to Ezechiel.

If now, according to Neh. 12:4, Iddo was among those who as priests went up with Zerubbabel to Jerusalem, and some sixteen years had passed from the time of this return until the time when Zechariah received his first prophetic message, viz., 536 to 520, all evidence would imply that Zechariah will have been comparatively young at the time he was called.

II. Historical Circumstances

The first word of the Lord came to Zechariah in "the second year of Darius." Since this king, also known as Darius Hystaspis, began to reign in 521 B.C., we get the year 520 for this first word.

The return from the Exile has become a reality. The unbelievable had happened: a people torn loose from its soil had not taken permanent root in the land of captivity but, when permission came by the decree of Cyrus, had returned to the land of their fathers, at least almost 43,000 of them had.

These had almost at once begun the erection of their Temple as Cyrus in his decree had permitted and ordered them to do. The difficulties of this undertaking were increased by the opposition offered by the Samaritans (Ezra 4ff) who, when they were refused a part in the building of the Temple, stirred up all manner of difficulties by rousing the suspicions of the Persian officials. As a result, the generous assistance that Cyrus had guaranteed was not forthcoming. Yet some progress had been made by the new colonists. They had succeeded in quite a number of instances in building for themselves rather substantial dwellings (Hag. 1:4). Still the work upon the Lord's house had come to a complete standstill.

Then it was that Haggai had appeared upon the scene as the first messenger from God to induce the people to resume building operations upon the Temple. To be exact, his first message was received in the year 520 B.C., in the sixth month, about two months before Zechariah's first "word." What Haggai demanded was promptly agreed to by the people, who displayed a very laudable zeal in completing the construction of the Temple. However, theirs was the fortunate lot of having two prophets to support them, for Zechariah ably seconded Haggai's effort without specifically commanding the people to build the Temple. How clearly it was recognized that these two prophets were cooperating appears from the passages Ezra 5:1 and 6:14 which represent the two prophets as joint supporters of the people in their difficult task.

III. The Prophet's Message

It might be well to regard the particular message of Zechariah as being supplementary to Haggai's. In Haggai's message the thoughts stand out that the Temple will be finished, and that God will make it glorious, also that Israel shall be made glorious; Israel's foes, however, shall be brought low. Such a message was rich in encouragement but would have been adequate only for a people who were zealously eager to obey the Lord's word. There were in Israel those who might be termed "Israelites indeed" as well as unworthy hypocrites, men who had cast their fortunes with God's people returning to Palestine largely because of carnal pride or advantage, men who had not sanctified the Lord God in their hearts. For each of these groups a word of God was necessary. Those who were sincere of heart needed more encouragement and direction than they had received. Those whose sincerity was defective needed special counsel and admonition and an earnest call to repentance.

All these elements are offered in rich measure in Zechariah's book. In fact, since, in the providence of God, prophecy would soon lapse into silence because Israel had received all that it needed under the circumstances, it appears that toward the close it pleased God to let a rich and mighty outburst of it ring out to indicate that prophecy was not dying a slow and gradual death due to a dearth of the Spirit's gifts. It seemed eminently proper to have prophecy die in a mighty blaze of glory, strong at its death as it had been at its birth. For prophecy, though it has a human background and is pronounced by human agents, is also entirely a work of God's Holy Spirit. Prophets did not speak by self-inspiration. The measure of their might was not conditioned by the spiritual level of their age. The mightiest of the prophets might well arise in any age or under any set of circumstances.

This is one of the facts that must be particularly borne in mind lest the richness of the material offered seems strange to us and induces us to claim, as for the most part the critics do, that not all that the book contains in its fourteen chapters can be the product of one pen.

Particularly prominent in the book is the Messianic element. With the exception of Isaiah, there is no other prophet whose book contains such a wealth and variety of this element, not only in proportion to the total amount of material offered, but also as a sum total of passages. New items in rich measure, presented in rich colors, appear at every juncture in the book. The emphasis of this feature, of course, rests entirely on the thought that for every situation developing in Israel's history there is nothing more necessary than faith in the Messiah of God. That faith is so many-sided and so entirely adequate to every situation that arises that, when new problems appear, all the nation needs is a fuller revelation of what the Messiah is and does, and it will discover at once that its help lies entirely in Him. With such deep insight did the prophets draw Israel to the Messiah in every time of crisis. The Savior of Israel was mighty to save in every emergency.

It is true, the message of Zechariah has a very generous admixture of visions and of that element which we term the "apocalyptic." The explanation for this phenomenon does not lie, as seems to be the opinion of some, in the unclearness of youth on the part of the young prophet (*Lange*), nor does it in any sense constitute a defect as so many seem to imply. A better explanation is that, since all other modes of teaching have been most generously employed, it pleases the wisdom of God to use this figurative mode of presenting truth to give man an added inducement to search the Scriptures. As Christ's parables are another and later form of instruction that reveals their truth to those who earnestly seek to arrive at their meaning but conceals it from others that seeing, they might not see, and hearing, they might not understand and be saved (Matt. 13:10–15), so we have a similar situation in the case of these visions of Zechariah.

It is true, the Jewish commentators have made some very strong statements on the obscurity of our prophet. Some Christian commentators have said equally harsh things. The attitude of the Jewish writers is quite readily explained. Since there is so much material concerning Christ in this book, and since several of the prophecies presented have met with such a striking fulfillment in the life of Christ, it is very difficult for these Jewish commentators to avoid drawing the patent conclusion that Christ is the Messiah. In an effort to rid themselves of the necessity of drawing this conclusion they must needs toil with all the ingenuity at their disposal to offer another interpretation; and this is the chief source of their difficulties. Nor can such efforts to avoid the evident truth leave the impression of being a satisfactory interpretation of a book.

In regard to present-day critics the situation is but little different. To be sure, on the part of many there is no attempt to avoid conclusions that point them to Christ, but they, too, approach the book with certain preconceived notions such as, for example, that a writer is of necessity bound to one type of prophecy, or again, that if several widely divergent types appear, they are indications of different authors. With such criterions of criticism which cannot be maintained even on purely naturalistic ground or in regard to any type of literature men place an insurmountable barrier in the way of arriving at a satisfactory understanding of a book.

We are not advancing the claim that it will be easy to solve the problems of this book. It is still one of the most difficult of the Old Testament books. But since God gives revelation in such a manner as actually to put it within the reach of the earnestly seeking soul that trusts in Him, we have every reason for believing that a faithful use of such revelation as the rest of the Old Testament offers will enable us to arrive at solutions that are clear and sufficiently well established to allow us to believe we have not missed the point of God's revelation though, indeed, we may be obliged to admit that certain minor problems have remained unsolved.

Two further items may be mentioned here. The first is the claim, set forth emphatically by *Horst* (p. 206), that there is unusual emphasis on the transcendence of God. He says: "Above all things else it is characteristic of Zechariah to stress the transcendence of God. No one has access to the invisible and hidden God beyond the world except the angel only who as mediator . . . must transmit to the world the acts of revelation coming from God. Just so on the other hand he has all prayers and happenings in the world laid upon him that he may bear them to the throne of God." This statement applies only to the first six chapters and grows out of the purely visionary character of the contents of these chapters. What *Horst* notes is not so much a characteristic of the prophet's thinking as it is a natural concomitant of visions that have an angelic interpreter. In chapters 7–14, which are, of course, not attributed to Zechariah by *Horst,* God is in direct contact with His prophet and communicates His word to him again and again. There is obviously less emphasis on the transcendence of God in such a situation.

We need not be unduly impressed by *McFadyen's* claim (*The Abingdon Bible Commentary,* p. 819) that "in their present form they [the visions] are the work of conscious art." This implies that, "though some real experience lies behind them," the literary form in which they are now cast reflects more of the prophet's literary skill than of precise historical record. We do not question that inspiration allows for the free use of the natural literary style of an author. But we feel that what artistic sequence or literary form may appear could very well have been inherent in the visions themselves. Why should not the God of beauty have clothed the visions which He granted the prophet to see in a native beauty, order, and elegance that called for no further elaboration on man's part?

IV. The Unity of the Book

It is quite obvious that the Book of Zechariah is composed of two parts. It is equally obvious that the subject matter treated in each of these parts is not one and the same. Part I offers a series of visions (1–6) that are followed by a question addressed to the prophet on the subject of fasting, which is followed by the prophet's answer (7 and 8). Part II consists, on the face of the evidence presented by the two headings, of two "burdens" (see 9:1 and 12:1). The subject matter of these two burdens may be summarized in the heading we shall use: "The Future Development of the Kingdoms of This World and of the Church."

In addition to this difference in subject matter there is a formal difference which cannot be denied, viz., that the materials of the first part are dated (see 1:1, 7 and 7:1); the material of the second part is not.

Furthermore, it must be conceded that there are differences in style between the two parts of the book. Other points of difference have been stressed by various writers. To these we shall allude as we proceed.

On the basis of the differences between the two parts of the book the majority of writers on the subject have arrived at the conclusion that these differences are so pronounced as to preclude the possibility of unity of authorship. Many think that at least dual authorship is to be accepted as one of the assured results of modern critical study of the Scriptures. In consequence of this position, depending on the dating that is given to the second part, not a few writers regard this part as a separate book that is not to be considered under the name of Zechariah.

It may be helpful in getting our bearings on this matter to examine the arguments offered by *Orelli,* one of the more moderate of the critics. He claims that one of the more common arguments against the unity of the book is the difference of literary form and style—briefly, visions vs. burdens. He admits that this argument cannot be decisive. We suggest: it is far from decisive. Otherwise one would have to set up such artificial canons of literary criticism as: If a writer once uses visions as the medium for conveying his message he must always use visions.

In this argument there would be involved another, which is the argument from vocabulary. For there is bound to be a difference in vocabulary in a portion that uses visions over against a portion that deals in portrayals of the future. Though this matter has been argued at great length, and some have shown that similar terms and expressions are used in both parts of the book, and others have pointed out differences of terms and vocabulary, it cannot be denied that neither type of argument has strong probative value. Subjective opinion usually enters into this form of argument so strongly as to make purely objective treatment extremely difficult.

Orelli's second argument deals with the difference of the subject matter found in the two parts of the book—already alluded to above: opinions vs. burdens. He admits that this argument is equally indecisive.

He then lists one of the arguments that he believes is decisive against the possibility of Zechariah's authorship of chapters 9–14, namely, that the historical situation found in these chapters is not that of Zerubbabel's time. This argument is based on the assumption that any historical or political allusions made by the writer must correspond with the historical or political situation which prevails at the time of writing. Generally speaking, this is true. But there are situations—and this is one of them—where the nature of the subject matter treated lifts the material in question above this requirement, especially where, as is the case here, the *future* development of things is treated. We hope to show that the references made to Greece (9:13); to Syrian and Philistine cities (9:1–7); to Syria (11:1); to Josiah (12:11); to Uzziah (14:5); to Assyria and Egypt (10:11) offer nothing that can be shown to be in conflict with authorship by Zechariah, all the more so since an *ideal* picture of the future Messianic age is being presented.

In fact, another aspect of the argument based on the historical situation should be considered. It cannot be denied that the historical situation to which a given passage refers must be carefully evaluated. But the assumption that *every* statement must in some way reflect the historical situation is erroneous. For example, "three shepherds" are mentioned in 11:8. To go on the assumption that contemporary personages are referred to and to date the passage accordingly has led to those many efforts referred to in the treatment of this verse (infra), efforts that lead to no assured result. There is great likelihood that Zechariah is not referring to any historical situation; he has no three distinct individuals in mind.

It should also be noted that, when the approach that stresses the historical situation is used, it dare not operate on the assumption that out-and-out prediction of future events is impossible or improbable. Too often in interpreting passages like 9:1–7; 12:10 ff.; 13:1; and chapter 14 this fact is ignored, and the passages in question are treated as if they cannot foretell future happenings, or, if they do, all that is involved is the immediate future which the prophet happens to be able to analyze more precisely than did his contemporaries. Much of what Zechariah writes in the first and the second parts of the book is pure prediction, long-range in character besides.

Orelli then lists as one of his irrefutable arguments the claim that *Israel's* situation is not the same in the first part as it is in the second part. Our counterclaim is: How could it be? Chapters 1–8 deal with the concrete historical present of Zechariah; chapters 9–14 deal with a highly idealized representation of the Messianic age. Failure to recognize the distinctive character of Part II leads to the claim that a different situation is involved. Of course there is, and it is the prophet's intention that there should be. One illustration of what is involved: on the basis of 11:3 it is argued that the Temple is still standing; chapters 1–6 assume it is destroyed. However, if chapters 9–14 describe the Messianic age, 11:3 cannot be used as proof that the Temple was standing at the time of the writer.

Lastly, *Orelli* claims that the moral irregularities referred to in chapters 9–14 are not those of the Exile, that is to say, those found in the earlier chapters. The approach we suggested above answers this claim. The second part of the book refers to matters that will occur largely in the far distant future. How could the moral issues be the same as those presented previously?

Examining the arguments of another writer, *Koenig*, we note that he emphasizes what no other interpreters seem to consider important, viz., that in chapters 1–8 the writer uses the Hebrew word *'ani* as the pronoun, first person singular whereas in chapters 9–14 he uses the parallel form *'anokhi*. With two forms at a writer's disposal, it is quite reasonable to assume that, quite by accident, he uses the one at one time in his life, the other at another. To insist on uniformity of usage in matters of this sort means to set up arbitrary canons of style.

Much of the same stripe is another of *Koenig's* arguments to the effect that Part I gives dates, Part II does not. Since when is an author committed to the responsibility of giving dates for all that he writes if he has once done so in the past?

We find another argument of his unconvincing when he claims that in Part I the language is poetic and picturesque, in Part II it is not. The difference will be due to the subject matter. In the very nature of the case, if they are impressive and of an exalted character, visions call for a vocabulary that is more poetic and picturesque. In any case, to deny picturesqueness and poetry to Part II is arbitrary. To demand a uniform level of poetic and picturesque style of an author is hardly reasonable. Style fluctuates with moods and with age. The second part of the book could have been written much later than was the first part.

Since the problem of the unity of the book overlaps with the problem of authorship to some extent, we shall consider the second of these in this connection.

After dual authorship was beginning to be commonly assumed, it was quite the fashion, for the most part, to attribute the second part of the book to an earlier writer—perhaps the Zechariah of Isa. 8:2—the assumption being that chapters 9–14 must refer to predictions about Israel's future prior to the Exile. *Hengstenberg* demonstrated rather effectively that the second part of the book obviously made use of Ezechiel and Jeremiah and other earlier prophets.

Stade—in an essay that we shall have occasion to refer to again[1]—freely conceded that *Hengstenberg's* statement was irrefutable on this point. Driver[2] (*Introduction to the Literature of the O. T.*, p. 351, footnote) lists many passages. We give a sampling: "Comp. 9:2b–4, Ez. 28:3, 4, 8b—9:5, Zeph. 2:4—9:5b–7, Amos 1:7–8—9:10, Mic. 5:10f.—9:12b, Is. 61:7—10:3; Jer. 23:2b, Ez. 34:17 (the he-goats),—10:5a, Mic. 7:10;

[1] ZATW, 1881, pp. 1-96.
[2] ILOT, p, 351.

10:5b (riders on horses), Ez. 38:15—10:8b, Jer. 23:3b—10:9a, Jer. 31:27—10:10a, Hos. 11:11—10:10b, Mic. 7:14b—11:3a, Jer. 25:36—11:3b, Jer. 12:5," etc.

A new argument on the unity of authorship is offered by *Moeller,* (*Einleitung in das Alte Testament,* p. 161) which stresses Zechariah's strange predilection for the use of the number *four* throughout the book. He points out that there are "four times two night visions; four horses; four horns; four smiths; four chariots; four winds; four subordinate clauses (3:7); four persons 6:14); four fast days (8:19); four admonitions (8:9f); a fourfold guilt (7:13f); fourfold punishment (8:10); four pronouncements (8:12a); . . . The same fondness for the number four is met with in chap. 9–14. In 9:1f there are four cities, also 9:5; 9:13; 9:14; 9:15b (four verbs); 9:17 . . . ; 10:2 (Teraphim, diviners, dreams, idle comfort); 10:4 (cornerstone, nail, battle-bow, ruler); 11:2f (four lamentations); 14:5 (animals), etc." Though no finality can be ascribed to arguments of this sort, they are effective in offsetting counterclaims.

We believe we have shown the untenableness of *Driver's* claim [3] when he summarizes his position in the words: "That the author of Zechariah 1–8 should be also the author of either chaps. 9–11 or 12–14 is hardly possible. Zechariah uses a different phraseology, evinces different interests, and moves in a different circle of ideas from those which prevail in chaps. 9–14."

It seems to us that an unexpressed assumption determines the approach of the critics, an assumption which needs only to be put into words to show how untenable it is. It amounts to this, that the historical situation which prevails in chapters 1–8 must be the same as that which is found in chapters 9–14. This is identical with the claim that the two parts of the book must date from the same or practically the same time and situation. In other words, most of the claims regarding differences between the two parts of the book could be accounted for by the simple assumption that some twenty or thirty years

---

[3] *ibid.,* p. 354.

might have elapsed between the time that the prophet receives his "visions" and the time when he is given his "burdens" to pronounce.

Again a parallel and very simple assumption is this, that after a fair lapse of time—say again some twenty or thirty years —quite a different cycle of ideas could have controlled the prophet's mind. We offer this as a more reasonable claim than the contrary assumption that so many seem to operate with: that if a writer has developed a certain area of thought he must continue to stay within, or almost within, this area if he later resumes his writing. This approach allows for no growth, no new ideas, no development. It condemns the prophet to stay within the scope of the ideas he set forth when he first spoke. This further forces writers to being one-track-mind men all their days. What a wide variety of subject matter engages the attention of some writers in our day! Why not *then?*

Another matter. If the critical approach rejects the authorship of Zechariah for chapters 9–14, what substitute does it offer? One may well hesitate to answer, for there is no one answer. The critics cannot agree as to their findings. Up till the time of *Stade's* famous essay just referred to (ZATW, 1881, pp. 1–96) the majority assigned an earlier date to chapters 9–14 than to chapters 1–8. *Stade's* arguments, based largely on *Hengstenberg,* carried the day. Very few ventured to champion the earlier date for chapters 9–14, as for example *Koenig,* who assigned chapters 12–14 the date 600. But then *Stade* veered into the other extreme of arriving at a date between 306–278 B.C. on the basis of historical allusions that he had discovered. If we were to list the variety of opinions on this subject, the array would be most bewildering and confusing. If a clear-cut case can be made against Zechariah as the author of chapters 9–14, why cannot they who say this arrive at definite results? Their lack of agreement is the refutation of their position.

Moeller (Einleitung, etc., p. 159) very correctly makes the following observation: "More effective than any criticism [of negative views] or rather the best criticism is the enumeration of these various conflicting opinions: chap. 9–14 are a unit, and to be exact pre-exilic or postexilic, but at least not to be ascribed to Zechariah; or 9–11 date from the eighth century B.C., but 12–14 are to be fixed at the end of the seventh century or the beginning of the sixth; or they are to be referred to the time of the Seleucidae or that of the Maccabees; or the entire portion 9–14 stems from an apocalyptic writer of the third or second century B.C., who wrote assuming the guise of a pre-exilic prophet, allowing for the possibility that 9:1–10 dates from the time of Isaiah, and that the apocalyptic writer simply used the name of Zechariah the son of Jeberechia found in Isa. 8:2 or the portion 9:1–10 is actually to be traced back to this Zechariah (Note: this man mentioned in Isa. 8:2 is not designated as a prophet and according to the connection it is hardly to be claimed that he was one!) Others again abandoned both the unity or the twofold character of chap. 9–14 and advanced to the opinion that it must be ascribed to four separate authors. In the face of such confusion it is simply out of the question that any of the views listed should claim any validity for itself."

On the positive side of the matter it is quite proper to stress the similarity of the materials found in the two parts of the book.

V. Outline

THE INTRODUCTORY EXHORTATION TO REPENTANCE (1:1–6)

I. *The Visions* (1:7–6:15)

1. The First Vision (1:7–17)
   The Rider under the Myrtles
2. The Second Vision (1:18–21; Heb. 2:1–4)
   The Four Horns and the Four Smiths
3. The Third Vision (2:1–13; Heb. 2:5–17)
   The Man with the Measuring Line

—It is an outstanding victory and consists
  (a) in her true penitence (12:10–14)
  (b) in her true sanctification (13:1–6)
b) The Lord's Victory (13:7–14:21)
  —the purging of God's people occasioned by the shepherd's death (13:7–9)
  —the deliverance of Jerusalem occasioned by the assault of her foes (14:1–5)
  —the new state of things after the Lord's day (14:6–11)
  —the confusion visited upon all enemies (14:12–15)
  —the submission of the nations (14:16–19)
  —the new state of holiness (14:20, 21)

VI. Bibliography

A. COMMENTARIES

Barnes, W. Emery, in the *Cambridge Bible*, (vol. Hag. Zech. Mal.) Cambridge: the University Press, 1934.

Chambers, Talbot W., in *Lange's Commentary, The Book of Zechariah*. New York: Charles Scribner's Sons, 1874.

Hengstenberg, E. W., *Christologie des Alten Testaments u. Commentar ueber die Messianischen Weissagungen*. Berlin: Ludwig Oehmigke, 1856.

Horst, Friedrich, in Eissfeldt's *Handbuch zum Alten Testament, Die Zwoelf Kleinen Propheten,* by Robinson and Horst. Tuebingen: J.C.B. Mohr (Paul Siebeck), 1938.

Keil, Carl Friedrich, *Biblischer Commentar ueber die Zwoelf Kleinen Propheten*. (3rd. edition) Leipzig: Doerffling und Francke, 1888.

Nowack, D. W., in Nowack's *Handkommentar zum Alten Testament, Die Kleinen Propheten*. Goettingen: Vandenhoeck und Ruprecht, 1897.

Orelli, C. V., in Strack and Zoeckler's, *Kurzgefasster Kommentar, Die Zwoelf Kleinen Propheten*. Muenchen: C. H. Beck, 1908.

Rignell, Lars Gösta, *Die Nachtgesichte des Sacharja*. Lund: Gleerups, 1950.

Sellin, Ernst, *Das Zwoelfprophetenbuch*. Leipzig: Deichert, 1922.

Smith, George Adam, *The Book of the Twelve Prophets,* in *The Expositor's Bible.* New York: George H. Doran, (n. d.).

Feinberg, Charles L., *God Remembers.* Wheaten, Ill. Van Kampen Press, 1950.

Mitchell, Hinckley G., *A Critical and Exegetical Commentary on Haggai and Zechariah,* in the *International Critical Commentary.* New York: Charles Scribner's Sons, 1912.

Pusey, E. B., *The Minor Prophets with Commentary;* Vol. VIII Zechariah. London: James Nisbet and Co., Ltd., 1907.

B. Dictionaries

Buhl, Frants, *Gesenius' Handwoerterbuch ueber das Alte Testament.* Leipzig: F.C.W. Vogel, 1905.

Brown, Driver, Briggs, *A Hebrew and English Lexicon of the Old Testament* (based on Gesenius). New York: Houghton, Mifflin Co., 1907.

Koehler, Baumgartner, *Lexicon in Veteris Testamenti Libros.* Leiden: E. J. Brill, 1951.

Koenig, Eduard, *Woerterbuch zum Alten Testament.* Leipzig: Dietrich, 1922 (2nd and 3rd edition).

C. Versions

Holy Bible, Revised Version, American Standard Edition, 1901.

King James Version.

Luther's *German Bible.*

Smith, J. M. Powis, *The Old Testament, An American Translation,* (Zechariah by J. M. Powis Smith), Chicago: University of Chicago Press, 1927.

    Hebrew Bible (Leteris) also *Biblia Hebraica,* edited by Rud. Kittel. Leipzig: J. C. Hinrichs, 1906 (Zechariah by M. Loehr).

Rahlfs, Alfred, *Septuaginta.* Stuttgart: Privilegierte Wuertembergische Bibelanstalt, 1935.

Kautzsch und Weizsaecker, *Textbibel, Das Alte Testament* von E. Kautzsch. Tuebingen: J. C. B. Mohr (Paul Siebeck), 1906.

D. Miscellaneous

Stade, Bernhard, *Zeitschrift fuer Alttestamentliche Wissenschaft*. The article "Deuterozacharja," pp. 1–96, 1881.

Stade, Bernhard, *ibid.*, p. 151ff., 1882.

Eckardt, R., *Zeitschrift fuer Alt. Wissenschaft*. The article "Der Sprachgebrauch von Zach. 9–14," p. 76ff. 1893.

Sellin, Ernst, *Journal of Biblical Literature*. The article "Der Stein des Zacharja," p. 242ff. 1931.

May, Herbert Gordon, *Journal of Biblical Literature*. The article "A Key to the Interpretation of Zechariah's Visions," p. 173ff. 1938.

One Volume Commentaries such as *The Abingdon Bible Commentary*, *The Old Testament Commentary* (Alleman and Flack), etc.

Textbooks on Introduction to the Old Testament like Koenig, Moeller, Young, and Weiser.

Koenig, Eduard, *Die Messianischen Weissagungen*, pp. 176–186 and 261–272. Stuttgart: Belser, 1923.

By way of comment on the commentaries mentioned above we add the following suggestions.

Hengstenberg and *Keil,* though no longer up to date, offer much solid material that has not been superseded or improved upon. The latter, building on the former, is the most helpful guide on the minor prophets. *Chambers* is of much the same type and still valuable. So is *Orelli,* though more recent; and *Barnes,* though not quite so conservative. *Smith* has critical leanings but has not lost his sense of the inspired character of the prophetic revelation and, always treating it with reverence, gives evidence of commendable insight into the prophet's message. *Pusey* is soundly conservative and scholarly, in the best Anglican tradition, although inclined to be too dogmatic.

Nowack represents those who deal very critically with the text. Though *Sellin* is more moderate in this respect, his view is influenced by Babylonian parallels which are often no more than a remote analogy and in the last analysis have little, if any, bearing on the text under consideration. *Mitchell* is very critical and offers little that is constructive. *Horst* represents the extreme of license taken by the exegete with a text that is largely unimpeachable and resorts to emendations and restorations and at the same time is dominated by the thought that Hebrew prophets knew and utilized Babylonian lore.

Feinberg's book is surprisingly helpful though seldom original and is also marked by a moderate millennial hope before the final Parousia. *Rignell,* though interpreting only the visions, has the courage to defend the integrity of the Masoretic text—a task which he fulfills very successfully—without ignoring the result of critical findings. His interpretation is also very solid and conservative and done with utmost thoroughness.

Chapter I

THE INTRODUCTORY EXHORTATION
TO REPENTANCE (v. 1-6)

In the visions that follow many rich and glorious promises are to be unfolded by the prophet. He will be showering his people with all the riches of divine treasures that God is wont to bestow upon His people. Such riches, however, can be received rightly only if a man has repented sincerely in the sight of his Lord. Only the poor in spirit shall have the kingdom of God. In fact, if a prophet should have dared to speak only words of grace and none of rebuke, perverse human nature in the hearers would have led in most cases to false security. As *Luther* already indicated, this is the reason an Exhortation to Repentance is the introduction to Zechariah's book. *Luther* says: "Because this prophet purposes to administer comfort very freely, therefore he strikes a very sharp and earnest note at the outset."

✠

vs. 1-6   ¹ In the eighth month of the second year of Darius the Word of the Lord came to Zechariah, the son of Berechiah, the son of Iddo, saying: ² The Lord was thoroughly angered at your fathers. ³ And now you shall say to them: Thus says the Lord of hosts: Come back to Me—utterance of the Lord of hosts—and I will come back to you, says the Lord of hosts. ⁴ Do not be like your fathers to whom the former prophets preached, saying: Thus says the Lord of hosts: Come back now from your wicked ways and from your wicked doings. But they would not listen nor give heed to Me—utterance of the Lord. ⁵ Your fathers— where are they now? And the prophets—are they still living? ⁶ But My words and My statutes, which I commanded My servants, the prophets—have they not overtaken your fathers? So they turned and said: Just as the Lord of hosts purposed to do to us, according to our ways and doings, even so He has done to us.

Verse 1 is in the nature of a title to the whole book and not properly a part of the exhortation though the indication of time refers only to the visions following.

Which year this was we stated above under Historical Circumstances. Such information as bore upon the identification of the prophet was discussed under the Person of the Prophet. See the *Introduction*.

It remains only to add that the term "the prophet" after "Iddo" is not in apposition with Iddo. Grammatically this would indeed be possible. But quite manifestly Zechariah is under discussion, and the term "the prophet" naturally describes him. This is simply another instance to show with what certainty of conviction in regard to their calling these men of God spoke. They were God's ambassadors and knew that the Spirit of God did speak by them.

Only a hypercritical approach could lead men to question so simple, natural, and inoffensive a superscription. Several attempts have been made to detect the hand of a later editor or to point out an error of omission. Some critics, acting on the unproved assumption that the verse was originally shorter because they feel it should have been, regard the words: "the son of Berechiah, the son of Iddo," as a later addition. The tendency behind the correction is manifestly an attempt to create support for the theory that we have in this book the writing of two Zechariahs, one from Isaiah's time, the other postexilic. Since in Isa. 8:2 a certain "Zechariah, the son of Jeberachiah," is mentioned, the claim is made that a later hand added the appositions in our verse. Our Zechariah is almost identified with Isaiah's contemporary, who, it is claimed, may have written the earlier part of this book. In this way the Israelites in days of old regarded the two writings as one and let them pass under a common name. A welter of unfounded suppositions leading to no tangible results!

In the second place, since some commentators felt that they themselves would have made the designation of the time of this word more exact they find fault with the statement as here given. Some determine the very day of the month by taking *cho'desh*, "month," in the sense of "new moon," or the first day of the month. But with the numeral "eighth" it is not likely that the term would signify anything but "month." Further, in all similar statements where the date is exact, and the number of the month is given, the numeral *'e(ch)chadh* is regularly appended to indicate the new moon or "first day of the month"; see Exod. 40:2, 17; Gen. 8:5, 13; Num. 1:1; 29:1; 33:38. The claim that the numeral was overlooked by copyists and the support of that claim by the further claim: "The first word of a Hebrew book is easily overlooked" (*Mitchell*), ought not to be taken seriously. Why should the first word of a Hebrew book be overlooked more readily than any other? The long and the short of the matter is simply this: The prophet felt that for his purpose the time was marked with sufficient accuracy if he said: "eighth month, second year of Darius." From this we can readily compute, comparing Hag. 1:1, 15, that this word came two months later than the word that Haggai received, according to chapter one of his book, and about one month later than Haggai, chapter two (Hag. 2:1–9). Knowing these facts, we see how closely Zechariah followed upon the heels of Haggai.

To be as exact as we can, this notation takes us to about November, 520 B.C.

Verse 2. We might have expected the very first word to voice the summons to repentance. Yet such an expectation does not rule out every other mode of approach as unsatisfactory and indicative, besides, of some tampering with the text. This is the critical approach, which then leads to various reconstructions. Such, e.g., is *Sellin's* method, who, after his realignments are completed, arrives at the conclusion that after 1–6a should be added 8:14, 15, with 6:15, however, inserted between these two larger portions, and the whole brought to a conclusion by 6b, namely, after 8:15. If our Hebrew text were so unreliable—of which unreliability no proof has ever very doubtful product and ought at best to be esteemed no better than lumps of clay which can be fashioned according been adduced—surely, our whole Old Testament should be a to the peculiar fancy of the individual critic.

We purpose to show that a reasonable approach can find a

natural sequence of thought and a message very much to the point for Israel at that time.

The burden of this opening message is the summons: "Repent" or "return." Note the frequent recurrence of the word. But this message is cast in a form that is most appropriate for Israel at that time, for it says: Profit by the example of your fathers and repent, (*Orelli*). It is for this reason that v. 2 begins: "The Lord was thoroughly angered at your fathers." This ought to be classed as a most effective mode of beginning on the part of the prophet. The land, after the exiles had returned in 536 B.C., had recovered but little from the general state of ruin in which Nebuchadnezzar's thoroughgoing devastation and depopulation had left it. Many, if not most, houses and cities were still in ruins. The walls of Jerusalem had not been raised again. The Temple was still but half reconstructed. The land, in its devastated state, bore eloquent testimony to the fact that "the Lord was thoroughly angered at your fathers." Every day the ruins stared those who had returned in the face. The prophet begins by interpreting this state of affairs to the people and adds to it the very effective application: All this was caused by the failure of the fathers to do what I am now exhorting you to do. Such a beginning, therefore, as v. 2 prefixes to v. 3, rather than being subjected to criticism, ought to be commended as being a very telling way of making a plea effective and concrete. Every last ruin in the land bore mute but clear testimony to the prophet's message.

There is no valid reason for emending the text according to the Septuagint by adding *gadhol* to *qétseph,* namely, adding the adjective "great" to the noun "anger," making the verse read in literal translation: "The Lord was angered with a *great* anger." For it is commonly known that without such an emendation the Hebrew would have this meaning. A verb that is supplemented by a cognate object, as here *qatsaph qétseph,* in the very nature of the case means: "The Lord was thoroughly angered."

Verse 3. Now comes the burden of this first sermon: "Return unto Me." From our point of view this might be rendered: "Repent." However, the original has a far simpler way of stating the case. For us the term "repentance" requires definition and explanation. To the Hebrews the term employed is already descriptive of what is involved. *Shûbh* signifies nothing other than "to return." When such an admonition is addressed to him, man's state is that of being turned away from God. That being man's position relative to God, every day carries him farther away from God. His basic need at such a time is that he cease turning his back to God, that he cease ignoring Him, and, having turned about, take such a position that every step in life carries him nearer to God.

This was Israel's primary need at the time. Only those who met this requirement would be able rightly to appropriate all the rich promises that were to be offered thereafter. The history of Israel during the next centuries shows that this warning was very necessary at this time. All those who failed to give serious heed to it but tried, nevertheless, to glory in God's rich promises were in the same class with the Pharisees of Christ's time, who had carnal hopes and carnal zeal for the kingdom, but had not even, sad to say, entered in at the gates of the kingdom.

This demand to return seems to agree rather poorly with the assurance that Haggai had given the people shortly before by the Word of the Lord when he declared (1:13): "I am with you saith the Lord." However, the two thoughts are to be harmonized in this fashion: A preliminary and earnest repentance on the part of God's people had been in evidence when Haggai spoke two months before. But every repentance, every return unto the Lord is imperfect at best. It is an experience which requires deepening; it must be done more sincerely and thoroughly. A godly life, in a sense, consists in perfecting repentance, always doing it more effectually. So what Haggai claimed was true: the people had God on their side because they had returned to Him. But what Zechariah claimed was also true: Israel needed to return with more sincere devotion if God's promises for the future were to become a reality.

This verse has a unique emphasis to assure those that heard it of the intense earnestness of the Lord's demand in asking

that they return unto Him: it states a thrice-repeated claim
to the effect: this is in very deed the *Word of God,* for it contains the words: "thus says the Lord of hosts" and "utterance
of the Lord of hosts" and "says the Lord of hosts." The second
of these terms differs materially from the first and the last,
which are identical. It reads *ne'um Yahweh,* which means
"utterance" or "oracle" of the Lord. All this is not wearisome
repetition but as solemn an assurance as can possibly be made
of the fact that it is indeed *God's* supreme demand that is here
being presented. In each phrase the solemn covenant name,
Jahveh or Lord, appears; and in the first and the last instances
the assertion is added that the Lord is the "God of hosts." He
has the heavenly armies and the host of all created things at
His beck and call. The demand of such a monarch should be
heeded with trembling earnestness. In regard to these repetitions *Smith* remarks: "Later hands have exaggerated the repetitions and ravelled the processes of the original." Not a very
sympathetic treatment of a good point!

A very gracious promise is given as to the blessed consequences that shall follow upon sincere repentance; God says:
"I will return unto you." The verb is the same one that was
used in the demand: "Return unto Me." These are two acts
that mutually determine one another. We, of course, in no
wise impugn the valid truth that no return on man's part is
possible except God turn to man and help him. But only when
man, who has been taken in hand by God, in all sincerity
turns to God, will God on His part turn to man and bestow
the full measure of grace that He is so eager to impart. For a
sinner to hear—after he has become aware of the fact that God
was very averse to him because of his sins—that God no longer
turns His back but has His kindly attention and the warm
glow of His love turned upon the unworthy sinner, is a prospect that might well induce any man to make his return unto
God as wholehearted and sincere as possible.

The second word of v. 3 is a *constructio ad sensum* and, like
all Biblical instances of this kind, readily understood. *'ᵃlehem*
(written without a *yodh*) would strictly refer to the antecedent
"your fathers" (v. 2). In a way, since v. 2 is a kind of prelimi-

nary parenthesis, v. 3 attaches itself to the close of v. 1, "saying." Only carping critics find the construction disturbing or
unclear.

Verse 4. The grave danger is that the traditional form
of conduct, inaugurated by "the fathers" and perpetuated
through centuries of history, might be followed by the
prophet's generation. In reference to these fathers history had
a very solemn lesson to teach. Everyone knew what that lesson
was. It stared every man in the face whenever he looked about
him at the ruined state of Israel. Not all, however, were duly
taking it to heart. Therefore the prophet calls to his generation to make a distinct break with this cursed tradition. He
says: "Do not be like your fathers." He then proceeds to
describe distinctly just what form their sin took in reference
to the prophets' messages that had been delivered. The
"former prophets" had preached to them. By this term Zechariah refers to all the messengers of God in Israel's past since
Moses. They had all been inculcating the same basic principle
of repentance, and they had stressed it as the solemn word of
the Lord—"thus says the Lord of hosts." These messages are
very aptly summed up in the word: "Return, pray," *shûbhû
na'*, the term "pray" indicating how fervently the prophets
pleaded with their hearers in God's name. That from which
they were to turn aside is aptly described by the double term:
"your wicked ways and your wicked doings." That covers the
whole compass of a man's life: his "ways" designate the direction and bent of his life; his "doings," the individual deeds
done as he travels along this wrong road. If the "ways" are
"wicked," the deeds done in these ways must naturally be
"wicked," too. This indictment has not said too much because, if a man is turned away from God, nothing truly good
can be produced by his life. The prophets roundly condemned
the whole of life as long as its basic trend and direction were
wrong.

What was the attitude of the fathers toward all such sermons
that demanded a return? The prophet introduces it by a
solemn: "Thus says the Lord of hosts" because the indictment
is not to be understood as a conclusion arrived at by the

prophet but as a part of God's own charge. It is stated thus: "They would not listen (*sham⁰ʿû*) nor give heed (*hiqshîbhû*) to Me." The former term implies giving heed in a general way by listening. The latter suggests the thought of paying close attention, literally, "pricking up the ears." What the prophet says is practically this: the fathers never listened; least of all did anyone ever pay close attention. Here lay the cause of Israel's sad plight and its present misery. At this very point would the author have his hearers mend their ways. Solemn and reverent listening to, and heeding of, the prophet's message were the first steps toward breaking with the fathers' evil ways.—Note: the *kethibh* (the text as written) *meʿᵃlîlêhem, min* plus the plural of ʿᵃ*lîlah,* is perfectly acceptable.

Verse 5. The prophet seems to sense an objection that his hearers might raise. He seems to note that his emphasis on the fathers and their experience is leading his audience to say: "Well, the fathers have passed off the scene; that's all a matter of history, and the whole issue is closed." He is ready to grant that. Nor is that his real issue. He can make their thoughts his own and voice their very words and so lead up to the matter that he would primarily emphasize. The fathers and the prophets are only incidental to the major consideration. That consideration is *the eternal Word of God* which is an abiding verity and always true. The adversative *'akh,* "but," introduces this contrasting thought in the verse that follows.

Verse 6. Two terms are used to describe this immutable Word: *dᵉbharay,* "My words," and *chuqqay,* "my statutes." They are "words" insofar as they are utterances of God. They are "statutes" insofar as He has definitely fixed and ordained them. Both these features of the divine Word come into consideration here. The great Lord has spoken these utterances, and they are firmly and unalterably decreed. These He then laid by commandment upon His prophets to utter, "I commanded," a correct description of the situation, for it was not of their own choice that they brought their messages or by virtue of unusual foresight that they divined the truth. Their message was God-given, and they had to deliver it as a matter of obedience. "Words and statutes" are not references to exhortations to repent but to God's threats; cf. Ezek. 12:28; Jer. 39:16; Zeph. 2:2.

But one thing this new generation cannot deny, even if it will relegate these happenings to a somewhat dim past, and that is that these words "overtook their fathers." This furnishes a guarantee of the inviolable character of these words. The fathers thought they could escape; but the Word set out in pursuit and caught them. This is a prominent feature of the divine Word; it is inescapable. That fact the prophet would burn into their conscience.

To encourage his generation still more to make haste and obey the Word and repent or "return," the prophet reminds it how, at least in the case of some, the fulfillment of the Word in the Exile stimulated repentance. These were the better among the fathers, men like Daniel (Dan. 9:4ff) and Ezra (Ezra 9:6ff) who earnestly confessed their own and their people's sins. This constitutes a motive for repentance. There were among the fathers those who admitted that God did no idle threatening; as He "thought to do unto us, so hath He dealt with us." That sacred Word is not to be trifled with, cf. Lam. 2:17.

Those interpreters who do not accept our present text of the Sacred Scriptures as being reliable amend it with the claim that it includes a contradiction. Verse 4 states: the fathers did not return; now v. 6 tells us: they did return and confessed that they could not escape God. However, our interpretation above shows both aspects of the case to be true. No one can deny that, generally speaking, the fathers refused to hearken and repent when the prophets addressed them. After the full measure of God's wrath had been poured out upon Israel, and the Word had overtaken it, there were at least some who felt impelled to make a full and free confession of guilt; and so they did return. These were exemplary in their attitude; those constituted a warning example. *Sellin* goes so far as to declare this apparent contradiction a piece of "nonsense" which is supposed to have been uttered by the prophet if we allow the present form of the text to stand. Such criticism is, however, farfetched and unfair to the prophet's statement.

THE VISIONS (1:7–6:15)

The First Vision (1:7–17)

The Rider under the Myrtles

In a series of visions the prophet now unfolds the message of divine comfort. We may rightly expect that there is going to be a sequence of thought, or that these visions will be built up in a well-ordered series. This can, for example, be made apparent by considering the following facts. In the first vision the emissaries of the Lord present a report that nothing has been done. Then follows a set of intermediate visions that portray the preparations for the realization of the Messianic kingdom. Then, as the visions draw to a close (6:1ff), the emissaries of the Almighty are seen going out to carry into effect all that has been indicated in the preceding vision, and which that vision indicated as unfulfilled.

All the visions were apparently received in one night—4:1 leads to this conclusion. So does the manner in which the visions follow one another.

It will scarcely be permissible to regard the visions merely as literary forms chosen by the prophet as the most convenient vehicle for the expression of thought. When he says (1:8), "I saw" and many times thereafter uses statements such as, "I lifted up my eyes and saw" (1:18; 2:1; 3:1; 4:2, etc.), there can be no valid objection to the most natural of all interpretations that, namely, the prophet, in a state of prophetic ecstasy, was actually shown certain visions. In fact, that is the only interpretation that does justice to the words employed. Commentators who do not understand this testimony of the prophet literally appear to be doing so largely that they might feel free to alter a purely human word, as they deem it, by as many conjectures and emendations as they may feel inclined to make. We do not here have "a series of conscious and artistic allegories . . . the deliberate translation into a carefully constructed symbolism of divine truths with which the prophet was entrusted by his God" (*Smith*). Nothing in the text or the fact portrayed is in the least at variance with the claim that the thought as well as the form in which the thought was cast was given by God.

If the general questions be raised, why apocalyptic visions, and why such a preponderance of them? we can venture but one suggestion that, to us at least, seems adequate to meet the needs of the case. It is this: God employs every possible form of revelation to drive home truth. In the past the plain prophetic word had been employed. Dreams had sometimes been used. Visions had been an occasional means of expression. Now to exhaust every approach in bringing home to men the word of guidance and the Messianic hope in all its fulness, a type of vision is employed that by its relatively new feature—the apocalyptic element—challenges attention anew. All this comes under the head of the "divers portions and divers manners" (Heb. 1:1) by which God of old time spoke unto the fathers by the prophets. Nor shall we overlook the fact that, though incidental difficulties appear in this form of revelation, all its main features are surprisingly plain, and we can rest assured that we may apprehend them aright.

One further feature of the visions deserves brief attention. This is the fact that the framework of the visions is somewhat sketchy—not fully elaborated, not worked out with fulness of details, but stated rather in as concise a form as possible. *Barnes* describes this feature thus: "The visions are of the nature of parables, or similitudes. The story told or suggested by any one of them is of the slightest. Few or none of the details can be treated as significant." Again: "The visions are slight and incomplete in the telling, but the Word of the Lord is delivered plainly and with authority." We may say, "As little is made of the narrative of the vision as possible; but the message conveyed by the vision is elaborated sufficiently to make it as plain as need be." Visions like Isaiah's inaugural vision (Isa. 6), or those of Ezekiel (Ezek. 16, 17, 19, 23, 37, etc.), or the parables of Jesus are an obvious contrast to Zechariah's method of presentation of his message in chapters 1–6.

✣

vs. 7–11   ⁷ On the twenty-fourth day of the eleventh month (which is the month Shebat) in the second year of Darius, the word of the Lord came to Zechariah, the son of Berechiah, the son of Iddo, the prophet, saying: ⁸ I saw by night, and there was a man mounted on a brown horse, and he halted among the myrtle trees down in a hollow, and behind him there were brown, sorrel, and white horses. ⁹ And I said, My Lord, what are these? And the angel that was talking with me said: I am the one who will show you what these are. ¹⁰ But the man standing among the myrtles answered and said: These are the ones whom the Lord has sent to patrol the earth. ¹¹ And they answered the angel of the Lord, who was standing among the myrtles, and said: We have patrolled the whole earth, and lo, the whole earth is quiet and at rest.

This vision comes to Zechariah in the eleventh month. The opening word of his book came to him in the eighth month. *Luther* surmises that the prophet spent the intervening time expanding upon and enforcing the message that he had first received. Since it is the *twenty-fourth day* of the month that is so specifically indicated, we cannot but be struck by the fact that on two other occasions the twenty-fourth day of the month is specified during this period after the Exile, viz., Hag. 1:15 and 2:10, 18, 20. This was the day when the work on the Temple was resumed. We, on our part, cannot help but feel that the day that marked Israel's new obedience is thus singled out by the Lord and made memorable by further revelations.

"The eleventh month, which is the month Shebat," corresponds roughly to our February and is a month that is marked occasionally by very pleasant weather and many signs of oncoming spring. To secure a kind of harmony between the weather and the nature of the prophecy, some interpreters associate the month with a bitter type of weather after the example of Jerome (died 420).

This word comes two full months after Haggai's last message, cf. Hag. 2:10. It is February, 519 B.C.

When the prophet is here identified as fully as he was in v. 1, that is neither an indication that the book originally began at this point nor that the first seven verses were prefixed later. Nor is it proof, in any sense, that these words are later interpolations. The fact commonly observed, that formulas are occasionally repeated in the *more solemn style* of days of old, is a sufficient explanation for all who aim to explain things as they are and are satisfied with reasonable explanations.

Here we must indicate that in the verses lying before us there is no reason for questioning the integrity of any one word of the text. If the *subjective* canons of criticism are to be followed, of which *Sellin* is a moderate exponent, we feel that our subjective reactions, backed by valid reasoning and objective textual criticism, are also a scientific canon of criticism and far more satisfactory than the so-called scientific point of view. To us the entire section seems a very coherent whole. Approaching it from this point of view, we hope to demonstrate that the very form of presentation that the text offers is the most skillful way of presenting the very thought that is set forth. The critical attitude succeeds by omissions and emendations in securing a picture that is different from that which the author portrays and in so far fails in meeting the first requirement of all fair exegesis. The type of criticism that operates with conjectures as to the possible form of what is called the *original* statement of the text is one of the most specious methods of discrediting a dependable Scripture text that has been devised by theologians. Imagination runs riot, and all scholarship is built on sand, if vs. 16, 17 are classed as later additions, and the entire section vs. 7–17 is described as being "distorted by glosses" (*Sellin*). We are hoping for a day in the near future when such methods of scholarship will be branded as *"utterly unscientific."*

Though in this verse the revelation received is called "the word of the Lord," yet we understand that that word may assume most varied forms as also, for example, the form of the "vision." The vision speaks to us and so becomes a word. It is for this reason that it is directly introduced by the word customarily employed in introducing indirect discourse, viz., *le'mor,* lit., "saying," here equivalent to "thus" or "as follows."

Verse 8. "I saw" (*ra'îthî*) is the regular verb for "seeing." When God granted the prophet the sight of these things, this was what his eyes "saw," whether with the inner eye or with the eye of the body. We are in no wise pressing the word "saw" as "literalists," nor will "the inadequacy of that method in interpretation become increasingly apparent" (*Mitchell*). We shall rather find that thus alone do we do justice to these marvelous visions. The seeing is done in the night when, after the disturbing sounds and sights of the day are removed, the recipient of these visions can sense to the full the import of what is revealed to him. *Halláyᵉlah* is accusative of duration of time (*Keil*) and does not mean "this night" as though Zechariah were writing on the following morning.

We do best to consider the vision as it now consecutively unfolds itself, noting why only a part is disclosed at a time. The prophet is apparently narrating exactly what transpired. He is not as a literary man aiming to secure certain effects by a skillful portrayal. He faithfully records just what God showed him. The effect created is just what God wants it to be; and the vision as given is the best agent for securing this effect.

The first vision is to be particularly regarded as are all the rest; therefore, "behold" (*hinneh*). We have no good and sufficient reason for identifying this "rider" with any of the individuals who later appear on the scene. All efforts to regard any two of those appearing as being identical are based on insufficient proof. We prefer to translate as above, "a man mounted on" rather than "a man riding upon," for *rokhebh,* because otherwise an unnecessary difficulty is created. For in the latter case he is first *riding,* then practically in the same breath he is *standing* among the myrtles. This difficulty is partly removed by rendering the latter verb (*'omedh*) "halted." But the fact is simply this: *rokhebh,* the participle, "riding," describes the rider. If a man is said to be a "rider," that by no means implies that he must always keep his horse going. He may halt ('amadh, lit., "stand") at any point. By this use of 'amadh no one becomes involved in the singular contradiction of being described simultaneously as "riding" and "standing."

The color of the horse must be established at once. 'Adhom, it is true, usually signifies "red." But since that color is less apt as the description of a horse, we adopt the meaning "reddish-brown," which is established by Gen. 25:30.

The "myrtle trees" and "the bottom" are not merely colorful details that are added to make a more complete picture. In visions, where all things are significant, these must be interpreted. It is quite proper to let "the myrtles" typify the *Jewish Church*, for the myrtle is a small evergreen, never exceeding a height of eight feet. Cedars and oaks are stately trees. They, however, are not chosen here, for the church of God ranks among the insignificant things in the eyes of the children of this world. So the symbolism of the burning bush (Exod. 3) pointed to Israel in distress. World kingdoms and rulers are represented by mighty trees (Dan. 4). The fact that these myrtles are "in the bottom" or, as we have translated, "in a hollow," (*bammetsullah*) typifies the low estate of God's people in these days of the restoration. (This word signifies low-lying land, a "hollow" or "bottom" rather than a "shady place," by almost common consent of dictionaries.) Cf. *Koehler,* p. 556. The article, "the hollow," implies nothing more than that particular hollow where the trees stood in the prophet's vision, according to one usage of the Hebrew article. It is like our: "Let us go out into *the* field."

As he begins to take in the rest of the picture the prophet sees behind the one rider a multitude of horses, "brown, sorrel, and white." It follows from v. 11 that in reality a great number of *riders* is involved. However, this is not stated, only the color of the horses is stressed for the present because that was the noticeable feature in the picture and the significant factor for the purpose of the visions. The colors apparently typify the mission of the cavalry squadrons. *'Adhummîm,* predominantly "red" (therefore we said above "reddish-brown"), is the color of blood. *Siruqqîm*, "sorrel," or German *fuchsrot*, fox-red, seems to suggest fire and blood mixed. "White" is the color of glory and of victory. Thus almost any reader would be inclined to interpret. Rev. 6 clinches this interpretation.

Here we find represented those agencies that God employs for the correction and punishment of men: war, fire, and victory on His part. Mounted *angels* represent all these (we see they are *angels*, for as the scene develops, all are discovered to be angelic characters) because the angels are God's agents for performing the many things He desires to have wrought on earth. (So also *Rignell*.) The fact that these hosts are "behind him," i.e., the rider, indicates that the first angel observed is the leader of the host. Mark again, the chief factor is not that hosts of angels appeared. That is a secondary though and becomes apparent later. We are rather to notice that *God's punitive agents are on the scene, embattled and under competent leadership*. The fact that horses also appear signifies that these agents of God are also swift and ready to hasten wheresoever God may want to dispatch them. *Rignell* calls these riders "messengers of vengeance and of victory" for "the good of God's people Israel."

The views of some commentators do not improve this interpretation. Because 6:1 presents chariots and *four* colors is not a reason for altering the picture presented in this chapter so as to make it conform to the latter. Had chariots and horses of four colors originally appeared here, the still greater difficulty encountered by those who favor such a view would be to explain, first, why anyone should have attempted to mar such an agreement between chapter 1 and chapter 6; and second, how any scribes or the careful Jewish guardians of the Sacred Scriptures could have suffered such an alteration to displace the original setting. Or to claim that the colors of the horses "represent the four different quarters of the sky toward which they are riding" (*Nowack*) appears to be a claim that is entirely unsubstantiated. Why not follow the helpful lead of Rev. 6?

Verse 9. Continued reflection might have suggested to the

prophet what these things that he saw typified. But the eager desire to know at once together with the surprise that the vision occasioned prompted the impulsive question: "What are these?" On the order of the words in the question see *K(S)* 338d. He who is addressed had not, however, been previously introduced. The prophet reports things rather in the order in which they actually transpired on that memorable night. He observed an angel standing near by. He surmised that this angelic being could furnish the desired information. He addressed him respectfully as "my lord" (not *'adhonāy*, "my Lord") the address of respect. From this point forward this angel will be regularly designated as "the angel that talked with me," *hammal'akh haddobher bî*, the *angelus interpres*. The expression *dibber bᵉ* signifies a peculiar intimacy of communication, for the expression "to speak unto" is *dibber 'el*. We dare not translate, "to speak in," for that is not the thought intended, cf. Num. 12:8. There is no convincing reason for identifying this interpreting angel with any one of the other angels appearing on the scene.

It is the interpreting angel's task to convey the meaning of all these things to the prophet whenever the prophet is unable of himself to discern what is meant. The prophet could have conveyed the meaning of the vision by expository remarks. He can do it by letting the various characters involved in the scene tell what the scene would lead them to say, and their words can serve as an equally satisfactory solution of the questions requiring an answer. The latter method is employed here.

Verse 10. "The man standing among the myrtles" is the same person whom the prophet noticed first as the vision began to unfold itself (v. 8). He is the leader of the squadron mounted on the variously colored steeds. On the strength of the material offered in v. 11, where the angel of the Lord is also described as "standing among the myrtles," to identify this leader with the angel of the Lord is not permissible, at least not necessary. This leader furnishes the prophet with some of the information he needs. He tells him: these steeds—plus their riders, of course—are the ones whom the Lord sends

abroad "to patrol the earth." In fact, they had just been commissioned to some such task (*shalach*, perfect) and had come
back. Their general business on this occasion had been to "patrol the earth." *Hithhallekh* is best rendered thus, meaning
"to go to and fro," here, naturally, for purposes of exploration
and investigation. The thought is not that God requires agents
to investigate for Him and keep Him informed. By virtue
of His omniscience He knows, yea, even foreknows, all things.
In the vision the use of many scouts is, as it were, a picturesque
way of conveying the idea that He is most fully informed at
all times. A thought of *Fausset's* is not out of place here: since
the same word "traverse" or "patrol" is used in Job 1:7 in
regard to Satan's restless going about, we are reminded that
over against all demoniac forces that are abroad to harm
God also has numberless hosts of angels to protect His own.

Attempts to make the scene in this vision more precise will
apparently help us little, for nothing more is indicated than
that there was a "man standing among the myrtles." Some attempt to fix details of location where none are given, saying:
"The scene of the prophet's vision [is] the neighborhood of
Jerusalem. The angel is seen by the prophet close to the city,
though concealed from the eyes of ordinary men." This
identification of the exact location may have been inferred
from the next two visions. But there is nothing to indicate
that the locale of the successive visions remains the same.
Each new vision seems to be a complete entity.

Of less help is the attempt to place the scene of the vision
far beyond the sea at the entrance to the heavens. *Horst* states
quite positively, referring to the "man standing among the
myrtles": "A man stands at the gate of heaven and behind him
are horses of various colors. . . . The description of the scene
of the vision is to be determined by mythologic-cosmological
conceptions of the Old Orient. According to the text of the
Hebrew Bible there lies a grove of myrtles in the East far
beyond the depths of the ocean which surrounds the earth; and
in or beyond this grove the deity dwells in seclusion. . . .
Here at this Eastern entrance to the heavens, Zechariah observes the figure of a man."

This interpretation ascribes many things to our text that are not to be found in it. *Horst* has arrived at this result by a rather specious use of facts. For, as he says, "mythological-cosmological conceptions of the Old Orient" must guide us in our interpretations. This being presupposed, attempts are then made to make the material of the vision conform to the thinking current in the Orient during the prophet's age. But to assert that such an interpretation is given by "the text of the Hebrew Bible" is a case of begging the question, and this approach must be rejected as being fantastic.

Others (*McFayden, Sellin*) prefer to follow a mistranslation of the *Septuagint,* which rendered *hadhasim,* not as "myrtles," but as "mountains." These "mountains" are then thought of as standing at the entrance to heaven and constituting a kind of gate. It may well be questioned whether the prophets were ever influenced by such mythological lore of the Orient, popular as that approach is in our day.

From the report now submitted (v. 11) it appears that these angelic hosts had, according to the vision, just completed their traversing of the earth and had returned. Their report is given in chorus—"*they* answered and said." Such a thought should not seem preposterous, for we have here a vision, not actual occurrences. A parallel would be the chorus responses of the old Greek tragedies. In the vision the prophet actually heard such a chorus report.

This report is delivered to "the angel of the Lord," *mal'akh Yahweh.* He appears suddenly without previous indication of His presence. This fact should not lead us to assume that the reason for His not being specially introduced here is that He has already appeared, namely, as one of those who are previously mentioned. "The man riding on a red horse" is usually selected for this purpose. In that case, however, the squadron would be reporting to its leader, whose most natural duty it is to conduct them on their way as they go to and fro. The situation is simply this: As the various actors in the scene consciously come before the prophet they are mentioned. The chorus report is delivered to one who also stands among the myrtles. Him the prophet observes more closely at this point and discovers in Him the Angel of the Lord. By divine illumination Zechariah is enabled to detect His identity.

We shall not at this place conduct an exhaustive investigation as to who this Angel of the Lord is. Two well-established reasons lead us to believe that wherever "*the* Angel of the Lord" appears and not merely "*an* angel" we have the second person of the Holy Trinity appearing in angelic form before the incarnation. The one reason is that He consistently identifies Himself with the Lord and is recognized as divine by those to whom He appeared, cf. Gen. 16:7ff; Josh. 5:31ff; and many more instances. The second is that Mal. 3:1 (according to the preferred interpretation) plainly identifies the Angel of the Lord with the One for whom John the Baptist prepared the way.

The Angel of the Lord had not been appearing to men for a long time. In the days of the patriarchs, in the Exodus and the days of the wilderness wanderings, in the time of the judges, even until David's time (II Sam. 24:16) and Hezekiah's (II Kings 19:34) He had gloriously manifested His presence. Now after 200 years He appears again to the particular joy of all of God's people who remember His marvelous person and deeds. It is for that reason especially mentioned that He was "standing among the myrtles," for He does not despise to be found among those of His church, whose appearance is so lowly.

We now consider the chorus report, which, by the way, excellently portrays the perfect unity that exists in the ranks of these angelic messengers: "We have patrolled the earth, and, lo, the whole earth is quiet and at rest." The word for "is quiet" is *yashabh,* here used in the same sense as in Mic. 5:3: originally "sit" or "dwell," here "dwell in peace." Our translation "is quiet" captures this thought. This fact is to be regarded as something marvelous, for a "lo" introduces it. We should be inclined to regard it as marvelous, too, from one point of view. That there should have been even a brief period of complete peace throughout the world in those warlike days surprises us. But here the situation is radically different. We have here a beautiful instance of how the activity of one prophet supplemented that of another. Hag. 2:6, 7, 22 had indicated four months before (cf. Hag. 2:1) that a tremendous upheaval of the nations should occur with the overthrow of thrones and kingdoms, and that in "a little while." Since this had been promised and was a just measure of divine retribution, Israel was naturally anticipating it. But nothing was coming of it; "all nations" were not "shaken." In fact, what had looked like the beginning of the colossal upheaval had come to a rather sudden collapse. For as *Sellin* remarks: "A great uprising was raging in the Persian Empire in 520. It is certain that by February, 519 it had long been known in Jerusalem that this uprising had failed of its purpose, and that Darius had subdued the Medes, the Babylonians, the Armenians, etc."

The historical details involved are set forth somewhat more fully in the words of *Barnes:* "The historical situation supposed by the visions is that of the beginning of the reign of Darius. The Persian king, after crushing Gaumata, or Bardiya (Pseudo-Smerdis) in Media, passed the Tigris, defeated Nidintu-Bel, the claimant to the Babylonian throne, in two battles, and captured Babylon. He thus repeated ca. 520 B.C. the achievement which Cyrus had performed in 538 B.C. in chastising the 'north country.' . . . After this capture of the capital of Western Asia, Zechariah might well say, 'All the earth sitteth still and is at rest' (1:11)."

Peace had been established. This fact seemed to challenge the veracity of God's promise. It was necessary to know, therefore, that God was well aware of this fact and was reckoning with it, and that His plans, as shall be further unfolded, have undergone no modification but shall be carried to a most successful completion.

There follows *the comforting prospect* (v. 12–17) that the prophet is allowed to set before his people.

✠

vs. 12-17   12 Then the angel of the Lord answered and said: O Lord of hosts, how long will it be until Thou wilt have pity on Jerusalem and the cities of Judah which Thou

hast scolded these seventy years? **13** Then the Lord answered the angel that talked with me kindly words, comforting words. **14** So the angel that talked with me said
unto me: Proclaim, saying, Thus says the Lord of hosts:
I am stirred by great jealousy in behalf of Judah and in
behalf of Zion, **15** and I am very much angered with the
arrogant nations; for where I was a little displeased, they
on their part helped forward unto disaster. **16** Therefore
thus says the Lord: I have turned back to Jerusalem with
kindness; My house shall be built in it—utterance of the
Lord of hosts—and the surveyor's line shall be stretched
over Jerusalem. **17** Again proclaim, saying, Thus says the
Lord of hosts: My cities will again overflow with prosperity; and the Lord will again comfort Zion, and will
again choose Jerusalem.

Some interpreters think it strange that the Angel of the
Lord should pray to God, especially if He Himself is considered divine. This is no more strange than the fact that
Christ prays to the Father in the days of His flesh (John, chapter 17). To the Angel of the Lord, too, it is a matter of concern that God fulfill His promises. Therefore He intercedes
with the Lord. However, in His prayer He dwells exclusively
on the positive side of the matter, on the favor to be shown
to the people of God. Prayer for the punishment of God's foes
and the foes of His people could always be misconstrued as
growing out of a wrong spirit.

The condition of Jerusalem and the cities of Judah, which
were more ruins than cities, clearly indicated that they stood
in need of divine mercy. Yet no substantial visible tokens of
such mercy were anywhere in evidence. It still looked as
though God "had indignation" against them. One special plea
that was perfectly valid could be based upon the expiration of
the "seventy years" that Judah and Jerusalem were to lie waste
(cf., Jer. 25:11 and 29:10). The seventy years could be
reckoned as extending from the first deportation, 605 B.C.,
to the time of the first return from the Exile, 538 (*Mitchell*),
or from the destruction of Jerusalem to the very time of
Zechariah, 587–520 B.C. (*Orelli*). In any case, the attempt to
compute an exact "seventy" has its difficulties as the views

above, cited as examples, indicate. We, therefore, do best, on the one hand, to regard "the seventy years" as a round symbolical number; and in the second place, we need not insist that the expiration of this period coincided with the time of the prophet's speaking. If the reckoning were made from 605– ca 536, the prayer spoken in 519 could very safely state that God's years of wrath had extended over seventy years, for they had, in fact, extended rather far beyond that time.

One of the effective means of helping His people that the Angel of the Lord employs is intercessory prayer. He had not previously appeared as employing this means for their good. Now as the New Testament times draw nearer, this mode is employed. In the "how long" of His prayer the many kindred cries of God's people are reflected, who were often compelled to utter similar pleas before God (cf., Ps. 74:10; Jer. 12:4, etc.).

Verse 13. The prayer of the Angel of the Lord was, indeed, made in all sincerity as a prayer for the good of Jerusalem. He is, however, in the vision shown as uttering this prayer so that the godly might take comfort from this fact. It is for this reason that the Lord answers *the interpreting angel* rather than the *Angel of the Lord,* for the former will communicate the results of the prayer to the prophet that he might publish them to the people. Though it is apparent that this angel receives an answer, its contents are not revealed. Still, from the Lord's manner it was evident to the prophet that in substance it consisted of "good words, even comforting words." The apposition *nichummîm* is particularly emphatic, being a noun, "comforts" (*G.K.* 131c). Interpreting thus, we see the apparent irregularity of procedure solve itself very acceptably, and the objection need not be raised: "We know nothing of the answer."

This (v. 14) is the sum of "the comforting words" as the interpreting angel himself communicates them to the prophet. They constitute a message that deserves to be proclaimed loudly, therefore, "Proclaim," *q^era',* a verb also used for "preaching." The message is of momentous import and is, therefore, to be introduced by, "thus says the Lord of hosts."

The substance of it is that God has given a token of divine
jealousy for His people. The verb *qinne'thî* is perfect, not
imperfect. It can scarcely be rendered, "I am jealous" (*A.V.*).
A Greek perfect would come nearer to expressing the shade
of meaning intended: "I have given a token of My jealousy
and am now eased" as the *Septuagint* translates—ἐζήλωκα. This
implies that, since others had wronged Israel whom He loved,
God had been stirred by a righteous desire to avenge the cause
of His people. He claims He has now done this and displayed
"great jealousy." The reference is apparently to some very
evident act of God's that is now completed. This must be an
allusion to that signal work that God did in bringing back
His people from captivity. With the Gentiles, who had sinned
very heavily in bringing Israel into the captivity and in many
things that they had done since that event, God here assures
Israel He now feels "very much angered." This is God's continuous attitude, for the present (*qotseph, Kal* active participle) has this force. This attitude on the part of God is in
itself a matter of sober comfort to Israel. For it had appeared
for some time as though the immunity of the heathen from
punishment would continue indefinitely. They were "at ease"
implies "carnal security," "proud ease." Their self-confidence
was in itself sinful.

Verse 15. The particular sin because of which the Gentiles
merited God's displeasure was that, when he was somewhat
(*me'aṭ*) angered at Israel and called upon the Gentiles to be
instruments for venting His wrath, "they on their part helped
forward unto disaster," spoken ironically. It was as though
He had summoned them to deliver Him from His people, but
they had done it in such a manner that it tended to evil
(*lera'ah*). They not only inflicted merited punishment; they
let their cruel ill-will rage till it was satiated, going to such
extremes that much evil had resulted. As a result there were
unsettled scores against the Gentiles. God gives assurance that
just retribution, that is to say, justice, shall prevail.

The positive favors that Jerusalem shall receive as a part of
the adjustment to be made must yet be unfolded more fully
in the following verses 16, 17.

Notice that there is a somewhat modest tone about the things promised to the people. All of them are blessings, very substantial blessings besides, but there is nothing about these promises that rises to the heights of the marvelous promises spoken by Isaiah in the latter part of his book and even, for that matter, by Haggai, who set forth rather glorious achievements. However, this attitude of Zechariah's is to be explained as follows: the rich fulness of God's blessings held in store for His people God does portray through Isaiah and Haggai. The people, none too expert in spiritual understanding, often failed to discern that Isaiah included everything in his portrayal, even the ultimate fulfillment in the new heavens and the new earth. Some of Zechariah's contemporaries, filled with a kind of religious enthusiasm, which was in a measure fired by Haggai's words, apparently expected every last promise to be realized at once and, when this fulfillment failed to appear, were tempted to question whether anything would be achieved. God, therefore, lets Zechariah depict largely that part of the future which the next years up to the Messiah's coming would realize. Everything is stated very soberly and so tempers the extravagant opinions that some, who misread prophecy, held.

These are the blessings to be expected in hope: "I have turned back to Jerusalem with kindness." This is the substance of all that follows. God had previously turned from His people in strong disfavor. That attitude of His is now at an end. Like the warmth of the sun when it shines directly on a man, so is the warmth of God's mercies when He regards a man with favor and causes His face to shine upon such a one. His face is here described as being turned back toward Jerusalem. The individual blessings that will be received are: a) "My house shall be built." On this matter Zechariah continues and supplements the efforts Haggai, and all who share in this work of building the Lord's house have the promise of success. And b) "the surveyor's line shall be stretched over Jerusalem." The surveyors will measure where streets and houses shall be located. The miserable heaps of ruins shall be a thing of the past.

Verse 17. Two additional blessings are touched upon in this verse in which '*ôdh,* "yet" or "again," appears four times to signify, that though everything points to the contrary, *yet* God's purposes shall be achieved.

In the series of four blessings which are mentioned in v. 16, 17 the third is c) "My cities will again overflow with prosperity." This blessing is separately set forth by the introductory words: "Again proclaim." *Q*ᵉ*ra',* "proclaim" or "preach" or "cry aloud." If cities are to experience such a transformation that from being wretched, half-inhabited ruins they become actual cities, even cities which God claims as His own (*'aray,* "My cities"), cities, furthermore, overflowing "with good" (*miṭṭobh*), or as we should say, "with prosperity," then, surely, such a prospect merits proclamation for the encouragement of the downcast. In addition, this proclamation is reinforced by a solemn: "Thus says the Lord of hosts."

The fourth blessing, d) is a double one. It includes a double comfort for Zion-Jerusalem. The two parts of it are closely synonymous, and we, therefore, list them as one. The first is: "the Lord will again comfort Zion." Words of this type are spoken when a nation stands in need of them. Zion was comfortless. God assures her that His comforts will not be wanting. The second: He "will again choose Jerusalem." This does not indicate something absolutely new. Jerusalem had been chosen as the city of God in David's day. This choice was annulled by the Babylonian Captivity. It is now spoken of as again being put into force. In reality it is no new choice but the old one again or "still" (*'ôdh*) prevailing. The promise practically means: My choice of this city still prevails.

The first vision concludes with a heartening prospect for God's people. They are at the same time made aware of the fact that supernatural agencies have been set into motion to bring God's good promises to fruition.

We also sense behind the face value of these statements references to truths of a most enduring character. These supernatural agencies are always at work to correct evils and to mete out justice to wicked offenders. The angel of God always intercedes for the people of God. God is jealous for His Holy City and His people, and Jerusalem continually remains the object of His choice.

Many writers are inclined to regard vv. 16 and 17 as a later insertion, whether from earlier words of the prophet and made by the prophet himself, or as supplementary material by a later redactor. This conclusion is based partly on the fact that to convey the word of the Lord v. 16 and 17a speak of the Lord in the first person whereas 17b uses the third person. However, such a change of persons is rightly described by *Rignell* as a "a common occurrence in Hebrew." The unity of the passage is the best guarantee of the integrity of the text.

The Second Vision (1:18–21; Heb. 2:1–4)

The Four Horns and the Four Smiths

Thus far nothing definite has been revealed concerning the fate of Israel's enemies except that the Lord is "very much angered" with them (1:15). A fuller revelation of what this implies is in order. This vision provides it. The close coherence of these visions appears in the fact that this second vision unfolds negatively one of the features of the first. Therefore no specific date is affixed: 1:7 includes also this vision (*Mitchell*).

If it be shown very distinctly just what God is able to do to those who in bitterness oppose and harm His people, such a revelation serves greatly to encourage the faith of His people, for it shows how entirely God knows the outcome of all issues, and how completely all results lie in His hand and His purpose.

There is about this vision also something that lifts it above the purely local and temporal. With a very definite revelation for Israel in its difficult situation at that time is combined an element of timelessness, which makes these visions repositories of truths that are equally valid for all times.

✠

vs. 18–21   [18] And I raised my eyes and looked, and lo, there were four horns. [19] And I said to the angel that talked with me, What are these? And he said to me: These are the horns

> that have scattered Judah, Israel, and Jerusalem. [20] Then
> the Lord showed me four smiths. [21] Then said I: What are
> these going to do? And he spoke, saying: These are the
> horns which scattered Judah, so that no man dared lift
> up his head; but these have come to frighten them away,
> to throw to the earth the horns of the nations which lifted
> up their horn against the land of Judah to scatter it.

A good approach to all these visions is to regard them as to the scenes and the action they represent as being like unto clear-cut pictures thrown upon a screen with a certain amount of action on the part of the characters and a certain amount of conversation portrayed, but all shown and done with the express understanding that deeper truths are being revealed in a kind of pantomine, if you will. But lest man fail utterly in apprehending rather clear visions a handy interpreter is provided to answer each difficult question as it arises.

Much needless confusion is caused in an interpretation of this vision by trying to identify certain of the characters mentioned with certain others of those appearing on the scene. By keeping each one named distinct, we keep the whole vision more nearly in the sphere of the simple sequence of things that is in reality offered. Again textual criticism causes needless difficulty. As soon as the method of making questionable corrections of the Masoretic Hebrew text comes to be the favorite method of removing difficulties, commentators are indeed in harmony with the prevalent procedure of the day but are not safe guides. In no case does the result they arrive at recommend itself as more feasible than does a sober Scriptural exposition of the very text as we find it. Textual difficulties are not to be removed by violent excision but are to be reverently expounded. Occasionally, of course, good textual criticism can be of help.

Verse 18. "I raised my eyes" is a common formula for introducing new visions (2:1; 5:1; 6:1; Dan. 8:3, etc.). The particular item that challenges attention first is "four horns." Attempts to secure more facts than the vision offers have led to interpretations such as a) conceiving them as being attached to steers, or b) as growing out of the ground, or c) as being alone visible because the cattle are grazing in tall grass which hides all but the horns. The vision purposely shows only horns in order to make fewer but more distinct impressions. Generally speaking, "horns," when used figuratively, typify power and strength (Amos 6:13; Jer. 48:25). True, in Daniel, for example (Dan. 8:3), they specifically stand for mighty world-powers. But in this passage the difficulty would be to pick out the four powers that "*have* scattered Judah." Many labored efforts have been made to make the findings in Daniel tally with this vision, but not very successfully. Or even if four is taken as the number of the world and is thought of as embracing the world-powers from every quarter of the globe, whether an exact four or fewer or more happen to be found engaged in harming God's people, even then not everything is included that the figures embrace. The best interpretation is that which, like *Buhl's*, lets qe'ren be "the symbol of world-*power*," not "*powers*." Then not only the nations as such are to be thought of but also every power, or resource, or effort that the world at large mobilizes to harm or destroy God's people. Our vision is all-embracing enough to include all this.

The prophet might have ultimately arrived at a solution of what the horns stand for by himself, but the fuller certainty that is so much desired would have been wanting. Therefore he appeals to the interpreting angel, who, it now appears, is discerned by him as also being present and is not specifically introduced because the question addressed to him indicates sufficiently that he was there. He affirms: "These are the horns that have scattered Judah." *Powers doing destructive work on God's people*—that is the substance of his explanation.

More difficult is the group of names chosen: "Judah, Israel, and Jerusalem." Even if one wanted to think of the divided kingdom and of the harm done by heathen powers to both its parts, it would be impossible to see what "Jerusalem" was to signify in that connection. More difficulty is occasioned by the fact that no connective stands between "Judah" and "Israel" though there is one between "Israel" and "Jerusalem." Also by the fact that the sign of the accusative appears before "Judah" and "Israel" and not before "Jerusalem." This situation is fully met by the following explanation: "Israel" is here used as *a name of honor* for Judah (therefore *'eth* before each and no connective); and with Israel, Jerusalem is coupled (by the connective *waw* and by placing one *'eth* before both) as the center against which all hostility was primarily directed. That the term "Israel" is used not infrequently for Judah even after the division of the kingdom appears from passages such as II Chron. 12:1; 15:17; 19:8; 21:2, 4; 23:2; 24:5, etc. (*Keil*).

Verse 20. That it is now said, *"The Lord* showed me," merely stresses the fact that the entire experience is not simply a work of self-originated reflection on the prophet's part. God is throughout the originator of the whole experience of Zechariah. *"Four* smiths" most manifestly correspond to the *four* horns, and they must represent mighty agents whose ability extends over the wide world. They represent the powers God puts into the field in opposition to those which the world devises to harm His people. As the four horns are not limited to some world-powers but include them all, so the four smiths are, least of all, to be limited to world-powers such as, for example, punish other world-powers by overcoming them, but include such agents and much more besides, namely, also God's resources for Israel's protection. Again, not only Israel and its immediate needs are under consideration but all God's people for all time.

Charash, the word for "smith," may mean a worker in wood as, e.g., the *Septuagint* translated, or a worker in stone or in iron as the circumstances here would make a more desirable meaning. *Koehler* gives as the first meaning *Handwerker*, "artisan." The two schools of thought here involved are represented respectively by the A.V. which translates "carpenters" and *Luther* who renders the word *Schmiede*. Those who advocate the former interpretation (cf., *Barnes*) feel it necessary to introduce an extraneous element in that they assume that the "carpenters" have come "to finish the work of panelling the House." The very earnestness of purpose which marks their coming and is stamped on their entire attitude is then supposesd to frighten away the opposition: "before this display of resolution the 'horns' are put to flight." Such an approach does not carry conviction. The one we advocate above, following *Luther,* is more in conformity with the other features of the text.

Verse 21. One of the most noticeable features of the vision is the fact that the smiths do not merely appear on the scene but come with the manifest purpose of doing something. They come for action, which we might visualize by suggesting that some gesture of theirs, like hammers raised ready to fetch a blow, was very prominent. (That they are equipped with hammers may well be inferred from Isa. 44:12). For the prophet, having been shown the smiths, at once inquires: "What are these going to do?" *Luther* translates: *"Was wollen die machen?"*

The answer the prophet receives is not, in its first part, acceptable to the critics. Because they set the fixed canon that every answer must at once refer definitely to the chief issue raised in the question, and since they do not find that to be the case here, they surmise that we here have a corrupted text. However, the matter is so very natural as it is reflected in the answer given. In order to stress the fact that some action on the part of God or mediately on the part of the smiths is necessary and so to answer the double question of Why? and What? the reply indicates first how cruel was the work of devastation or "scattering" wrought upon Judah. It had, in fact, advanced to the point "that no man dared lift up his head." *Kephî,* "so that," is, indeed, here used consecutively, *K (S)* 395, d. The figurative expression, "not lifting up the head," signifies utter dejection and hopelessness. So low was Judah brought that men despaired and sat, as it were, with bowed head, not caring what happened, nor expecting that anything favorable to them would happen. Nations, like Judah, may deserve punishment. They do merit it so certainly that God's agents are pictured as being ready to administer it.

Now comes the answer to the *"What?"* "These have come to frighten them away." "Fray" (*A.V.*) has the same meaning. Because they expected a different reply, those who are critically minded almost with one accord sense some textual defect. A satisfactory explanation has long ago and repeatedly been offered. It requires but moderate intelligence to discover that there is something inappropriate about *smiths terrifying horns*. But that is so self-evident that even careless copyists would scarcely have written this had they not sensed that the explanation of the vision plays over into the interpretation of the vision. *Koenig* (W) framed a very adequate formula for this when he labelled it *aufklaerendes Interpretament*, i.e., "explanation plus interpretation." Everyone notes the thought unless he is bent on displaying ingenuity along the line of conjectural criticism of the Hebrew text. It is this: First, God's agents of vengeance, when they come, will strike terror into the hearts of those who grievously afflicted God's children.

In the same breath, without the insertion of a conjunction—to indicate how directly this second work attaches itself to the first—we are told that the smiths are come "to throw to the earth the horns of the nations." This, in a way, is the most direct answer to the question, "What?" Smiths, no doubt equipped with hammers, facing each man a horn, will without doubt crush the horns and utterly beat them to the ground. This all interpreters understand; but the rest of the answer does not have confused issues as is claimed. It has made the strict necessity of such an act apparent. Clever emendations like that of *Orelli*, following the *Septuagint*, have very serious deficiencies. *Orelli* suggests for "to terrify them," "to sharpen their swords." Five separate vowel changes in the Hebrew text are necessary to get this meaning. But see the incongruity. Instead of suggesting how easily and adequately God can rectify wrongs it represents God's agents as being somewhat unready for the tasks God assigns them: they must needs first sharpen (!) their swords. Besides, swords used upon horns—a certain impropriety is involved; this is not the proper tool for such an act. The most charitable thing we can say for the translation τοῦ ὀξῦναι of the *Septuagint* is that it misread the Hebrew.

The words, "which lifted up their horn against the land of Judah," especially the phrase "lift up their horn," suggest arrogance on the part of Israel's oppressors.

Those interpreters who believe that much of what the Bible offers is, like the ancient literature of other nations, the outgrowth of a legendary and mythical past find here (like *Sellin*) in the smiths an indication of "a cursed trade" (*fluchbeladenes Handwerk*) according to a "fixed mythological conception." Nevertheless, by these same interpreters the smiths are supposed to be, according to Zechariah's conception of them, "angelic beings." The gods of antiquity are also referred to, who carry hammer and axe. Such views reduce the Scriptures to the level of literature such as other nations produced, at least as far as its method of origination is concerned.

One feature of the vision, its chief purpose, however, can scarcely be misunderstood. God has adequate resources for curbing all powers wheresoever on this world they may appear in an effort to harm His people. As little as horns can hold their own before powerful smiths, so little can God's enemies lastingly prevail over God's people.

Chapter II

The Third Vision (2:1–13; Heb. 2:5–17)

The Man with the Measuring Line

The positive side of the first vision (1:7–17) indicated (1:16, 17) that God would in due time bring about the rebuilding of Jerusalem and days of prosperity for her. Few who heard or read this prophecy interpreted it in terms of spiritual values or had an adequate conception of the greatness of the truths involved. Therefore, the fuller interpretation of these items for the purpose of removing misconceptions was very much in order. The third vision provides the needed elucidation. From this it is again evident how closely the visions belong together. The difficulties involved are again largely matters of detail.

The verses 6–13 are not to be regarded as a later appendage to the vision. They are the section in which the spiritual greatness of God's city is unfolded to the full, the substance to which the vision was largely introductory. It will always be a precarious contention to assert that a certain section is not an original part of a passage but was added later. Such decisions are so largely dependent on subjective viewpoints that men should readily discern how impossible of convincing proof such assertions are.

✠

vs. 1–5

¹ And I raised my eyes and looked, and lo, there was a man with a measuring line in his hand. ² Then said I: Where are you going? And he said: To measure Jerusalem to see how broad it is to be and how long. ³ And, lo, the angel that talked with me went forth to meet him, ⁴ and said to him: Run, speak to the young man yonder, saying: Jerusalem shall be as open villages by reason of the multi-

52

tude of men and cattle therein. **5** For I will be to her—
utterance of the Lord—a wall of fire round about, and
I will be the glory in the midst of her.

A new vision begins; cf., "I raised my eyes" with remarks on
1:18; also introductory remarks on 1:7. For the shortened form
wa'ere' see *GK* 49, 2b and 75, 6, Re.

Attempting no unwarranted combinations, we observe that
the one whom the prophet discovers is described merely as "a
man" (*'îsh*). Though this may mean about as much as "an individual" and may designate an angel as the "man" in 1:8 by
virtue of his position is discovered to be; here, however, the
reference is unclear. We shall do best, therefore, to consider
him only "a man," all the more so since the angels appearing
later are so distinctly labelled as angels.

This man has a "measuring line in his hand." Though the
word used (*che'bhel middah*) is different from that used in
1:16 (*qaw*), yet the difference is unimportant. The Hebrew
word used in this passage designates a cord as a means of bind-
ing (*chabhal*); the word used in 1:16 indicates a cord as a
twisted thing (*qawah*). To prevent all misconception the cord
is here distinctly labelled as a "cord for measuring."

The prophet's interest is aroused. It is so clearly the man's
purpose to do some measuring that the prophet feels impelled
to ask, "Whither goest thou?" implying, of course, "to do your
measuring." What the prophet implies the man states when
he says: "To measure Jerusalem." This is clear enough, but
the following words have occasioned much investigation. The
question arising is: Is the Jerusalem to be measured the actual
or the future city? Or is he measuring Jerusalem as she now is
or as she is to be? Very much depends on the answer. The actual circumstances give us the proper directives. We found the
time of these visions to be February, 519 B.C. Jerusalem's walls
were not going to be rebuilt until the year 444 B.C., when
Nehemiah returned. Before the walls of the city are completed
and their position defined, no one can measure them even
though it be claimed (*Keil*) that, "to measure what is the

breadth and length" must apply to a city as she is. This last contention is not an entirely exact translation. The expression is not "to see what," etc. (*lîr'ôth mah*) but "to see *about* what," etc. (*lîr' ôth kammah*). He is going out to compute about how large the city of the future *is to be*. This point of view agrees with what follows.

Verse 3. Thus far two characters have appeared on the scene in the vision—if it be permissible to class the prophet among those appearing in the vision—the man with the measuring line and the prophet. Two more appear: first the interpreting angel, then an angel that goes forth to meet him. There is nothing unusual about this, for the angel that goes forth with authority assigns a task to the interpreting angel, who has repeatedly been speaking to our prophet. Why should he (the interpreting angel) not speak to another man? The critical approach first creates an unnecessary difficulty, then alters the text to escape the difficulty, and finally offers a new thought that is foreign to the text. The insurmountable obstacle to a correct understanding is said to be the fact that two angels going forth "meet" one another. The difficulty grows out of the failure to make proper allowances. If the basic demand is laid down that the word "go forth" (*yotse'*) of necessity demands that both men went forth at the same point, then a satisfactory solution is out of the question. But if these two angels met, the assumption is forced upon us that they went forth, as it were, from opposite sides of the stage.

Verse 4. The second angel is apparently clothed with authority to direct the interpreting angel. This suggests a higher rank on the part of the former. As this Scripture passage unfolds, especially in v. 11, it appears as though the angel speaks in the name and by the authority of the Lord. He might be the Angel of the Lord, yet he prefaces his statements with "says the Lord" (v. 5, 6, 8) so that every instance following may also be explained on the score that we have direct discourse in the words of God. No definite conclusion can apparently be arrived at. The main issues are certain: the angel delivers his message, and the Lord adds His promises. These facts remain the same whether this angel is the Angel of the Lord or not.

One of the major issues of the passage is to determine the identity of him who is to be the recipient of the message given through the interpreting angel, namely, the personage designated as "the young man yonder" (*hannă'ar hallaz*); on *hallaz* see *GK* 34, 2R2. Many commentators take him to be the prophet himself and on this designation base their supposition that the prophet must have been comparatively young at the time he received these messages. However, if this were the case, "the man with the measuring line" would have appeared on the scene and disappeared without a definite purpose. We should be able to make scarcely anything of his role in the vision. It would be as though one of the characters introduced were lost in the shuffle. *G. A. Smith* remarked in regard to the first vision: "We must not expect lucidity in a phantasmagoria like this." Besides, the prophet would become almost a major character in the vision whereas his role is throughout only that of a spectator who never advances into the vision beyond the point of inquiring for or of receiving needed elucidation.

Far more appropriate is the interpretation which has the angel's message given to "the man with the measuring line." He who was first called "man" (*'ish*) is now more closely described as a "young man" (*nă'ar*). Besides, a very excellent agreement is established between what he purposed to do and the directions that deter him from doing it. He wants to measure the city as he thinks it will be or is to be. But that is unnecessary. The walls that mark the city's boundaries will not be needed, for the city "shall be as open villages," (*perazôth*, an accusative of specification; *vid. GK* 118, 5; cf., Esther 9:19; Ezra 38:11). These are not strictly "villages without walls" (*A.R.V.*); they are the open country which never needs walls.

The "young man," therefore, represents the average opinion of the day. He believes that the city will be rebuilt. But his conception of the city of God is poured into too small a mould. He fails to discern the far greater things that God has promised. He cannot as yet see that God has destroyed the historic Jerusalem in order to build "the Jerusalem that is above." He must learn to think of the Jerusalem of God in far grander terms. Walls cannot confine her "by reason of the multitude of men and cattle therein." Many more creatures shall inhabit her than Zechariah's contemporaries ever dreamed of. We gain little by claiming, as *Barnes* does, that, when the city lay without walls for another sixty years, Zechariah's policy was being followed. Not policy but weakness determined that situation.

We misunderstand the prophet if, on the one hand, we believe that he taught that the walls of the city would not be needed in the immediate future. That is inexcusable literalism attributed to the prophet in spite of v. 5ff. Equally wide of the mark is the literal understanding of the "men and cattle" as though the prophet thought that a tremendous multitude would cover the land. In days of old cities did harbor cattle as well as people; cf., Jer. 33:10, 13; Jonah 4:11; Ps. 144:13. Zechariah is speaking of the ideal Jerusalem—the church—and of an ideal dwelling in her—membership in the church of God. *Luther* certainly offered a queer interpretation when he tried to press a meaning out of the term "cattle" by suggesting that it meant Christians who are less sturdy in their faith. (Similar passages would be Isa. 2:2–4; Ps. 87; Isa. 60, etc.).

Verse 5. The fact that spiritual issues are involved and not material growth and external prosperity is best established by this verse. God's indwelling explains why walls shall no longer be needed: He is Zion's full and adequate protection, being like unto "a wall of fire about her." Surely, the Lord is a far more adequate protection than is fire. His omnipotence is perfect safety. What the pillar of cloud was for Israel when it came and laid itself between Israel and the Egyptians at the Red Sea (Exod. 14:19) that will God be in richest measure. That is an abiding reality which holds good for the church for all times. Her protection against foes is perfect. Besides, her glory is splendid. God in the midst of her is her glory. Even as the pillar of cloud was identical with the "glory of the Lord" in the wilderness days, so God's mere presence with His people is in itself unspeakable glory.

Not a few narrow-minded Israelites of Zechariah's time had too limited a conception of the future glories of Jerusalem. Those interpreters, too, offer an unsatisfactory interpretation of this passage who, like *Smith,* allegorize the walls to mean dogmas, etc.

One peculiar misunderstanding of the problem of this section, v. 1–4, is that of *Sellin* who first identifies the "man" with an angel and then, when another angel is sent to rectify the limited and erroneous conception of the angel (!) with the measuring line, reasons that this fact affords ground for a new contribution to our doctrine concerning angels, namely, that the angels' having a degree of independence of action may result in occasional errors on their part and, besides, result in the need of correction by angels of higher rank—a view which is practically only a repristination of the errors of *Dionysius,* which *Luther* condemns.

The future greatness of Zion is too important a subject to be quickly dismissed. Various aspects of it should yet be unfolded; therefore verses 6–13 follow, which are very much in place at this point, and for just this reason. The mere fact that such a continuation of the subject is no longer cast in the form of a vision does not militate against our contention. The use of one style of portrayal does not bind a man irrevocably to that style. The claims of all who, like *Mitchell,* contend that to treat v. 6–13 "as part of the preceding vision must be abandoned" are not solidly grounded but grow out of the tendencies of divisive criticism.

✣

vs. 6–13   **6** Ho! Ho! flee from the land of the north—utterance of the Lord—for I shall spread you abroad as the four winds of the heavens—utterance of the Lord. **7** Ho! Zion, escape, thou that dwellest with the daughter of Babylon. **8** For thus says the Lord of hosts: After glory He has sent Me to the nations which plundered you; for he that touches you, touches the apple of His eye. **9** For, lo, I shall wave My hand over them, and they shall be a spoil to their subjects; and you shall know that the Lord of hosts has sent Me. **10** Exult and rejoice, O daughter of Zion; for, lo, I will come and dwell in the midst of thee, says the Lord. **11** And many nations shall attach themselves to the Lord in that day and shall be My people; and I will dwell in the midst of you, and you shall know

that the Lord has sent Me to you. **12** And the Lord shall
inherit Judah as His portion in the holy land and shall
again choose Jerusalem. **13** Be silent, all flesh, before the
Lord. For He has bestirred Himself from His holy
dwelling.

The purpose of this passage is most readily understood if
attention is fixed on the sentence, "I shall spread you abroad,"
v. 6. The Hebrew has *a prophetic perfect;* it is, therefore, not
to be rendered, "I *have* spread you abroad." Back of this rendering lies the mistaken conception of its meaning. *Paras,* almost without exception, signifies "to spread out" like a
garment or like the hands. Whether the meaning "to scatter"
is ever proper is doubtful. Therefore we do not here have a
reference to the dispersion of Israel which took place in the
past but an amplification of the idea expressed in 1:17 and 2:4
of the *future expansion* of the people. God's people shall be
spread out, the true Israel, of course, "as the four winds of the
heavens." This is not a phrase which "refuses to yield sense"
(Sellin) but a forceful way of stating that, as the four winds,
when they spread out, reach every part of the world, so extensive shall be the expansion of God's people.

If these are the gracious purposes that He holds in store for
them, the exhortation given in v. 6, 7 falls into its proper place.
Since God desires to spread them abroad, they should flee from
the impending destruction of Babylon so that they may be
available to be spread abroad. "The land of the north" is without doubt Babylon as Jer. 1:14; 6:22; 10:22, etc., indicate. For
though it is not directly north of Palestine, invasions coming
from Babylon always had to enter the land from the north.
The subsidiary thought is in this instance the certainty of the
destruction of this outstanding foe of Israel.

Our interpretation is further established by the fact that the
summons addressed to those of Israel who still dwelt in these
lands is not a summons to return to Jerusalem but a summons
to "flee" and "escape" as from impending ruin. The thought
receives double emphasis by the use of a double *ne'um
Yahweh,* "utterance of the Lord." *Hoy,* "Ho," is hortative;
"anfeuerndes," Sellin; it is not to be translated *Schmach,*

"shame," *Lange*. "Zion" in v. 7 by metonymy signifies all true believers of the Word of God in Israel. "Daughter of Babylon" signifies the people of the realm of Babylon in an ideal personification of one figure's representing a race.

From this point onward throughout the chapter there is a peculiar change of subject; sometimes the Lord speaks as the Lord; sometimes concerning the Lord. Apparently, *Hengstenberg* suggests, this is for the purpose of indicating, on the one hand, the identity of this "Angel of the Lord" with the Lord and, on the other hand, a personal distinction from Him. But the fact that the Angel of the Lord speaks frequently in v. 6–13 does not yet identify Him with one of the angels mentioned in v. 1–5, particularly with the "other angel," v. 3, for everything that is stated from v. 4 onward may be the word of the Lord as the interpreting angel conveyed it to Zechariah.

In verse 8 the statement, "thus says the Lord of hosts," introduced by a *koh,* does not refer backward, for *koh* is seldom a retrospective "thus." This statement is the solemn introduction of what follows.

It must plainly be the Angel of the Lord who says: "After glory hath He sent Me." But what is "after glory," *'achar kabhodh?* The Angel of the Lord is speaking, and He says that He was commissioned to "go unto the nations which plundered Israel" and acquire glory through vanquishing and subduing them. One of the proper works of the Savior is "to put all His enemies under His feet," and those who are enemies of His people are enemies of His. To subdue such and put to naught their wicked devices is a work that redounds unto His *glory*. This is the glory He refers to.

We observe how very dearly the welfare of His people concerns the Lord. It is here stated thus: "He that touches you touches the apple of His eye." Because whatever touches the eyeball is felt to be very painful, and every man most sedulously guards this organ, therefore is this figure chosen. The rash handling of Israel pains God, and, therefore, He protects His people.

Verse 9. In the acquisition of this glory for which He is sent the Angel of the Lord will not need to toil at subduing His foes. It will be only a matter of waving His hand. He merely indicates by a gesture what He wills, and it is done. Such is His omnipotence. As a result, those who had been the victors now become a spoil to those who had served them as Israel had. If the status of nations is radically altered with such ease, surely that is "glory." By such achievements of His which those who know the Lord can understand as being wrought by Him whom God hath sent, they on their part recognize His divine mission. This does not refer only to political deliverance but more essentially to spiritual deliverance, by which, whenever it is achieved, God's own are made aware of His mighty works.

It is not necessary to depart from the more basic meaning of the verb *menîph* (from *nûph*) which means "to wave," "to move to and fro." That conveys the thought of how simple a thing such restitution of His own is. Other meanings like "shake" (*A.V.*) and "brandish" (*BDB*) are well enough established but lose the simplicity of the thought. Nothing essential is gained by connecting this gesture, as *Sellin* does, with gestures of sorcery: "the waving of the hand is originally (*von Haus aus*) a gesture of the sorcery trial," or for purposes of healing or warding off demons (*Horst*). Such gestures can have meanings entirely their own apart from sorcery.

The blessings that God achieves for His people are of such a kind as to make the recipients of them exceedingly glad. Therefore v. 10 brings this forcibly to our attention. The greatest blessing of all, that is the source of all the rest just mentioned, dare not be lost sight of. It is the one that is the supreme cause of joy: "I will come and dwell in the midst of thee, says the Lord." Immediate fellowship with God is the glorious prospect. It is pointed to with a "lo" and emphasized by a *ne'um Yahweh*, "utterance of the Lord." For mortals, who are sinners, to have such favors promised is surely sufficient to stir up rare jubilation. But the Lord, knowing the slothfulness of the human heart rightly to praise Him for His greatest mercy, prods men unto a proper readiness. As *Keil* well remarks: this coming begins with the incarnation and completes itself in the last judgment.

Unnecessary distinctions are made when it is claimed that

v. 10 is a word of the Lord, but v. 11–13 are a word of the prophet. In fact, from v. 5 onward to the end of the chapter we have the word of the Lord as the interpreting angel revealed it to the prophet. Nor may we class this one verse (v. 10) as "a lofty conception but narrow withal" on the score that "the new temple at Jerusalem is the shrine and the only one of the God of the whole earth" (*Mitchell*). Verse 11 alone would suggest a broader point of view. When there is no longer only one nation but "many nations" that "shall join themselves unto the Lord in that day," one would naturally expect such other limitations as were characteristic of the old covenant days to pass away. Indeed, the second half of the verse specifically asserts that, when these many nations join themselves to the Lord, God's Angel or the Lord shall, indeed, dwell in the midst of "thee," Israel. Israel shall hereby recognize that the Angel of the Lord was definitely one commissioned by God. The mighty results shall prove the presence of the mighty author of them all.

But v. 13 just as certainly pictures Him as going forth out of His holy habitation. In early days it had pleased Him to let the sanctuary at Jerusalem be the only place where His presence was guaranteed to His people. The Lord was pleased, for Israel's good, to limit Himself thus. This last verse of the chapter pictures the end of that economy of grace—God *leaving* "His holy dwelling." The fact that this involves all flesh and is not of special moment to Israel only appears from the summons to "all flesh" to "be silent before the Lord."

Nor does v. 12 stay within narrow limits as might at first seem to be the case. Standing between the two verses just discussed, v. 12 must regard "Judah" and "Jerusalem" as a designation of His people wherever they may be found. So also "the holy land" is not specifically Palestine but every place where God manifests Himself. So the verse becomes a glorious testimony that the Lord's unwavering faithfulness shall be displayed toward those who truly merit to be called His.

In commenting on these verses *Lange*, rightly says: "The very mystery of salvation is that He has bestirred Himself out of His holy habitation and has already left the limitation of the Temple in order to reveal His honor also unto the Gentiles." It is for this reason that v. 13 summons all flesh to behold and to give heed to this solemn opportunity in reverent silence. Such an event is for all Gentiles a rare good fortune which should not be lost.

Ne'ôr is Nifal from '*or*, G.K. 72, 9.

Chapter III

The Fourth Vision

The Vindication of the High Priest, Joshua

Before we proceed, note how little confidence men have in the Hebrew text as it now stands. This may be judged from the following example: *Barnes,* who is for the most part conservatively minded, suggests a "general scheme for the rearrangement" of the material of the visions from this point onward as follows:

4:1–6a
10b–14
6b–10a
3:1–9a
6:9–15a
5:1–11
3:9b, 10
6:1–8

One marvels at the supposed carelessness of Hebrew scribes who shuffled portions of the text around indiscriminately and without apparent reason. Evidence is available that no copyists ever did their work more meticulously than did the Hebrew scribes. From such rearrangements as the one here indicated it is evident that one can make passages mean almost anything. One clever arrangement is as good as another, depending on what one supposes a writer should have said. Such procedures are not valid exegesis. One's real concern should be first to enter sympathetically into the meaning of the text as it now stands.

Manifold comforts and guarantees of the future success and prosperity of Israel had been provided by the preceding visions. But from still another angle Israel needed reassurance. When the nation regarded its own moral state, its hopes might well have been dashed to the ground because there was first the heavy weight of accumulated guilt of past centuries that had finally driven Israel into captivity. Then there were many instances of individual shortcomings that marred life and character. The serious-minded among the people might well have felt that their personal holiness did not merit any of the Lord's great promises, in fact, might even frustrate the realization of them. Timid consciences needed comfort and the reinvigoration of their hope. This is what this vision provides, in fact, provides through the Messiah to come.

At first glance, however, the vision seems to be concerned only with Joshua and his specific needs. It might also seem unreasonable to expect that among visions that have had a broad bearing upon the whole nation one vision should be furnished that specifically applies to an individual whose role in Israel's life was not signally important in any sense and important only because he was a high priest.

We are, therefore, under necessity of looking for broader aspects of the truth. We find them in the fact that the high priest held a position that was representative of the people. The fact that he is here under consideration in this representative capacity is clear from the double use of the full title "the high priest" (v. 1 and 8) in this chapter. He represents and practically impersonates Israel in his holy office. For the nation he prays; for it he enters into the Most Holy Place; he bears the nation's guilt. We must, therefore, not refer the issues and the implications of this chapter to Joshua as an individual, nor merely to Joshua, the high priest. We must conclude that *his* condition is *Israel's* condition, *his* acquittal a typical way of expressing *theirs;* the words of comfort and assurance given to *him* apply with equal validity to *them.* On the other hand, just as true as it is that he typifies the people, so true it is that he may at the same time consider the words he hears as being applicable also to himself. It will be best to offer a translation of the entire passage.

✠

vs. 1-10   ¹ And He showed me Joshua, the high priest, standing before the Angel of the Lord, and Satan standing at his right hand to oppose him. ² And the Lord said to Satan: The Lord rebuke you, O Satan: yea, the Lord that hath chosen Jerusalem rebuke thee! Is not this a brand snatched out of the fire? ³ Now Josua was clothed in filthy garments and was standing before the angel. ⁴ So He answered and spoke to those standing before Him: Take away the filthy garments from upon him. But unto him He said: Lo, I have removed your iniquity from you, and clothe you in splendid robes. ⁵ And I said: Let them set a clean turban on his head. So they set a clean mitre on his head and put clothes on him, and the Angel of the Lord was standing by. ⁶ And the Angel of the Lord solemnly testified to Joshua, saying: ⁷ Thus says the Lord of hosts: If you will walk in My ways and keep My charge, then also you shall govern My house and have charge of My courts, and I will give you free access among those that stand here. ⁸ Hear now, O Joshua, high priest, you and your friends that sit before you, you are men of a marvelous sign: for, lo, I am bringing forth My servant, the Branch. ⁹ For, lo, the stone that I have set before Joshua, upon one stone are seven eyes: lo, I will engrave the engraving of it—utterance of the Lord—and I will remove the iniquity of that land in one day. ¹⁰ In that day—utterance of the Lord of hosts—every man of you shall invite his neighbor under the vine and under the fig tree.

The person that showed this vision to the prophet (v. 1) is certainly the Lord Himself and not the interpreting angel, whose function it is rather to expound that which was previously shown the prophet by the Lord. Since every feature seen is a part of the vision, it is of deeper import; for that reason Joshua may also represent the people. Add to this argument and the remarks above the following: in v. 2 a reason for refusing to countenance the charges preferred is that God has chosen Jerusalem. Again, in v. 8 Joshua and his "fellows" are addressed, and a like position and like honors are ascribed to all of them. Lastly, v. 9 indicates that those who are to benefit by what is being set forth are the entire nation, for it is said that the iniquity of "that *land*" is to be forgiven.

This Joshua was the high priest at Zechariah's time as we learn from Hag. 1:1 and Ezra 5:2, and we shall meet him again in 6:11. Attempts to center the vision exclusively on Joshua and his person lead to certain other unnecessary difficulties. Thus, when it is observed that he is solemnly charged with misdemeanor, attempts are usually made to fix on some specific deeds. These attempts are, however, quite unsatisfactory, for we know little of his history. But when his representative position is kept in mind, we can more readily sense what the charges might involve: they are the current sins of that era.

Somewhat too much is made of the words that follow—especially "standing before the angel of the Lord" and "Satan standing at his right hand"—in an attempt to create a formal trial scene by regarding these as technical terms that are descriptive of juridical procedure. "Standing before the angel of the Lord" is said to be a phrase that is descriptive of a court scene on the basis of Ps. 109:6, "Let an adversary stand at his right hand." The oft-made claim that the plaintiff regularly took his place at the right hand of the defendant during a trial had better be dropped, for this is the only proof passage that can be adduced; especially since whatever proof v. 6 seems to offer is within the Psalm cancelled by v. 31. Besides, the first verb used, "to stand before," 'omedh liphney, in so many instances suggests the thought of standing at hand to serve the person who is named after liphney so that BDB gives as a rendering of this phrase "attend upon," "be(come) servant of"; see I Sam. 16:22; I Kings 1:2; in reference to the Lord: I Kings 17:1; 18:15; II Kings 3:14; 5:16; Jer. 15:19; in reference to priests: Deut. 10:8; Judg. 20:28; Ezra 44:15, etc. To this well-established usage the other, which is purely problematic, must yield. Rignell rightly remarks that "nothing in the terminology employed points to the idea that Joshua is on trial."

What the vision does represent is Joshua ministering unto the Angel of the Lord. How the prophet could detect that Joshua was engaged in the duties of his office need not trouble us—detect it he did, and he reported it. Nor does the fact of his ministering give us a clue as to the scene of the vision. Some interpreters think it to be heaven, others the Temple, others the city gate (where a trial might be held), this, however, the gate of the heavenly city. All such surmises are unimportant and without value. They merely encumber a picture which lets only the essentials appear.

While Joshua is engaged upon his ministration (*'omedh—* active participle) Satan is standing (also *'omedh*) and preferring his charges. Though *satan* has the article it is to be regarded as a proper noun; *K(S)* 295K. The noun and the verb used have the same root, which might be rendered: "the adversary was standing to play the part of an adversary"; (*lesiṭno,* with (*i*), see *G.K.* 61, 1R1). At Zechariah's time the designation "Satan" was well understood. Job 1:2 and I Chron. 21 throw light on the term. "Satan" does not, therefore, suggest "the justice of Jehovah as contrasted with His mercy" and so "the reproof of the adversary by the angel of Yahweh . . . the triumph of the milder attribute" (*Mitchell*). Such an interpretation is a guess and has well-established Scriptural usage against it. Besides, the verb *saṭan* implies *attack,* not *accusation* (*Rignell*).

It is a futile effort to try to determine what charges were raised by the adversary. The sins that characterized the age are plain enough. These the high priest as the people's representative certainly bore officially. Let each interpreter recall what he may; the text mentions none. There is, however, one feature that is rather noticeable: the silence of Joshua implies that he has nothing to say by way of defence; silence in the face of charges usually signifies guilt. Nor does God proclaim Joshua's innocence, for such a proclamation was apparently impossible. Yet the Lord can save the case of Joshua.

Verse 2. We meet the same situation that we noted in regard to 2:6–12, namely, that two characters appear who are, on the one hand, identical, on the other, distinct from one another. One is the earthly representative of the Lord, the Angel of the Lord; the other is the Lord Himself. Their identity is clear from the fact that they have the same authority, and that the Angel of the Lord does what God does. Their difference is chiefly a difference of work. It is like the intertrinitarian difference between the persons of the Trinity. What is so plainly set forth even in the Old Testament ought to be accepted.

There is no need to revise a good text by leaving out these very significant references to the Angel of the Lord and following the less competent guides who made the *Septuagint* translation. This type of textual criticism is governed by the maxim that is rightly repudiated by all textual critics: The *easier* reading deserves the preference. An example: To the first "the Lord" criticism prefixes the word "angel," because it would avoid the implications of the received text and claims that the statement involves an impossibility.

The person who replies to Satan's charges is very properly the Lord Himself, first, because it is *His* servant who has been attacked; second, because His servant stands helpless before true charges, the Lord must help him if Joshua is not to be proved guilty of them. We recognize "the Lord" in this case to be the Angel of the Lord, God's earthly representative. The fact that it must be He follows from His words which predicate in solemn double assurance what God will effectually do with the adversary. The Angel of the Lord does not take it upon Himself to visit the deserved punishment upon Satan, whose misdeed consists in viciously opposing God's servant. Such punishment does not fall in the category of duties devolving upon the *earthly* representative; it is not something that occurs in the earthly sphere. As each of the three persons has distinct operations, each works in His own sphere. Speaking in New Testament terms, the Son asserts that the Father will rebuke the adversary.

The repeated assertion indicates the certainty of the fulfillment of it. The imperfect *yigh'ar,* "he will rebuke," is to be regarded as a future rather than as an optative: "*may* he rebuke." Still better, since there is no emphasis on the fact that such a rebuke is to be administered at some future time, we do best to regard this as a present: "He rebukes." Yet God's rebuke is not a mere sharp word of displeasure, for His Word is "quick and powerful," and so it is the same as though actual punishment were inflicted upon the adversary, the plaintiff, and not on Joshua, the defendant. If some interpreters prefer the future rendering of *yigh'ar* they will see in it a reference to the overthrow of Satan by the Son of man in the days of His flesh.

The proof that Satan is in the wrong and Joshua is to be justified lies in the statement: "Is not this a brand snatched out of the fire?" God gives proof that what He does is proper by pointing out that the high priest stands under His favor: he has already been rescued, and that recently, from grave peril. Because of such a rescue the man must stand in God's grace, else God would not have shown him favor. This grace is Joshua's hope. Referring to him personally, we notice that Joshua had, as it were, experienced a narrow escape in the Exile. His grandfather, Seraiah, had been killed by Nebuchadnezzar, II Kings 25:18ff; Jer. 52:24ff. His father, Jehozadak, had been dragged away into exile, I Chron. 5:41–6:15. All those whose parents or who themselves survived the Exile were practically "brands snatched out of the fire," rescued, as it were, in the very last moment. These Joshua typifies. Now those to whom God had granted distinct favor are not to be victims of malicious slanders of the adversary. He wrongs them since God favors them. He charges God with having made a mistake in rescuing these "brands" and virtually asks that they again be cast into the fire. Let it not be overlooked that the state of the *people* is at stake. Joshua typifies the nation. He stands charged with the people's sins in a preliminary way even as does our Great High Priest at a later time.

In v. 3 the state of Joshua as he "was standing" (*'omedh— Kal* active participle, expressing continuation) before the angel is described as "being clothed" (*labhush*—also *Kal* participle) in "filthy garments." In both instances the participle draws attention to a continued state of being which seemed the more unseemly the longer it lasted. If one is but freshly "snatched out of the fire," how can he appear otherwise than as a man having many a mark of defilement upon him? The delivery from the Exile had restored Israel to its land, but the experience had left many a filthy stain on unworthy Israel. Because of a full measure of iniquity the Exile had finally come. During the Exile there were fresh occasions for contamination. Though the people had repented, marked traces of sin were still in evidence. In the vision this would appear on Israel's official representative, Joshua, as "filthy garments." God's answering (*wayya'an*), v. 4, is in reply to this *situation*, not to any remark or question that precedes. *'anah* often has this force.

Verse 2 had indicated God's readiness to show mercy unto Joshua and thus unto the people. Verse 4 now shows God actually bestowing this mercy. The act that follows is symbolical of the forgiveness of sins. As completely as a man whose filthy garments disfigure him is cleansed by their removal, so completely does God's pardon remove the guilt of sin. As the bestowing of garments of beauty makes a man presentable, so does the garment of imputed righteousness make him worthy to appear before God and man, only, however, by virtue of the "rich apparel" that God has granted him. This is God's own interpretation of His act as He addresses Joshua: "Lo, I have removed your iniquity from you." Strange to say, criticism has regarded this interpretation as an interpolation (*Mitchell*) that "betrays its origin by the disturbance it creates in the order of thought." Not only does it not create a disturbance in the order of thought; it is in reality the clearest feature of the thought, the key to the interpretation of the passage, and the gem verse in the vision. It offers a safeguard against an externalistic interpretation of the passage.

The passage and its purpose are obscured by the approach which finds at this point a reference to the Babylonian Adapa myth, an approach traceable to *Gressmann* (*Der Messias*, Göttingen 1929, p. 260). The approach is based on the fact that both passages contain a reference to filthy garments. Adapa, a mythical figure, is brought before the god of heaven to be tried for having in anger broken the wing of the southwind. For the whole tale see *Pritchard's, Ancient Near Eastern Texts*, (Princeton University Press 1950, pp. 101–103). Aside from this accidental similarity these two texts have nothing in common, and a reference to the Adapa myth is an obvious case of a reference to purely extraneous material.

Equally unsatisfactory is the approach of *Mowinckle* who,

referring to the obscure and unbiblical New Year's festival, cites the Babylonian custom of having the king on New Year's day deposit his insignia of office before the throne of Marduk and, clad in the garments of a penitent, make confession of his own sins and those of his people. Priests would then treat him in a humiliating fashion, and he would finally receive an absolution. *Mowinckle,* although he has no proof for it, says this unusual custom was observed also in Israel and assigns Joshua the role that the king would normally have. But, as *Rignell* quite properly emphasizes, it is not the prophet's purpose to describe something that constituted an important part of Israel's cultus but an occurrence that transpired in the counsel of Jehovah and was transmitted to the prophet and has bearing upon the new era into which Israel is about to enter.

Also unacceptable is the claim of some interpreters that, since sacrifice and offering are not mentioned, therefore God is able by the exercise of His sovereign will to cancel and forgive sin. They overlook the fact that the vision aims only to stress the truth that God is gracious and will pardon but does not aim to dwell on the question: How is this pardon made possible? Silence on this score is not a point of doctrine but an indication only that no one figurative presentation of a matter can exhaust all sides of it. This is one instance when the *argumentum e silentio* is misleading.

Another point must be noted—those who are commissioned with the removal of the filthy garments are described as "those standing before Him." Again we have the phrase *'omedh liphney,* signifying as it did in v. 1, "attend upon" or "be servant of." This serves as further corroboration of our interpretation of the phrase above (v. 1). Those referred to are the angels.

Deductions should not be made on the basis of this statement as to who are the agents that cleanse from sin. To assign a certain function to angels in this action would be without analogy of the Scriptures. Such features are only the scaffolding of the figurative passage and can afford no ground for doctrinal deductions.

But let us not lose sight of the fact that the symbolic clothing is a lesson for the *people* that, as their official representative is thus accepted by God, so are they.

The infinitive absolute (*halbesh*) continues the line of discourse after a finite verb, *K(S)*, 218b.

Machalatsoth correctly designates "splendid robes" or "rich apparel."

The completeness of that acceptance on God's part is to receive added emphasis in the verse that follows (v. 5).

A pleasant little episode is attached to this transaction. Though no mention had been made of a clean headdress or turban of the high priest as an item of clean raiment, we may well assume that that item of dress was covered by the general term "apparel." The prophet, vitally interested in the transaction and sensing its importance, is carried away by his intensity of interest and makes a personal request that this item be added ("fair" [*A.V.*] means "clean"). This is eloquent testimony to the eagerness with which he shared in all that was being revealed and to the graciousness of God who does not rebuke such zealous participation. The prophet is not made to feel that he has become guilty of unwarranted and presumptuous interference. A divine summons to supply this turban is the answer. We have preferred to translate what we have referred to as a "turban" by the term "mitre," for it is really the official headdress of the high priest that is implied, (*tsaniph*, practically identical with *mitsnépheth*).

The fact that the verse should begin, "And I said," has disturbed students of the Bible from days of old as the Latin and the Greek versions indicate. For a prophet to inject himself into a vision is no more unnatural at this place than it is in Amos 7:2, 5. Compare also Isa. 6:5 where the prophet breaks into the vision; also Isa. 6:8 and Jer. 1:11ff may be considered. Among other considerations, this participation of the prophet in the action of the vision shows how little our usual conception of visions has reckoned with the many possibilities involved.

We are justified in assuming that complete cleansing lay within God's purpose, and that, therefore, in the symbolic act every necessary part of the priest's garments would be in-

THE FOURTH VISION 73

cluded because God had indicated (v. 2) that His full favor
was turned toward His people. That eliminates finding a distinct and separate interpretation of the "mitre." It is true that
upon the mitre was attached the plate with the inscription:
"Holy to the Lord," Exod. 39:30, 31, but this is merely the
other side of true cleansing. For all who receive with all sincerity of heart that forgiveness which God so freely bestows
do also "follow after that holiness without which no man
shall see the Lord." The mitre merely indicates the completeness of the act of pardon with all its necessary complements
and results. Or we may state it thus: The mitre indicated, not
what God's people received, but what they were to aspire
after. It was a continual reminder of the need of sanctification.

To give added solemnity to the transaction there is present
as a witness none other than the Angel of the Lord who "was
standing by." At the same time His presence lends divine
sanction to these proceedings. That is what His "standing by"
('*omedh*) indicates. For this verb does not mean "stand up."
Nor is the phrase in any sense an idle one as though we here
had an unfinished statement. His presence spells approval.

A significant example of the mode of procedure followed
by the critical attitude is to regard a part of v. 4 as interpolation, viz., the words: "Lo, I have removed your iniquity from
you." To establish this contention it is claimed that, if this
statement had been made, the result would have been "ridicu-
lous; for Joshua is left standing unclothed, not only while the
angel of the Lord makes this explanation, but until the
prophet himself had suggested the addition of a turban"
(*Mitchell*). There is no cogency in this type of reasoning. It
lays strained meanings into simple narrative. It is not stated
(v. 4) that, as soon as the commandment to take away the filthy
garment had been given, it was also carried out. Without in-
terrupting His speech, the Angel of the Lord expounds it, and
as His agents are about to carry it out, the man Zechariah
proffers his suggestion about the mitre. To express, so to say,
the perfect agreement of the Lord with the prophet's request,
the Lord lets his request be granted first (5b) and then His
agents proceed to "put clothes on him," but surely there is no

indication that the stripping off of the filthy garments occurred before this moment.

The matter presented is of some moment, for the Angel of the Lord Himself "solemnly bears witness" (v. 6). This is the sense of the *wayya'adh* which *A.V.* renders correctly, but rather in the older meaning of the word, as "protested."

Joshua is informed (v. 7) of the need of personal righteousness ("walk in My ways") and of official faithfulness ("keep My charge") if God's favor is to continue. That favor will, if these conditions are met, express itself in allowing the high priest full jurisdiction over the Temple and the administration of its affairs ("you shall govern My house") and continuance in office ("have charge of My courts"). He shall not be demoted as were high priests of the past; cf., for example, the case of Eli, I Sam. 2:27ff; and of Abiathar, I Kings 2:26, 27. The crowning favor to be shown him is that he shall have "free access among those that stand here." As an intercessor for the people he shall have the right of "goings (*mahlekhim*) among those that stand here." This somewhat difficult phrase is apparently best taken in the sense of free access in intercessory prayer before the very throne where God's angels stand; as freely as they may approach, so freely may he. This interpretation suggests itself partly because official "goings" of the high priest are, no doubt, referred to, and also because "those that stand here" seem to be those who are in God's presence. Behind all that is said there is the assumption that, as *Barnes* says: "Access to the sanctuary was of course open only to such priests as were in a state of ritual purity; Exod. 40:30–32."

All this is the strongest possible encouragement to live up to the requirement found on the plate of the mitre: "Holy to the Lord." The terms are stated; the advantages accruing from the faithful observance of the terms are shown in glowing colors. Since the official capacity of Joshua is under consideration, all this, no doubt, points also to the favors that God's *people* shall enjoy, particularly the privilege of "free access" to the throne of grace. Some interpreters have misapplied the idea of "free access" to the point of having it mean that Joshua was to have the privilege of associating with angels in heaven (*Gressmann*). After misapplying the idea they then proceed to condemn it as a rather useless thought, not noticing that such an interpretation proves itself incorrect.

There lay in the priesthood things that were prophetic of the future. They were to be even more glorious than any of those mentioned above. On these the priesthood as such as well as the people at large are to fix their attention. They constitute the climax of the vision, being the Messianic content. Because of this fact these verses (8–10) deserve most careful consideration.

Verse 8. Not a mere "behold" introduces this message, for it is something to which diligent heed should be given by hearing it in the obedience of faith; therefore "hear now," *shema'-na'*. Joshua is not being considered in his own person, cf., "the high priest"; also v. 1. Also his colleagues in office (this is the meaning of "your friends that sit before you") are addressed. The importance of the priesthood as a body is under consideration, for not the high priest alone is by divine ordination a "marvelous sign." Every member of the priesthood shares in this in a measure. We have translated *môpheth* "marvelous sign" and not "sign" only because the word originally means a "wonder," a "marvel," especially when it is joined with *'ôth*, the word for "sign." But *môpheth*, when used alone, often verges into the meaning of "sign." A *môpheth* can, therefore, signify something deeper as does a sign. It at the same time usually retains in part something of its original meaning as being a thing that leads men to marvel at what God is doing. Both meanings are in a measure covered by the translation, "a marvelous sign"; German: *Wunderzeichen*. The genitive relation (viz., "men of a marvelous sign") is then a genitive of description, or better, of apposition; for the priests *are* a "marvelous sign." This they are, not of themselves, but by virtue of God's having ordained them to be such. But not by virtue of anything that they shall achieve or produce but by virtue of what God will achieve: He "brings forth His Servant, the Branch." When Christ, who is in so perfect a sense God's Servant and in so eminent a sense the

Branch, shall have come, then these wider implications of the priesthood will become apparent.

The priesthood symbolizes something more than men had thus far discerned. Not that there had been no revelation concerning the priestly office of Christ (cf., Ps. 110 and Isa. 53) but that men needed to grasp more fully what this involved. For this reason the priesthood had been rescued and cleansed as "a brand snatched out of the fire" (v. 2). The true Priest was the One to come. He is here designated as "the Branch" "Shoot" or "Sprout." This term *tse'mach*, from the root *tsamach*, "to sprout forth," was frequently found in prophecy at Zechariah's time; cf., Jer. 23:5 and 33:15; see also Isa. 4:2; 11:1; and 53:2 for the same idea although this term is not found in these latter prophecies. The term "Sprout" receives a new meaning in this passage. The high-priestly house, whose hopes seemed extinct, shall blossom forth into glory when the Priest who fulfills all the marvelous achievements implied in the office appears on the scene and causes the glories to arise. The thought is akin to Isa. 11:1, where the Messiah is declared to spring forth from the lowly house of David, whose glories seemed extinct. Thus does He revive the glories of the extinct priesthood. Of all this the high priest Joshua and his colleagues are continual reminders or "wonder-signs." The other name which is here given to the Messiah is "My Servant" (*'abhdi*). In this passage this name does not stand forth as prominently as does the other. It, too, is familiar to the readers from prophecy: Isa. 42:1; 49:3, 5; 50:10; 52:13; 53:11; Ezek. 34:23, 24. It designates the One who in a preeminent sense serves God perfectly, fulfilling His will, as the Messiah does in the work of redemption.

Some critics refer to 6:12 at this point and use this passage as a correction by referring it to Zerubbabel rather than to Joshua; v. 8 is then interpreted to mean that Zerubbabel is the "Branch." It is then claimed that Zechariah believed Zerubbabel would be the Messiah but erred in believing this as the outcome clearly shows. This passage, however, gives no intimation of such an interpretation, and our interpretation given above has avoided these pitfalls.

Verse 8 might be summarized as follows, paraphrasing freely: I shall not let you, Joshua, and your fellow priests be removed from office nor your office be discontinued, for I have a destiny for you—you are a type of the coming Messiah, who will do my work perfectly ("Servant"), and who will bring the priestly office to undreamed-of glory ("Shoot") when He springs forth.

The interpretation of v. 9 is extremely difficult. Hence a variety of explanations has been advanced for the stone set before Joshua. In addition to what we ourselves shall advocate, let us list a number of them: a foundation stone of the Temple; a stone crowning the Temple structure; the stone that took the place of the Ark of the Covenant in the Holy of Holies; a symbol of Zion itself; a precious stone in the crown worn by Zerubbabel; a similar precious stone that adorned one of his royal garments; some sort of amulet; a signet in the ring of the Almighty Himself; a stone of remembrance like those found on the breastplate or shoulder of the high priest (cf., Exod. 28:9ff; 15ff).

We proceed to offer our own interpretation. The glorious outcome that shall be the result of the coming of the Servant and Branch has not as yet been sufficiently unfolded. He shall guarantee the glorious future not only of the high priesthood (v. 8) but more particularly of the church of God, which is the object of the care and the solicitude of the priesthood. For more important than priests are the people of God, the church, over whom the priesthood extends, or for whose good it is instituted. That is what is meant by the stone set before Joshua. This stone is not the Messiah as many claim, because that figure is used elsewhere (see Isa. 28:16; Ps. 118:22); thus *Luther* also contends: He is called the stone "because we are all founded on Him; He alone is our sure foundation."

Two major difficulties lie in the path of such an interpretation: 1) there would be a bewildering variety of figures employed to describe the Messiah—"Servant," "Sprout," "Stone," two that are quite familiar in prophecy, a third that is less so; 2) a confusion within the figures results: on the one hand the high priest himself together with his companions typifies the coming Messiah (v. 8), and at the same time the Messiah would be lying before the priest as an object of his care. This criticism applies also to *Pusey's* view; he says rather positively: "That the stone is the Lord Jesus Christ, the head corner-stone, elect, laid as a foundation; and that the seven eyes on the one stone are the sevenfold Spirit of God which rested upon Him, is or ought to be unknown to no one." Our interpretation has an analogy in Dan. 2:34 where the word *'ebhen* is also used. We claim the stone represents the *church.* In Dan. 2:34 it is the church which dashes against the figure representing man-made empires and destroys them.

Now the question: What do the "seven eyes" represent? They recur in 4:10 and are there described as being the "eyes of the Lord, which scan the whole earth." God's eyes are, therefore, regarded as resting upon "the stone." A *man's* eyes may rest upon something in order to take good care of it. Of God it is said that He has seven eyes to express the perfection of divine operations. His watchful care is, therefore, perfect, especially as it is directed toward His church. The church may be before Joshua as the object of his care, but in a truer sense it is God Himself whose perfect care guards His own. This meaning is more satisfactory than to refer to Rev. 5:6, where the seven eyes represent the seven spirits of God. That such a meaning was intended in our passage no one could have been able to detect from the evidence available.

Neither is anything helpful gained by making "eyes" represent *facets* cut on stone although the word as such may have that meaning. A black stone at Borsippa (of Nebo) with seven eyes (*Mitchell*) is an accidental parallel and useless for our purpose. When God emphatically draws attention (by a "behold" and by the remark, "utterance of the Lord") to the fact that He will "engrave the engraving" of this stone, that must refer to the work that God performs upon His church in making her crude and shapeless form an object of beauty carefully wrought by Himself. The comparison is very suitable. As "engraving" (*mephatté(a)ch*) is a work that requires careful effort but achieves permanent, long-enduring results that are characterized by fine beauty and symmetry, so is God's work done for His own. Note: *'enayim*—dual for plural (*K.(S)* 257d).

One other possibility of interpretation in reference to this "stone" calls for special consideration. It is that advocated by *Sellin* in the *Journal of Biblical Literature,* 1931, in an article entitled *"Der Stein des Sacharja." Sellin* advances a very plausible contention to the effect that one of the well-known *Kudurru* of the land of Babylon is referred to, i.e., boundary stones on which is inscribed the fact that a given grant of land is made to the individual who holds the land directly from the crown under the special patronage of the god whose name and seven eyes are inscribed on the edges of the stone together with the necessary descriptive and factual material on the faces of the stone. So then, argues *Sellin,* skillfully combining the following passages: 3:9; 4:7, 10, a stone is referred to that guarantees Zerubbabel, the lineal descendant of the line of David, full and free possession of the land of promise under the protection of Jahweh.

We offer two major criticisms of this rather brilliant presentation.

The first is that the three passages mentioned, which are considered jointly as necessarily belonging together in any interpretation of the above passage, do not refer to one and the same stone as *Sellin* maintains. He gets them to refer to the same matter by having "the top stone" (4:7) mean "stone of possession" according to the *Septuagint* and "the plummet" of 4:10 mean a "stone of separation," i.e., a stone that assures the land to Zerubbabel as possession or inheritance, which interpretation is a skilful conjecture that would bring the passage in line with the other two. Besides, there is no suggestion in the context that 3:9 has reference to Zerubbabel. A good deal of shifting of text and facts must be resorted to in order to arrive at this interpretation.

In the second place, though *Kudurru,* boundary-markers, may have been common enough in Babylon, that does not imply that the Israelites also set them up. Though they may have been seen by some Israelites in captivity, one would surely be justified in expecting that something of their purpose would find clear expression in 3:9 at the first mention of the stone. The meaning of the *Kudurru* stone cannot be so obvious to the reader as to require no explanation whatsoever. A statement of purpose does occur, but it is unrelated to the main contention of *Sellin*, "I will remove the iniquity of that land in one day." So *Sellin's* interpretation is another of those which lean too heavily upon some archaeological detail and draw sweeping conclusions from it as though archaeology were the chief guide and inspiration of exegesis. At the same time it assumes a free and indiscriminate use on Israel's part of the superstitious practices current in other nations, an assumption that is quite generally made in the field of Old Testament studies.

Whereas v. 9a offers the positive, constructive side of the Lord's work upon His church, what follows states the negative side: "I will remove the iniquity of that land in one day." This work is, no doubt, of major necessity. There is "iniquity" (*'awôn*, "guilt") in the land. It must be removed. God does this, but He does it in so perfect a fashion that there is no need of many repetitions. One day and one work suffice. The Old Testament sacrifices furnish the implied contrast. They required endless repetition and yet effected no actual removal of guilt. The sacrifice on Calvary holds good for all times. For all that has been stated is closely linked with the greater High Priest, the greater Joshua whose coming is predicted (v. 8).

In v. 10 a brief sketch to conclude the picture follows, a sketch that aims to convey the thought that outward prosperity runs parallel with inner spiritual attainments. For when sin and its guilt are removed, nothing can mar outward peace. Since Solomon's time (I Kings 4:25) "dwelling under one's vine and fig tree" was a picture of happy prosperity and contentment. Later prophets employed the statement thus, cf., Isa. 36:16; Mic. 4:4. Zechariah patterns after them by blending, as *Chambers* reminds us, the physical and the spiritual realities in one picture.

Chapter IV

The Fifth Vision

The Lampstand and the Two Olive Trees

How beautifully these visions supplement one another appears, for example, in the progression of thought from the preceding vision to this one! The vision of the removal of the filthy garments indicated how moral obstacles were to be removed from the path of God's people. The fifth vision shows how "political obstacles" (*Smith*) are to be overcome. Though this vision is concerned primarily with Zerubbabel, that fact does not limit its application to him. Beyond the personal message their is here, as in the preceding chapter, a lesson of truth for the whole people.

In some respects this vision, too, presents unusual difficulties; they do not, however, pertain to the major features of the vision. For the major thoughts can be traced with comparative ease if the analogy of the Scriptures is carefully followed. For the sake of greater clarity we shall present the translation of vv. 1–10 at once.

✠

vs. 1-10   ¹ Then the angel that talked with me waked me again, as a man that is waked out of his sleep. ² And he said to me: What do you see? And I said: I see, and, lo, a lampstand all of gold, with a bowl on top of it and seven lamps on it; there are seven pipes to each of the lamps on top of it; ³ and two olive trees by it, one on the right side of the bowl and the other on the left side of it. ⁴ Then I answered and said to the angel that talked with me: What are these, my lord? ⁵ Then the angel that talked with me answered and said to me: Don't you know what these are? And I said: No, my lord. ⁶ Then he answered and said to me: This is the word of the Lord to Zerubbabel, saying: Not by might, nor by power, but by My Spirit, says the

Lord of hosts. ⁷ Who are you, O great mountain? Before Zerubbabel you must become a plain. And he shall bring forth the top stone with shoutings of: Grace, grace unto it! ⁸ And the word of the Lord came unto me, saying: ⁹ The hands of Zerubbabel have laid the foundation of this house; his hands shall also finish it; and you shall know that the Lord of hosts has sent Me to you. ¹⁰ For who would despise the day of small things? For these seven shall rejoice and see the plummet in the hand of Zerubbabel; these are the eyes of the Lord which scan the whole earth.

Verse 1. It is simpler and more in conformity with Hebrew usage to translate thus rather than: "The angel came again and waked me," (*A.V.*). There is no indication that the angel had left the prophet. Furthermore, his leaving would be entirely unmotivated, and if it were mentioned, this fact would add no constructive thought to the vision. Lastly, the verb "he returned" (*wayyáshobh*), when it is coordinated with a second verb (here, "and he waked"), very frequently has only adverbial force, which is usually best rendered "again," (*G.K.* 120, 2a). That is plainly the meaning of the verb in 5:1 and 6:1. The only objection that might be raised would be that the prophet had not been waked previously, therefore not now "again." However, if our translation is correct, we receive the first direct intimation that the prophet had been waked after the preceding visions. Only in connection with this vision is specific mention made of it because the period between visions was very likely longer in this instance.

The correct understanding of "he waked" me makes our approach still more plausible. We do not here have a case of actual physical sleep, for it is very distinctly stated, "*As* a man that is waked out of his sleep." Actual sleep would not be described thus. The prophet remained awake throughout this memorable night. What the words do convey is that the state of mind essential to appropriating divine visions is so much above the ordinary waking state in a man's life as the waking state is above the state of sleep. Zechariah had to be raised to the ecstatic condition which is necessary for beholding and experiencing visions. By nature man is dull and obtuse to such experiences. On the mount of transfiguration even the disciples were overcome by drowsiness in a somewhat analogous situation (Luke 9:32).

Even when a man like Zechariah is roused he needs still further coaching in order fully to apprehend what is being shown to him. So little does human, sin-spoiled nature apprehend divine truth. The prophet must also be asked: "What do you see?" (v. 2). Thus the prophet's attention is focused on the vision. The next form in the text, *wayyó'mer,* "and he said," must be a textual error and is, therefore, usually read according to the marginal reading (*kethibh*) as *wa'omar,* "and I said." Attempts to use the former reading as though the angel without awaiting an answer rushed into a response to the prophet are rather artificial and therefore unacceptable.

The prophet's response begins *ra'i'thi,* which had best be translated, "I have gone into the state of beholding the vision," for that is what the perfect implies; otherwise the "I have seen" is not grasped as to its actual significance (*Orelli*). The outstanding feature of the vision, indicated by the "behold," is a "lampstand." That is what *menorah* means. "Candlestick" is the traditional translation, but since there were seven lamps on one stand and no candles, our rendering is more exact. Since this lampstand is of gold in all its parts and has seven lamps upon it it has its counterpart in the lampstand in the Tabernacle, described in Exod. 25:31ff; 37:17ff. If the Pentateuch is regarded as a composite work of rather late origin, and these references in Exodus are ascribed to a postexilic writer, then the Tabernacle and its furniture did not exist during the Mosaic days, and then what Zechariah beholds has no background in Israelitish tradition. Those commentators who hold such a view also assert that the lamps referred to as having been in the Temple of Solomon (I Kings 7:49) were not lampstands but individual lamps. Yet this passage in I Kings has the very same word as our passage (*menorah*). Consequently, the critical view which sends the prophets aborrowing and copying from Babylon is untenable though, since *Gunkel* raised this claim on this point, almost all critically-minded interpreters followed him (cf. *Sellin*).

There lies behind such efforts, whether commentators are aware of it or not, an attempt to discredit the inspiration or the reliability of the Biblical documents.

As *Keil* has rightly pointed out, though this lampstand is patterned after the Tabernacle or Temple model, it has three new and very distinctive features. First, there is above it (*'al ro'shô*, lit., "over its head") a rounded bowl (here called "its bowl," *gullâh* for *gullathâh*, middle syllable absorbed). Second, there are seven pipes running from this bowl to each of the lamps. Third, there are two olive trees, one on either side of the bowl.

First of all, the correctness of our interpretation of the second point needs to be established. The *A.V.* renders: "seven pipes to the seven lamps," a rendering that has one pipe run to each lamp. It must, indeed, seem strange to have seven pipes supplying oil from the bowl to each lamp. But visions are very apt to carry features that are not in accord with the things that we witness daily. The question must be only: "Just what does the text state, and is its statement clear?" No particular difficulty is encountered. It states, literally translated: "seven and seven pipes to the lamps." The *critical* solution of the problem is simple but unwarranted. Starting on the assumption that Zechariah must have said one pipe to each lamp, it crosses out one seven. Such a treatment of the text is unjustifiable. It reaches conclusions, then changes the evidence. The fact that the *Septuagint* translators retain but one seven is only one of many instances where *they* resorted to similar procedures.

"Seven and seven pipes" is the Hebrew mode of expressing the *distributive* idea of *seven each;* cf., II Sam. 21:20 and I Chron. 20:6, especially the latter passage. There a giant of Gath is described as to the number of his fingers and his toes: "six and six, twenty-four." Addition of "six and six" cannot be intended; that does not yield twenty-four. "Six and six" must mean on *each* hand and each foot there were six instead of five.

If the picture is somewhat unusual with a total of forty-nine pipes, it might well be possible that this represents one of the unusual features that are intended to convey an unusual thought as we shall see in a moment. Our prosy approach might at first be inclined to the impression that the vision is encumbered with an excess of plumbing. But it is clearly to be seen that the many pipes did not clutter up the vision nor mar its beauty.

The interpretation rests on a correct understanding of what the lampstand typifies. It plainly represents the church of God. Christ's use of the same figure is unmistakably clear. His own can be called "the light of the world," Matt. 5:14, from this point of view. They can be admonished to let their "light shine before men," Matt. 5:16, and to let their "lamps be burning," Luke 12:35; Phil. 2:15. Rev. 1:20 places this interpretation beyond the possibility of a doubt: "the seven candlesticks are seven churches," though this statement is obviously not a direct reference to Zechariah; yet the unity of Scriptural usage allows us to quote the passage from Revelation as confirming the usage of Zechariah. The oil is indubitably that which God supplies in order to enable the lamps to give light. That is without doubt His Spirit. In the Scriptures oil regularly typifies the Holy Spirit, not so much as He works moral results but rather as to physical achievements, cf. on the general thought Isa. 60:1; Luke 4:18, 19; Acts 10:38.

The popular modern interpretation that makes the candlestick the seven eyes of God by identifying the "seven lamps" mentioned in v. 2 with "these seven" in v. 10 may be mentioned as a typical instance of the method of interpretation adopted by critics. By large slashes of the accepted text such a result is attainable. A generous portion is cut away, viz., from v. 6a to 10b. No effort is made to reconcile the difficulties found in the Masoretic text. To interpret this text as it stands takes but half as much effort as must be put forth to make the new arrangement plausible—thus proving it to be the more reasonable as it stands. Besides, the critics owe us a satisfactory explanation as to how such corruptions as they have detected were ever allowed to creep into the text; and if but one man had made these extensive changes of a logical original, why no one in those days ever detected what to the critic's eye seems so self-evident.

Those interpreters who maintain that the items appearing in the vision must be in the way of each other need only to use their imagination a bit more freely and they will find ways of placing each in its correct position. Nor should it be forgotten that the entire vision presented a scene of great beauty and splendor. In regard to ornamentation the lampstand may have been patterned after the style that had been devised for the original Tabernacle lampstand.

Verse 4. Though the prophet had been speaking he, nevertheless, according to the Hebrew idiom, "answers," for 'anah is used in the broader sense of taking issue with any problem that confronts one and seems to address a question to one. He might have hazarded an opinion but is glad to avail himself of the angel's presence to secure an authoritative statement. The fact that the angel asks (v. 5), "Don't you know what these are?" does not as yet indicate that *every* Israelite could easily have discerned what the original lampstand or, for that matter, all the rest of the Temple furniture represented symbolically. We go too far when we assert that human ignorance is enough to amaze angels. But at least this much is true; Men of old were able to discover the meaning of the divine symbolism employed by God in the original Tabernacle. Zechariah is reminded that he could have known had he made a sincere effort to do so. There is not so much of humility and sincere desire to learn in the prophet's reply as there is an admission of ignorance. On *lo'* as equivalent of "no" and not as negativing a particular word see *K(S)* 352f.

It now developes (v. 6) that all that had appeared in the vision thus far was to convey a specific message to Zerubbabel, the chief civil ruler over Israel (Hag. 2:4, 5; Ezra 2:2, etc.). He was the man before whom all manner of obstacles piled up, both in the administration of the civil affairs of the nation and in the directing of the work of constructing the Temple. This work and these difficulties were not his only but those of the entire nation. It will presently become clear that the specific reference to him just as did the one to Joshua in chapter 3 will lead up to a Messianic prophecy. Affairs in Israel were in such a tangle and difficulties so numerous as to seem to threaten the very future of the nation.

The message to be delivered to Zerubbabel assumes an unusual form. It seems to ignore the preceding vision whose interpretation it aims to be. But such departures from what would seem to be the regular course of procedure prevent the prophecy by vision from deteriorating, as it were, into a stereotyped form. We expect 1) a vision, 2) the details of the features involved, 3) an explanation of each feature, and perhaps 4) something in the nature of some general principle that sums up the whole in an emphatic fashion. In this case the sequence is not 1, 2, 3, 4 but 1, 2, 4 of the series just outlined. Item 3 is explained by item 4 and by the concluding portion, vv. 11–14. In fact, since the epigrammatic form of the principle involved is so striking, the interpretation is all the more pronounced.

This principle is an elliptical sentence: "Not by might, nor by power, but by My Spirit, says the Lord of hosts," a kind of motto, as it were, to guide all endeavors and enterprises of the nation in these evil days. If we were to complete the ellipsis we might formulate the statement somewhat after the following fashion: If success is to be gained in the achievements of the people of God it will not be secured by what man can do but by the Spirit's work. No additional light can be thrown on this statement by searching for the difference in force between "might" (*cháyil*) and "power" (*kó(a)ch*). These two words are so closely synonymous, although *cháyil* has the wider range of application, that no line of demarcation between them can be drawn. They represent every human resource and ability such as physical or mental strength, all material and spiritual resources—even armies for that matter. They represent everything that man can muster. All this is brushed aside as being inadequate in administering the kingdom. A greater agency must be secured; in a greater power must all confidence be placed. That agency—"My Spirit, saith the Lord." Him God sends where men hope to succeed by God's power. Or, changing the figure, He gladly enters the ranks where men in faith trust His promise to help, and He champions the cause of those who are of themselves weak. Thus victories are gained in the kingdom. That is the major lesson for success in kingdom work. Note the aptness of the word backing up this statement, namely, "says the Lord of hosts." The Lord puts all his resources at the command of those who hope to succeed through Him, and He has "hosts" to serve His cause.

We see, too, why item 3 of our sequence of parts in the vision was not necessary. Every attentive reader can make his own application of this vision. The "lampstand" was the church of God as she gives light through the seven lamps, that is—*seven* being the number of divine operation—by the power that God supplies. This power is the Spirit. A lamp fulfills its function when it shines in the power of the fuel or oil that it has. The church fulfills her function, not by man's striving, but by letting the Spirit make of her a light to the world. At this point we are confronted by an issue of faith: will we believe that an adequate supply of the oil of the Spirit will be provided by God? This so manifestly leads to the motto: "Not by might, nor by power," etc., that no reader can fail to see how the statement of the principle and the explanation of the separate items of the vision are in beautiful and most harmonious agreement.

Criticism again attempts an improvement of the text. Since it had established a canon of criticism which anticipated item 3 of the above sequence after item 2, and item 3 was omitted, the conclusion was easily drawn: corrupt state of the text. In this instance form criticism's canon of interpretation that all visions should be cast into the same mould was not broad enough. Bible students who are willing to accept the text as it stands readily discern how aptly v. 6 is the interpretation promised; however, an interpretation which has completely stripped off the preparatory framework and the props of the vision proper. The interpretation is no longer cast in terms of the original vision. *Orelli* has given a good refutation of the textual emendations supplied by criticism. Suggestions of rearrangement of verses at this point, for example, offer as an improvement the following sequence: v. 6a, 11–14, 6b.

Verse 7 assumes that Zerubbabel will be ready to act upon the suggestion that v. 6 gave him and the people. As a result that which towered before him as an insuperable obstacle will be reduced to a mere plain and will no longer present difficulties. But to be exact, what does the "great mountain" represent? To speak of the "mountain of difficulties or obstacles" lying in his path is to substitute a modern mode of speech for Biblical language. In certain instances in the Scriptures the mountains plainly refer to world-power. We point to Ps. 68:16, 17; 76:4, 5; Jer. 51:25. Other references to mountains may suggest the same thought. This interpretation is much broader than is that which understands the mountain in our modern way of thinking. The greatest power that arose against God's people in those days was certainly the world-power. At God's behest all that the nations and Gentiles devise against His own shall vanish when His own trust that they will achieve success by His Spirit, and shall vanish as completely as if a towering mountain had been converted into a level plain. Naturally, if that biggest of threatening dangers is disposed of with such ease, then all other obstacles and difficulties must in like manner disappear. Very emphatic is the word which removes the threatening danger; it must be conceived as a supreme divine command: "Before Zerubbabel, unto a plain!" It suggests at the same time instantaneous obedience: "He spake, and it was done."

The success that Zerubbabel will have as a result is concentrated on one instance. From this he may gather what the outcome will be in other cases of legitimate and necessary enterprises. The same promise is, of course, held out to the entire people. This bit of success is described: "He shall bring forth the top stone." "Bring forth" (*hotsi*') refers to the bringing forth out of the place where it was being prepared. The "top stone" (*ha'ebhen haro'shah*) or as it might be translated, "headstone," signifies the stone that in some way marks the completion of a structure; it is the last one to be fitted in place as would, for example, be the stone that marks the point of an arch whose upper masonry runs into a point over a door. Zerubbabel's bringing forth of the stone does not of necessity refer to his personal efforts at carrying the stone. What he does or has others do is covered by the word.

Unsatisfactory and unacceptable are explanations of the "top stone" that have mythological beliefs of other nations determine what this stone might mean. The presupposition of this approach seems to be that the Jews of Zechariah's time made a thoroughgoing study of archaeological material that is available to present-day research or at least were thoroughly informed on every detail of Babylonian and other mythology. Some again refer to the *Kudurru* stones (cf., our remarks on 3:9) and add the fanciful idea that Zerubbabel brings it forth from the mythical mountain of heaven and so establishes his right to rule the territory of Israel. We rightly ask: "What have we here: heathen tales and superstitions or valid prophetic visions of Israel?"

The attitude of the people on beholding the glorious consummation of the task will be one of jubilant rejoicing. There is nothing that makes the heart of God's people more ready to overflow with the truest joy than to witness success or the fulfillment of God's promises in the work of the kingdom. *Teshu'oth* are "crashing bursts of applause," *Getoese, Gejauchze.* By their very intensity these expressions of joy testify to the high degree of joy that will be attained: joy will wax vociferous.

The words, "Grace, grace unto it" (*chen chen lâh*) are a prayer for divine favor to rest upon the completed structure and upon what it stands for. Since this meaning of *chen* is so well substantiated by usage, the other permissible rendering, just as well established, that suggests the thought, "Fair, fair is it," is, nevertheless, less desirable. For on such occasions God's people, deeply moved, will be less likely to think of external *fairness* than of the need and the value of divine *favor.* Psychologically the latter has the decided preference. *Luther* suggests: "Good luck, good luck to it"—*Glueck zu, Glueck zu!*

We have here, then, a divine guarantee of the success of the endeavors of God's people if these endeavors are carried out, "not by might, nor by power, but by My Spirit."

The word of exhortation to Zerubbabel continues (vv. 8–10). This leads to the prophet's inquiry (v. 11 and again v. 12) concerning the remaining outstanding item of the vision. And so the vision receives a thorough exposition. Throughout we see the fine propriety that marks each step.

Verse 8 introduces another word that came to Zechariah. It is distinct from the former as the new formula of introduction indicates: "And the word of the Lord came unto me." At the same time it is closely attached to the preceding by taking up the promise of the completion of the Temple and restating it: "his hands shall also finish it." The new thought is added that from all this Israel shall arrive at a greater certainty of knowledge that the Angel of the Lord has in all reality been sent by God to His people and has been actively engaged in their behalf, the same Angel of the Lord of whose divine activity for Israel the fathers had experienced so much. For this is the meaning of the statement: "And you shall know that the Lord of hosts has sent Me to you." These words do not apply to the prophet, do not establish his divine commission. This is clear from 2:9, 13 and 11:11 where the reference must be to the Angel of the Lord. Since throughout these visions the Angel of the Lord and the Lord Himself appear frequently, either as the same person or as distinct in reference to certain functions, this interpretation ought to appeal to us as being the only correct one.

There is danger that the weaker in the faith will be able for the present to discern only "small things" as the eye of man views matters. *Qetannoth,* "small things," feminine for neuter, see *K(S)* 245d. This statement of the case is a warning not to fall into this error, for those who know God's manner of working are aware of the fact; no outward display accompanies it. To the unenlightened mind the greatest achievement both in the making and in its completion seems trivial. The force of the perfect (*baz*) in this construction, "who would despise," is that of an admonition. It is not a doubtful statement or the

equivalent of a denial, *monierend nicht dubitativ,* K(S) 171c.
On the form of *baz* see *G.K.* 72dd. We can, therefore, paraphrase the statement thus: "Do not despise the day of small
things." This is a plea not to run with the crowd and become
guilty of its foolish judgments.

What reason is there for not being disturbed by these days
of small things? Answer: the watchful care of God. For God's
seven eyes take joy in beholding even so trivial an action as
Zerubbabel's going about here and there, dropping the plummet to test whether the wall is being constructed true to the
perpendicular. If such minor activities of men are observed
by God and cause Him joy, what broad conclusions may men
not draw as to the extent to which God's zeal supports the
work?

The statement of this tenth verse is somewhat unusual as to
form. To give all possible emphasis to the remarkable feature
of the thought, the verbs are placed first and are followed
rather late by the subject—about as follows: "They shall rejoice and shall see the stone, the plummet in the hand of
Zerubbabel, viz., those seven—they are the eyes of the Lord."
This passage casts a definite light on 3:9, and our interpretation of that verse is established as correct. It would be impossible to use the demonstrative *"these* seven" if something had
not marked them before; 3:9 does mark them. The eyes of
God are represented as being seven in number to indicate
how far richer the divine forms of activity are than the human.
If they can "run to and fro" (*meshoṭeṭim, to scan at a rapid
glance*) they can discern all and select for particular attention
the things of actual moment, like the work of chosen servants.

There is lasting comfort for the church in this thought.
Small tasks faithfully performed in the church experience
God's watchful care and are a source of joy to the Almighty.
Then nothing in the kingdom is small, and the joy of standing
in His service grows tremendously.

Efforts to introduce the "seven" planets (*Sellin* and *Horst*)—
a Babylonian thought—to interpret the "seven" would not
have been made if interpreters had not been influenced by the

idea that nothing can be original in Jewish thought; it must be borrowed from Babylonia.

The matter of the olive trees requires a bit of attention, for an exposition of their meaning has not as yet been provided.

✠

vs. 11-14   ¹¹ Then I answered and said to him: What are these two olive trees on the right side of the lampstand and upon its left side? ¹² And I answered the second time and said to him: What are the two olive branches which are beside the two golden spouts that empty the golden oil out of themselves? ¹³ And he said to me: Don't you know what these are? And I said: No, my lord. ¹⁴ Then he said: These are the two anointed ones that stand ready to serve the Lord of all the earth.

These two verses (11, 12) contain two questions which are in reality one. Nor is it a clumsy presentation that makes a double statement of one question. One reason for stating the questions thus is that they were put after this manner by the prophet at the time when the vision and its interpretation were granted him. The second, that it is very natural to state the questions just as they are stated. The first statement (v. 11) recalls us from the interpretation, which had left the original vision far behind, to the actual vision and its general features, particularly the item that requires further elucidation. We see, as it were, the prophet himself concentrating his attention upon that part of the vision that had left him puzzled, and as he regards it more closely he discerns features that he had not himself at first been aware of. So he directs his question toward these and words it more accurately to conform to the new matters he observes.

The two olive trees are involved. Their relation to the lampstand is found to be this: They stand on either side of it; there are noticeable and prominent branches (*shibbalay*, lit., "ears" like those of grain) which are by the side of and overhanging two spouts or funnels; these funnels catch the oil which these branches drop into them and empty its rich golden fluid (*zahabh*, "gold" for the "oil") out of themselves and, doubtless, into the bowl mentioned in v. 2. The entirely new features are the branches, the golden spouts, and the golden oil. The most unique element of all is the fact that the branches freely drop their oil into the spouts. Olive trees have never been known to do such things. But in visions as in dreams most unusual things have been known to appear, and in this case, too, these unusual features make the thought to be emphasized so much clearer. The thought is that an inexhaustible supply is provided for these lamps: trees grow; they drop oil; the oil fills a reservoir-bowl; seven pipes lead from this reservoir to each lamp. A lamp so equipped will never lack oil. In fact, if the oil is symbolic of the Spirit, then a better picture for the generous measure in which God bestows the Spirit could hardly be found. In the Tabernacle and the Temple men were commissioned to tend and to fill the lamps. In the better dispensation that is to come God will Himself provide what is needed.

Nothing helpful is gained by creating a device whereby the oil is extracted from the olive berries. *Tsanteroth* appears to mean "spouts" not "presses" or unheard-of devices with sharp points to pierce the berries and extract the oil. The term appears to refer only to a device that is intended to empty the oil (*hammeriqim*, from *mariq*, "to empty"). We can best liken the device to a funnel-like contrivance that is broad enough at the top to catch all that the branches may drop, yet capable of carrying the oil to the *gullah* or "bowl." True, the fact that the branches are said to be beside (*beyadh*) the two golden spouts gives an unusual meaning to this compound preposition, literally, "by the hand," but that is not far removed from "by the side." The fact that the oil is called *hazzahabh*, "the gold," is easily understood because of its yellow color; the metaphor is quite natural.

Verse 13. For a second time (v. 5) the question is addressed to the prophet, "Don't you know what these are?" This suggests again only that he should have been able, in part at least, to understand the issues involved in this portion of the vision. It appears that, though the interpreter is ready enough to give needed information, he seeks to discourage the attitude which makes no strenuous effort of its own to penetrate into the meaning. Immediate readiness to supply answers might create the impression that it is quite impossible for any man to discern the import of this type of revelation, or that the visions were scaled on too high a plane. The dogmaticians rightly claim that one of the attributes of the divine Word is *claritas,* perspicuity. To give explanations before a man has done his best would serve to support a wrong attitude on man's part.

Verse 14. The literal translation of what we have rendered "anointed ones" is "sons of oil," *Oelkinder (Luther).* None of these translations alone brings us very far along the road to a correct apprehension of the term though the English translation offers the best interpretative rendering. The word "son" is used in a great variety of connections that are utterly foreign to our idiom. *Ben,* "son," is used as a *nomen relationis* "followed by a word of quality, characteristic, etc." Thus a "son of might" is a mighty man; a "son of death" is a man "appointed or exposed to death"—a very common use of the word "son." Here the term must refer to men who are supplied with oil or to whom oil has been generously applied. We cannot apply this to men except in so far as they act in a representative capacity in a divinely created office, men whose divinely appointed gifts are represented by anointing as an act of induction into office. Since this vision follows the very recent mention of Joshua, the high priest (3:1, 3, 9), and of Zerubbabel, the civil ruler (4:7, 10) who fills the place of a king, and since the incumbents of both these offices were anointed, Lev. 21:10; I Sam. 10:1, we take it that the office of the high priest and the king are typified.

If it appears to any reader that we seem to be attributing too much to human agencies, let it be borne in mind that God gave these offices to His people and filled the incumbents of them with the gifts of His Spirit so that in these offices they might be instrumentalities that were specified to enable the church to furnish the requisite light; in the last analysis it is God who is supplying the needed light through these means.

Since these two offices were functioning in the earlier days of the Old Covenant, it might seem as if this vision does not point to the future and the Messianic times as do the rest. Yet the two olive trees do point to that which is new. The fact that they were not provided for the original Tabernacle candlestick and do appear in this vision marks an advance upon the earlier economy of things. What God in fact promises is that the lamp (the church) will be enabled far more perfectly to fulfill its destiny than heretofore because two offices will distill a richer measure of the Spirit upon the church. This apparently points forward to the Messiah whose very name is "Christ," the "Anointed One," the true "Son of Oil," who unites in His person these two offices. No mention is made of the prophetic office, apparently for the reason that for a time it must recede into the background. To prepare for its temporary cessation the prophet makes no reference to it and its future.

These two are said to "stand ready to serve the Lord of the whole earth" literally "stand over the Lord, etc." However, 'al—upon or over—is used in such connections when the one near whom they stand appears as seated. In a sense they stand over him, but their presence indicates that they are at hand to obey the behest of him near whom they stand. The fact that He is here designated as the "Lord of the whole earth" shows what resources are at His command, and how it must, as a result, be an easy matter for Him to furnish His agents with the needed gifts to enable them to guarantee a successful future to His church. There is a type of interpretation which goes too far—the interpretation that suggests that these words mean that Zerubbabel and Joshua are to be thought of "as favored members of the court of heaven."

On the whole, a very encouraging vision: the golden lampstand (the gold indicating the very precious character of the church) shall not fail in her function of giving light because of the two offices which God gives to His church, a Spirit-filled king and a Spirit-filled priest. Whatever other gifts in the form of other Spirit-filled rulers and priests our Great Bishop provides, they, too, guarantee that the church shall not fail in her divinely given destiny.

Chapter V

The Sixth Vision

The Flying Scroll

One important problem in the life of Israel has not yet been touched upon: How shall the sinners and the ungodly be dealt with? Outwardly they belong to the nation but inwardly are not of Israel. They were the Israelites who prospered in their sins and were the cause of much suffering on Israel's part. They seemed to be having their day. It may have seemed that by their oppression of the poor and the helpless they were able to undo more than godly, constructive effort was able over a period of years to build up. Since every important feature of Israel's life is to be dealt with in these visions, this state of affairs is deemed of sufficient importance to be dealt with in the two visions of chapter 5. Though they are both concerned with much the same subject or with two aspects of one and the same subject, it is scarcely feasible to regard these two visions as two sides of but one vision. The two are too distinct for that. The vision of the Ephah is not the continuation of the vision of the Flying Scroll. This artificial construction on the part of some interpreters is an outgrowth, in a large measure, of the attempt to make the total number of visions seven. True as it is that the symbolism of numbers is quite studiously observed by Zechariah, in this instance this does not seem to be the case.

This vision of the Flying Scroll is closely related to that of the woman in the Ephah, and the relationship might be stated thus: as the one indicates the certain destruction of the individual sinners, so the other indicates the removal of the principle of wickedness from among the people of God. Both are necessary. When people are upset by the success of the ungodly (cf., Ps. 37 and Ps. 73) this may cause a very serious spiritual disturbance. Such people receive double assurance of the ultimate victory of the cause of righteousness when they are led to see, on the one hand, a very definite vision that the individual sinners shall fail; and, on the other hand, that the principle of ungodliness that seemed to pervade the land and animate men on every hand shall be overthrown.

✤

vs. 1-4   ¹ Then again I raised my eyes and looked, and lo, a flying scroll. ² And he said to me: What do you see? And I said: I see a flying scroll, its length is twenty cubits and its breadth, ten cubits. ³ Then he said to me: This is the curse that goes forth over the face of the whole land, for every thief shall be cut off according to the inscription on the one side; and every one that sweareth shall be cut off according to the inscription on the other side. ⁴ I will cause it to go forth, says the Lord of hosts, and it shall enter into the house of the thief, and into the house of him that swears falsely by My name; and it shall abide in the midst of his house, and it shall consume it with its timber and its stones.

The lifting up of the eyes indicates the beginning of a new vision. The literal rendering: "and I returned and lifted up," here, as in 4:1, is not feasible. The verb *shubh* is to be taken adverbially in the sense of "again," and this substantiates our rendering of 4:1. "A flying scroll" is in one sense equivalent to a flying "book," for all books appeared in the form of scrolls (Jer. 36:1ff). The *Septuagint's* translation δρέπανον, "sickle," the *Vulgate's, falx,* have overlooked the final *h* of the word. The fact that this scroll or book is said to be "flying" (*áphah,* feminine of the Kal participle, from *'uph*) indicates that the threat involved in the contents of this book is not only one that is being foretold but is already, like some bird of prey, winging its flight to alight on its victim. We are reminded of the statement, "Where the carcass is there will the eagles be gathered together."

In v. 2 the interpreting angel, desirous of leading the prophet to a correct understanding of what is involved, asks him a question. After all that has been observed it is scarcely

THE SIXTH VISION 99

necessary to give the *angelus interpres* a special introduction;
therefore the indefinite: "and he said" is unambiguous. The
angel's question demands that the prophet himself formulate
what he sees. The prophet's effort to do this is the first step
toward a correct apprehension of the vision. We notice repeatedly how the interpreting angel guards the prophet
against mental sloth. Only as he earnestly seeks will God let
him find according to the principle: They that seek Me early
shall find Me.

As the prophet answers he becomes aware as a result of
closer scrutiny of facts that had apparently not been observed
at first (4:11, 12; 3:3, etc.) namely, that the scroll was twenty
cubits (approximately thirty feet) long and ten cubits (*ca.*
fifteen feet) wide; and states these facts in answer to the angel's
question. On *ba'ammah*, "by the cubit," cf., *G.K.* 134,3,R,3.
How the prophet could at a glance note these measurements
of the scroll need not be investigated, for we lack data for the
answer. Yet he must have discovered this feature and been
sure of it, otherwise there could not have been such a definite
statement of the case on his part. The scroll does not go forth
from heaven (*Sellin*); it merely appears.

These dimensions of the scroll do not indicate merely that
the scroll was large. It was large, and its abnormal size indicates that the thing it stands for has become a prominent issue.
It is not a matter of trivial importance. But why just these dimensions? The debate as to whether they are derived from the
porch which Solomon had built before the Holy Place (I
Kings 6:3) of the Temple or from the Holy Place of the
Tabernacle, which was of the same size (Exod. 26:8), need
not be renewed. If these dimensions occur in these structures
they indicate a standard of the sanctuary. Measured by sanctuary standards, which is synonymous with measured by the
divinely sacred rule, a certain definite judgment of evildoers
is at once implied. This must indubitably be a verdict of disapproval and of condemnation, that is to say, "a curse,"
(*ha'alah*, with the definite article—generic—and yet to be
rendered: "*a* curse" according to our idiom).

Since this is certain, it is surely an idle pursuit to guess what might have been the very inscription on the scroll. If the interpreter labels it a "curse," then even such additions as "the volume is the record of the crime of the land" (*G.A. Smith*) are idle speculation. To determine upon the lack of actual clues of what was here written is well likened by *Lange* to "the effort to read an inscription on a book painted on some portrait." This can usually not be read and is not intended to be.

Verse. 3. The clause, "That goes forth over the face of the whole land," cannot mean that it "is flying from the land." *Kol-ha'árets* means "the whole land" because of the contrast with *'érets shin'ar* in v. 11. Nor do we here have anything that is patterned after superstitious practices. It may be that men did, as seems fairly well established, from days of old (*Sellin*) inscribe curses on strips of parchment in order to put them into operation against enemies, but the prophet does not avail himself of this "superstition" (*Mitchell*). Nor was there belief on the prophet's or on Israel's part in the magical efficacy of written or spoken curses. This occurred only where men had fallen prey to heathen superstitions. Since the Spirit of revelation never goes aborrowing at filthy sources to find the crystal pure water of divine truth, all we dare do when a vision like this has remote points of contact with superstitious practices is to label such coincidences accidental. They are not a source, either direct or indirect, of divine truth.

We hold to this contention even when men like *Sellin* remark: "The custom of curse-tablets (usually made of lead) or of curse-slips (of parchment) is proved widespread for all antiquity and especially for Palestine." The one point of contact that providence intended to use may have been this: As you set loose futile curses against your enemies, so I send forth effective curses that invariably accomplish their purpose; your efforts are hollow mockery, mine terrible reality. It is a libel upon divine revelation to state the case thus: "The prophet, taking advantage of this superstition, represents the penalty for sin as an inscribed curse that executes itself upon the offender, seeking him wherever he may be" (*Mitchell*). For such a procedure would be indifferent to the character of the means employed as long as an apparently salutary effect is obtained.

Two classes of evildoers are mentioned as being about to be cut off as a result of God's curse which is becoming operative—thieves and perjurers. These two classes are mentioned by way of illustration, not with the thought that all others would be allowed to continue in their sins. The reason for singling out these two classes appears to be that in a community such as that of the returned exiles these sins would be particularly in evidence on the part of all who oppressed Israel. The expression "everyone that sweareth" is not inaccurate or based upon a misunderstanding as if all swearing were sinful, for it specifies more closely (v. 4): "him that sweareth falsely" (lashshéqer—"unto a lie," cf., Lev. 19:12; Exod. 20:7; Isa. 48:1). Nor is the expression "everyone that stealeth" to be limited to those who refuse to give God their dues in tithes, etc., though such are mentioned, Neh. 13:10; Mal. 3:8 (Fausset). These must be included; but the others who are guilty of theft as the most brazen of offenders are presumably referred to primarily.

The expressions "on the one side" and "on the other side" refer to the scroll which is inscribed on both sides. In a general way it must then be asserted that the curse as such is the inscription on this book or scroll, but how it is worded, and whether any other features are incorporated in it is beyond our power to discern. The curse states the standard of procedure according to which judgment is inflicted; "according to it" (kamónah) is used twice. That the expression mizzeh—mizzeh is used correlatively and does not only have the literal meaning "thence" or "from thence" (A.R.V.m)—is to be translated as we have rendered it appears from other cases where the double use of the expression necessitates the translation: "on this side . . . and on that," (Exod. 17:12; Num. 22:24; Ezek. 47:7, Keil). Again too sweeping an inference is drawn if the inscription on both sides is taken as a direct reminder of the two tables of the law, which were inscribed on both sides (Exod. 32:15, Fausset).

The word *niqqah* should not be rendered "cut off"; it suggests the thought "purged out" or "to cleanse by purging," coming from a root that means "to be clean." *Luther's* translation has caused some confusion: *"alle Diebe werden nach diesem Briefe fromm gesprochen,"* "all thieves are by this scroll pronounced just." This translation is very misleading and is not at all made necessary by the verb *naqah.* It sets out from the wrong assumption that the scroll is the embodiment of false doctrine. *Naqah* in the Niphal appears in Isa. 3:26 in the same sense of "emptied out." The textual emendations resorted to at this point by almost all critics are quite unnecessary.

Verse 4. Regarding this scroll, which is already on its way ("flying"), the Lord of hosts solemnly asserts that He will cause it to enter into the very houses of the evildoers above specified, thus singling them out one by one. It shall not only cause these wicked men to perish—that is so self-evident that it is not even stated—but shall also consume the very "house with its timber and its stones." God shall do an unusually thorough work, giving notable tokens of His displeasure. A literal fulfillment of this threat is not required. It portrays chiefly the intensity of the divine aversion to such people and their acts. This verse reminds us of I Kings 18:38 where God in His wrath also did a very thorough work. Surely, the vision is a very solemn testimony to the truth that men should not "be deceived, God is not mocked."

Those interpreters speak ill-advised words who with *Sellin* claim in reference to the spirit of this passage: "The belief was characteristic of the religion of Israel from days of old that an absolute and downright mechanical efficacy inhered in the divine curse as well as in the divine blessing." The passages cited as proof, Deut. 11:29; 27:13ff; Jer. 51:49ff, afford no convincing proof. They indicate merely that God let solemn blessings and curses be spoken and written in order to cause the severity of His wrath against sin to be strongly felt. As a result Israel believed that His wrath was no light matter since the Lord spoke so sharply. But a belief in the magical efficacy of such curses or blessings never took hold

upon Israel. The claims to the contrary tend to reduce inspired prophecy to the level of human invention and superstition.

The Seventh Vision (5:5–11)

The Wickedness-Ephah

On the relation of this vision to the preceding one see the
remarks at the beginning of the chapter.

✠

vs. 5–11   **5** Then the angel that talked with me went forth and
said to me: Raise your eyes now and see what is this that
goes forth. **6** And I said: What is it? And he said: This is
an ephah [bushel basket] that goes forth. He also said:
This is their appearance throughout the land. **7** Then all
of a sudden a round lid of lead was raised, and there was
a lone woman sitting in the ephah. **8** And he said: This
is wickedness. And he thrust her back down into the
ephah and cast the heavy lead on the opening. **9** When
I next raised my eyes suddenly I saw two women appearing
with wings driven by the wind, and each had a pair of
wings like those of a stork. And they lifted up the ephah
between the earth and the sky. **10** Then I said to the angel
that talked with me: Where are they transporting the
ephah? **11** And he said: To build a house for it in the land
of Shinar. And when it is ready, they will set it there in
its proper place.

The interpreting angel had retired from the scene and now
again (v. 5) comes within the range of the prophet's vision.
This clearly indicates the beginning of a new vision. So little
is human nature capable of readily appropriating divine revelation that it is not only necessary for God to let the necessary
visions appear but also to stimulate the recipient's attention
step by step lest, overcome by the power of the heavenly, he
fail to appropriate all that God desires to offer. Therefore
the angel's admonition to the prophet: "Raise your eyes now
and see what is this that goes forth."

Was it that the prophet had absorbed all that could reasonably be expected; or that before asking: "What is it?" he had himself endeavored to the utmost of his ability to determine what it was that he beheld; or that he had, indeed, noticed that what he saw was an ephah, but that its deeper significance was as yet not apparent to him—at any event, he receives an immediate answer and no rebuke such as: "Knowest thou not what this is?"

The reply (v. 6) indicates, first of all, that the thing seen is "an ephah," *ha'ĕphah,* the article must be regarded as being equivalent to our indefinite article as in v. 3 above "a curse"— *G.K.* 126, 4—because the object, not mentioned before, becomes determinate as the vision progresses. The ephah holds "according to the latest authorities 38.86 American quarts" (*Mitchell*) and very closely resembles our bushel as to size. It may well be possible that the prophet's inability to answer what it was that he saw was due to the unusual proportions of the measure which is afterward found capable of containing a woman. But even as we might call a measure that is shaped as the customary bushel baskets are a "bushel" even though it is much larger than the average bushel, so we do here. Besides, the ephah, though not the largest measure known, was the largest in actual use. In shape it may even have more closely resembled a barrel as some state. *Sellin's* remark that, though the ephah was not capable of containing a woman, "such magician's boxes are capable of containing everything," is inappropriate.

Rather difficult is the statement: "This is their appearance throughout the land." The difficulty was felt by the first translators (LXX) who rendered the Hebrew word found here ἀδικία, "iniquity," lengthening the *yodh* of *éynam* to *waw* and reading *'awonam,* "their iniquity." But this, aside from having no basis in sound textual criticism, leads to a lame tautology: the ephah is first called "iniquity," then the woman in the ephah is called "wickedness." Further devices must then be resorted to to smooth out this new difficulty. It does not create insuperable difficulties to retain the *textus receptus.* The meaning "appearance" for *'áyin* is well established; see Lev.

13:55; Num. 11:7. The force of the pronominal suffix which is expressed by our possessive pronoun "*their* appearance" is to be determined from the context. Since we notice that the removal of wickedness from the land is the chief issue, the suffix refers to the perpetrators of wickedness, who are naturally involved when wickedness itself is removed. As *it* looks, so *they* look. It seems as though the days of wickedness were numbered and its doom sealed. So they also look. No matter where wickedness finds itself "in all the land," all of it shall be removed, for a thorough house cleaning is in prospect.

As in the preceding visions, the details become apparent as the vision is subjected to closer scrutiny. What the prophet successively discovers is successively revealed (v. 7). "A round lid of lead" is lifted, a piece which had served as a close-fitting cover of the ephah as a barrelhead closely covers a barrel. This "round piece," *kikkār,* meaning *a round,* may be a talent when it refers to gold and silver, but lead talents are unheard of; therefore our translation. Who or what may have lifted the lead cover in the vision is of no moment. It might have been the interpreting angel who might have lifted it to reveal what the ephah contained. But the sequences and the causalities of visions are not strictly after the analogy of everyday life. The *wezo'th* beginning the second clause may be translated literally "and this," but that necessitates a clumsy parenthesis in order to make the second half of the verse the continuation of the angel's explanation. It is better to regard *wezo'th* as a resumption of the *hinneh,* "behold," in the first clause of the verse, like *Luther's: und da,* "and there." The force of the *'achath* is somewhat like our English "a *lone* woman." The fact that she was but *one* was to be emphasized, for larger measures ordinarily contain quite a collection of individual items. As the cover is lifted, this woman appears to be "crouching" (*yoshébheth,* lit., *sitting*) within.

Verse 8. Her identity is of chief moment for the understanding of the vision. Therefore the interpretation follows at once. She is "wickedness" (*harish'ah*). The feminine noun appears to be chosen in preference to the somewhat more common masculine to designate the woman; and the female figure appears because, according to the almost universal habit of nations, vices and virtues, are by preference personified as female figures. It is the disposal of more than individual sinners that is aimed at. The very principle and essence of sin as such is to be eliminated according to this vision (vs. the preceding). *Rignell* very appropriately defends the idea that *rish'ah* here means "idolatry."

When the cover is raised, wickedness, confined, at once seeks to regain her former freedom. To have a fully harmonious vision, and to indicate how she is to be curbed in every way, the interpreting angel promptly casts her down into the ephah. To indicate that the conquest of evil is also to be permanent and absolutely sure, "the weight of lead," which is, of course, the heavy lead cover, is clapped down on the top of the ephah. The weight and the solidity of the lead cover are of such a kind as further to indicate that wickedness is secured so firmly as to preclude her escape. "The weight of lead" is in the Hebrew "the stone of lead," but "stone" came to be synonymous with "weight" because the weights employed in weighing were actually stones and were graduated as are weights for the balances today. "Upon the mouth thereof" naturally refers to the mouth of the *ephah* and not of the woman—a thought that is in every way unacceptable. *Luther* renders well for "mouth thereof," *oben aufs Loch,* "upon the opening." But the beginning of the verse he renders less fortunately when he translates, "This is the wicked doctrine" (*Lehre*). Wicked doctrine is but one of the pernicious evils to be removed.

In verse 9 we have what *Sellin* aptly calls *der Abtransport der Gottlosigkeit,* "wickedness is transported away." Two women come forth, that is, appear on the scene. Their appearance causes the prophet to lift his eyes to discern what they purpose to do. He notices first that they have a peculiar equipment for their specific duties. One part of their equipment is "wind in their wings." Lest we investigate too curiously this feature of the vision, let it suffice to note that, in addition to the ordinary propelling power that wings have, there is a blast of wind that speeds these women on their way. There is no further significance in the fact that the wings are like "wings of a

stork" than that this is a good and familiar comparison to indicate strength of wings. For the stork is very frequently seen in
Palestine and during the migratory season may appear in great
numbers. That he has a powerful wing is also well known.
Every feature of the vision indicates that every part of it is entirely adequate for the purpose which it is to serve. Wickedness is to be disposed of, and this disposal is to be carried out
in an efficient manner.

The question as to why *women* should serve as agents to
carry away the ephah containing wickedness is, perhaps, best
answered by defining them "as necessary adjuncts for an effective picture" (*Mitchell*). To claim that, since women carry
away a woman, this demonstrates that God punishes sin with
sin, is as unfounded as are all other such constructions that are
put upon this part of the vision, for what could suggest that
these two women, too, are wicked? If they were they would
very likely assist wickedness to escape. This, then, is a feature
of the vision that does not lend itself to interpretation. The
fact that "they lifted up the ephah between the earth and the
sky" carries out the picture in conformity with its adjuncts, for
when storks are migrating to distant lands they, too, take a very
high course of flight as all inhabitants of the land had frequently observed. Low flights served to carry them conven-
iently from one near-by place to another; a high altitude of
flight indicated that they were bound for distant parts.

Verse 10. Since especially the last feature of v. 9 had indicated that removal into distant lands was in prospect, the
prophet feels moved to inquire whither this might be, for he
feels that that feature of the vision will also be significant. It
actually is according to the answer given in v. 11.

The answer given by the interpreting angel is similar to
many answers that God supplies when man in his infirmity
asks questions. For God's answers often include not only what
man inquired about but also what he might have inquired
about had he had deeper discernment. Here the answer is for
the most part as if the question had been, Why? not, Whither?
The former is really more important. The latter might serve
largely to satisfy curiosity.

Since "Shinar" is the old name for the land where Babylon was located, it is significant that it is used. Prophets do employ it for Babylon, Isa. 11:11; Dan. 1:2; but it usually seems to have a connotation of what Shinar stood for when it first appears in the Scriptures. When it is first used (Gen. 10:10; 11:2) it reminds us of the ungodly attempts of Nimrod to found earthly kingdoms and of the heaven-storming projects of the men who built the tower of Babel. Since the land was marked by this spirit from its earliest days, it is not surprising to see the spirit of enterprise apart from God stamped upon all its endeavors in later years. That spirit is, however, the very essence of wickedness. Therefore it is quite appropriate that "wickedness" is transported thither. That is "its proper place." "Building a house for her" implies a fixed residence.

This vision may be interpreted very literally and thus limitations be placed upon it which are far from the intention of the Spirit of revelation. Of such a kind are all interpretations that limit the removal of wickedness to removal only from the Holy Land and in like manner thereafter confine her exclusively to the land of Shinar. As little as anyone cares to claim the latter, that, namely, it should at any time lie in the purpose of God to banish wickedness to one particular land, just so little do God's purposes single out only one land for purging as millennialists are wont to interpret at this point. Shinar represents the world, generally speaking, as contrasted with the church. It follows the principles of wickedness; it shall acquire more and more of wickedness. But on the other hand, God's work of cleansing His people or church goes on continually. It will ultimately be effective just as wickedness in the ephah is successfully banished. Though it pleases God to let this be consummated at the final judgment, nonetheless God does not let wickedness in any sense prevail.

Some of the latest developments in the interpretation of this prophecy, especially of the closing verse, are not an exegetical advance. Though "house" may be a name that is given to Babylonian temples or *ziggurats* (stage towers) in honor of divinities, and though a small chamber was found on the top platform which contained a shrine of the particular divinity whose tower it was, this cannot be what is signified by "her own place." Nothing suggests the apotheosis of wickedness. In fact, this latest find (*Sellin*) is another unfortunate application of the unproven hypothesis that Israel's thoughts are to be derived from the superior (?) culture of Babylon.

Somewhat more apropos is *Sellin's* other suggestion that there is an analogy with the setting free of the sin-bird (*Suendenvogel*) in the cleansing ceremony for leprosy (Lev. 14:1–7, 48–53). Equally unacceptable is *Sellin's* contention that as "the ephah goes forth" (v. 6), this must be from heaven, "in which also the sins of men are laid up" (*aufbewahrt werden*); and he offers in proof the passages Deut. 32:34; Hos. 7:2; 13:12, which prove only that the *remembrance* of unforgiven sins remains with God. Many of these finds of exegesis are unfounded attempts to degrade the character of Old Testament revelation by assigning to it crudities of which it cannot be proved guilty. All these efforts again have as their ultimate objective to give a warrant for rewriting Israel's history from the evolutionary standpoint.

The last two verbs used in v. 11 read literally: "And it shall be prepared, and she shall be set there." When the common Hebrew co-ordination gives place to the subordination which we employ, this is the equivalent of: "*When* it is prepared, she shall be set there." *Wehunnîchah* is a mixed form, half Hifil, half Hofal, which is best explained by *K.W.* as embodying *wehunnîchah* (Hof.) "and she shall be set" and *wehinnîchuha* (Hif.) "and a one shall set her" (LXX: καὶ θήσουσιν αὐτό).

Chapter VI

The Eighth Vision (6:1–8)

The Four Chariots

At this point we have a better opportunity than we had heretofore to discover the plan of arrangement of the visions. The first and the last have to do with Israel's relation to the nations. The six intervening center about the people of Israel and their peculiar problems. So then, after we know that God clearly discerns how the relation between Himself and the nations who antagonize His people stands, we yet observe that He postpones action. This is done that Israel might learn that, as far as it itself is concerned, the most important issue is not the punishment of the Gentiles but the building up of itself under the guidance of divine grace. After all the vital issues that relate to Israel are then touched upon, we find God's agents taking in hand the matters dealing with the nations. What the first vision seemed to delay, the last vision pictures as getting underway, and yet not in a way that might seem to nurture a spirit of revenge on Israel's part but merely as a matter of strict justice and fair play.

Though some (like *Orelli*) let their fancy play at this point and represent the first vision as coming at the beginning of the night—the horses coming in from every quarter—the last vision represent the thing that transpires as morning is about to dawn —the riders or chariots again go out; we must draw attention to the fact that nothing of a time element is indicated. It is just as thinkable that the entire body of visions required no more than an hour to reveal.

In any case, this last vision just as did the first does concern itself with "the universal providence of God" (*Smith*).

vs. 1-8   ¹ And again I raised my eyes and looked, and of a
sudden there were four chariots coming out from between two mountains; and the mountains were mountains
of bronze. ² Hitched to the first chariot were red horses;
and to the second chariot, black horses; ³ and to the third
chariot, white horses; and to the fourth chariot, dappled,
strong horses. ⁴ Then I answered and said to the angel
that was talking with me: What are these, my lord? ⁵ And
the angel answered and said to me: These are the four
winds of heaven, which are going forth after having
presentèd themselves before the Lord of all the earth.
⁶ The one with the black horses is going out toward the
north country, and the white are going after them. And
the dappled went out toward the south country. ⁷ And the
strong went forth, and sought to go and patrol the earth.
So he said: Go and patrol the earth. So they patrolled the
earth. ⁸ Then he cried out and said to me: See, they that
are going to the north country have put My spirit in the
north country.

On "again I raised my eyes" see 5:1. The beginning of a new
vision is clearly marked. The distinctive feature that characterizes this vision over against the rest is, as in each case heretofore, the very first thing observed, "four chariots." As little
as the riders in the first vision represented war but were God's
agencies for bringing to Him reports, as it were, of what was
transpiring, just so little is it necessary in this case to make the
"chariots" represent the agencies of war. For the term used
(*markabhôth*) means chariots used for display purposes as well
and may here particularly represent the agencies employed by
God to have something carried and transported to a certain
place as we shall especially learn from v. 8. The fact that their
number is four is to indicate that God's relation to the four
quarters of the world, that is, to the whole world, is being
portrayed, cf., 1:18, 20.

Which are the two mountains? A wide range of suggestions
could be collected. They must, however, be ideal mountains
and not real, for they are at once more exactly described as
being "mountains of bronze" (*harey nechósheth*). Since no
such mountains exists, these must be mountains of the vision

only. Even such suggestions as those of *Keil* must then be rejected. On the assumption, which he himself does not intend,
that the purpose of the coming of the chariots is for judgment,
he identifies these mountains as being respectively Zion and
Olivet because God is represented as coming to judgment
sometimes from the one (Joel 4:16), sometimes from the other
(Zech. 14:4). His reason for this view is largely that some
geographical center is assumed, for the different quarters of
the globe are spoken of in reference to this center, which would
then be the two mountains just mentioned. Without questioning the fact that the judgment of God is represented by
prophecy as issuing from this center—the Valley of Jehoshaphat
—we, nevertheless, refuse to identify these mountains with any
that are known, for none are of bronze.

Still these "bronze mountains" (*nechósheth* is *bronze* not
brass) must represent something; so prominent a feature of
the vision cannot at the very outset be meaningless. The chariots apparently come forth from the place where they have
been kept in reserve, the stables, as it were, where they are
stored; for they have not done anything as yet; they are *about
to do something*. The "mountains" represent the *gates* of the
enclosure that held chariots. The fact that they are hard
"bronze" represents what strong and invincible agencies God
must employ for His work; for in God's arrangement of things
every feature is in harmony with all the rest: as the chariots
are, so are the gates of the enclosure in which they are kept.
In advancing this opinion we would not identify it with the
view of those who say (*Mitchell*): "The prophet seems to be
borrowing from a popular mythological representation, according to which the approach to the dwelling of the Deity was
guarded on either side by a brazen mountain." The prophets
should not be expected to be acquainted with all mythological
representations of antiquity, they could occasionally give evidence of originality, although in this case the visions cannot
be of the prophet's invention but are divinely originated.

A brief canvass may be made of the various explanations
that have been offered for the "mountains of bronze." *Lange's*
suggestions are rather diffuse: they are "the two fundamental

forms of divine appointment (*zwei Grundformen der goett-lichen Stiftung*) represented by the actual hills Moriah and Zion, more recently by Joshua and Zerubbabel . . . and finally church and state." *Mitchell* goes into the opposite extreme: they are "ideal mountains in front of the abode of Yahweh." *Hengstenberg*, as so often, allegorizes: they are the spiritual mountains of divine protection which (in Ps. 125) surround God's people; "two" represents protection on two sides; bronze typifies that God encircles His kingdom with a protective wall of invincible strength. Notice how far such a view deviates from the substance of the vision. Two walls of mountains are no longer sufficient; a complete circlet of them is invented, and God's people are placed within this enclosure—a matter concerning which the vision does not offer even the faintest suggestion. *Calvin,* too, is very vague: the mountains are the agencies for concealing God's secret purposes until the proper time for their execution has come. *Luther* has the mountains be "the law and the prophets," a view for which proof cannot be adduced. All these interpretations put either too much or too little into the figure.

Let it also be understood that we cannot let the four chariots represent four successive nations after the manner of the four nations of Daniel. Readers who desire a full refutation of this view may find it in the remarks of *Keil,* who has so thoroughly disposed of this vagary that it ought never again to raise its head.

In vs. 2 and 3 the colors of the horses are, no doubt, significant yet not of primary importance. A relation of the colors to the work done is in no wise intended. For in v. 5 *one* explanation is given for all. "Red" may represent carnage and warfare; "white," no doubt, represents victory; "black" is the symbol of grief and death; "dappled" or speckled may be variously interpreted, suppositions ranging from famine to changing fortunes or even hail. This is not a matter of moment, and we shall not attempt to determine anything definite, especially since the last descriptive term does not suggest color at all, namely, "strong."

Nor is there need of making alterations of the original text.

Certainly for four chariots we should have expected *four* descriptive terms. We happen to find *five*. This proves that our expectation was not correct. Our expectation, therefore, stands in need of revision, not the Hebrew text. In fact, since we discover (v. 6) that the "dappled" are a separate team of a separate chariot we shall have to revise our expectation still farther so as to include the thought that four groups of chariots are referred to according to v. 1, or, perhaps still more to the point, along *four avenues of approach* come chariots, and on the last or fourth avenue come two distinct kinds, not necessarily side by side; perhaps one after the other. Even this arrangement is not vital to the understanding of the vision, for the prophet leaves it to us to arrange it in our thoughts. Other efforts to circumvent the difficulty of interpretation here involved are unsatisfactory. It is an unwarranted procedure to strike out the word "strong." To have it apply equally to horses of "four" chariots" (*Hengstenberg*) is the expedient of dire necessity, but surely the author would then have employed about as ambiguous a mode of expressing the thought as could have been devised.

Two recent efforts along this line may also be mentioned. *Rignell,* who offers about the most exhaustive treatment of the passage, cautiously attempts to have *'amots* be some color and finally suggests that it is a synonym for "red." But in that case the arrangement of the colors becomes very perplexing. *Ludwig Koehler,* in his *Lexicon,* gives *barodh* the meaning "speckled" and *'amots* the meaning "piebald," which merely creates a new difficulty by having two teams of speckled or mottled. Why this unique emphasis?

It will also be observed that no drivers are specifically mentioned. That does not imply that there are none. They merely do not have an independent significance. To make it appear that Christ must then be the driver, as *Luther* does, is correct only in so far as that He has control; but in a *vision* Christ could not occupy five chariots; nor has it in any way been indicated that Christ has a part in this vision.

Well may the prophet be puzzled as to what these chariots

signify, and so there is no implied rebuke but an immediate answer on the part of the interpreter. Still the answer is puzzling: "The four chariots are the four winds." One would at first be inclined to suggest with *Mitchell:* the prophet is "using figurative winds to explain imaginary chariots." But that would imply undue criticism. These visions are not the outgrowth of the fertile prophetic imagination; God displayed them to him. Better is *von Hofmann's* statement of the case: the prophet is interpreting figure by figure *(Bild)*.

But is the problem actually so hopeless? The wagons carry what God gives them to carry (v. 8). There is a certain imperfection about the figure—*omne simile claudicat*—wagons or chariots must lumber along slowly, consuming, perhaps, weeks till they arrive at their destination. Surely, what God would dispatch to this land or that does not move under such handicaps. The lighter and more mobile "winds" *(rûchôth)* emphasize this feature more adequately. Even as they bear many things abroad through the earth—heat, cold, moisture, pollen, etc.—so they can serve adequately as symbols of the agents that spread spiritual forces through the wide world even as it is written, "Who makes the winds His messengers," Ps. 104:4. To regard the winds exclusively as symbols of God's judgments *(Hengstenberg)* is to emphasize only a part of the truth. They are that also, but according to Ps. 104 and according to this passage winds may serve many more purposes figuratively.

All commentators who have "winds" equal *directions* or the four points of the compass by translating *'arba' rûchôth* "to the four winds" (adverbial accusative, which is, of course, grammatically possible) must face several strong points which militate against this translation: 1) an unnatural word order which is in the original doubly clumsy; 2) the answer which is fitting for the preceding question, "What are these?" fails to agree with it; and 3) the passages cited to prove that "winds" means the four points of the compass (Ezek. 37:9; 42:20; Dan. 8:8) fail to establish the point, for Jer. 49:36 is not a later passage than this one *(Mitchell)*.

Equally difficult is the position of all interpreters who, like the *A.V.*, translate: "These are the four *spirits* of the heavens." Though *rûchôth* could mean "spirits," there is nothing elsewhere in the Scriptures about the four spirits of the heavens. This passage would then stand alone without corroboration.

These "four winds" are designated as *four* because their influence is world wide. They "stand before the Lord," *hithyatstsebh 'al 'adhôn,* a phrase that signifies their readiness as servants who stand patiently and submissively awaiting the command of their master. *'Al 'adhôn,* literally, "over the Lord," has *'al,* the preposition, as in all cases where attendants stand about a master who is seated. He is called "Lord of all the earth" to remind us, even as does the "four," that His powers must extend over all the earth because it is all His.

Those interpreters who have the "four winds" (v. 5) mean the four cardinal points of the compass alter the text of these two verses (6, 7) accordingly till they have at least one chariot going to each. Others resort to textual emendations to gain conformity with a plan which they have beforehand determined. The simplest solution is to let the unusual situation depicted by the text stand unchanged.

According to it four of the five chariots go out; one remains behind—the red one. Two go north—the black and the white ones; one goes south—the dappled one; the strong one roams to and fro in the earth. There is nothing so unusual about this procedure except that it does not fit in with a plan that is determined to distribute five chariots (or four if the text was previously changed) to the four cardinal points of the compass. None go east or west.

There is, however, good reason for this distribution of the chariots. The north country is Babylon (see our remarks on 2:6, 10). Already in 2:6–10 Babylon appeared as a land that was ripe for God's judgment or at least as one that had reached the point where God should take it in hand. A double portion of God's agents is dispatched to the north. For what purpose we shall detect more clearly after we have examined v. 8. Another outstanding power which was to feel God's influence lay to the south—Egypt. The fact that the black and the white chariots go to the north signifies grave calamity as well as victory—God's victory. The going of the dappled chariot to the south seems to imply that changing fortunes are to be visited upon the people of the south. Other lands do not demand attention now. But wherever new situations arise that need to be taken in hand, there the minister of God is already, as it were, at hand in order to act at once: the strong ones are out patrolling or policing the land. To illustrate God's unlimited resources, one chariot is held in reserve. Even when the situation calls for action (Hag. 2:7), not all of God's agents are called upon.

The manner in which "the strong" are described in v. 7 adds a colorful touch: they abound in strength to such a measure that they are eager to get into action—"they sought to go." Their desire is met in that they are bidden to "go and patrol the earth"—vs. 6 and 7 are part of the angel's remarks which began in v. 5. "He said" (v. 7) refers to the Lord of all the earth.—*Yotse'îm* (v. 6), though referring to "chariot" understood, takes its gender from "horses" preceding.

This last verse (v. 8) offers a better key to the interpretation than does any other feature of the vision. It shows in one definite instance what the chariots accomplish. From this one case conclusions may be drawn as to the rest. The rest need not be mentioned since this one case shows clearly enough what is being done. For both chariots going to the north have done this: they have put down God's Spirit there. That means they have caused God's anger to cease there. The Hebrew phrase used in this case is a bit unusual. It reads: "They have given My Spirit rest." But "Spirit" frequently signifies any disturbance of the Spirit such as displeasure or irritation or even anger. For this use of *rûach* compare Judg. 8:3; Isa. 25:4; 30:28; Prov. 16:32; 29:11. The nearest parallels to the expression as a whole seem to be offered by Ezek. 5:13; 16:42, although in these instances the object of *henîach* is *chammah* and not *rûach*. Nevertheless, the point at issue is the one so commonly found in Scripture, namely, that Babylon had dealt so cruelly with Israel in bringing about the latter's captivity that Babylon had herself incurred God's wrath (cf., Isa. 14:5ff),

and God's Spirit could have no rest till it had vented its displeasure on the offender. Interpreted thus, the last vision ends
upon a strong note of judgment. This is also *Pusey's* view who,
having interpreted the phrase to mean: they "have made My
anger to rest," concludes: "as St. John saith of the unbelieving,
'the wrath of God abideth on him.'" Judgment upon the
heathen offenders was surely a necessity and a clear token of
the sovereignty of Yahweh and so, indirectly, a reassurance to
Israel that justice shall prevail, and God's purposes shall be
accomplished.

Though this is the traditional interpretation which is based
on the Greek translation and is well established, it appears
that we should not stop with a consideration of this one side
of the matter. For when God's Spirit, which is a most powerful
agent, has been brought to a place, tremendous results are
achieved. First of all, as we have seen, He is a Spirit of judgment (cf., also Isa. 4:4) and brings about much-needed judgment. He at the same time does constructive work, aiding and
strengthening His own. Note how manifold His powers are according to Isa. 11:2; 61:1ff. To expect only negative results
when He Himself appears would do Him little honor. *Rignell*
very correctly sums up this aspect of the case: "Yahweh's Spirit
in the time of salvation has a dual function—to bring judgment upon the heathen and salvation for the people of God.
The symbolism of the two chariots hastening northward with
the black and white horses is very appropriate."

True, God's Spirit needs no agent to transport Him from
place to place; He proceeds of His own volition. In fact, being
divine, He is omnipresent. But the vision sought to demonstrate in a drastic fashion that His power was to be felt in a
very prominent way at certain places, and it behooved God to
appear as the One from whom the Spirit goes forth inasmuch
as the person and the work of the Holy Spirit had not yet been
fully revealed in the Old Testament.

The interpreting angel cried aloud (*yaz'eq*) in addressing
the prophet in order to impress upon him this part of the message as being the most important, not because of the clanging

chariots or the whistling of strong winds, of which the vision knows nothing. Verse 8 is thus marked as the key verse.

Some modern exegesis undertakes an unwarranted shifting of the text at this point. *Sellin* strongly approves *Rothstein's* view, who was the first to suggest that v. 15a should be appended to v. 8. By such exceedingly clever but uncritical procedure a text may be made to assume almost any shape or form, depending upon the inventive genius of the commentator. But how, by all that is reasonable, should v. 15a have gone so far adrift? And by what actual and clear argument can the assumption that v. 15a should follow v. 8 be proved? All such conjectures are "farfetched," "ludicrous," and "utterly unscientific," not to say "dangerous" and "misleading."

The Crown upon the Head of Joshua (6:9–15)

This is not a vision. The introductory words indicate that it is a "word of the Lord." Besides, it lacks those elements which are characteristic of a vision: nothing was seen by Zechariah; he was only commanded to do a certain thing.

Yet this portion has a very direct connection with the eight preceding visions. It follows them so closely that it appears as a practical continuation of them. But there is also a deeper inner connection. The eight visions are to be divided into two groups of four each. An interruption at the close of the fourth is indicated by 4:1. The first group comes to a climax in the Messianic thought concerning the Branch, who is typified by Joshua. As the portion 3:6–10 is attached to the fourth vision, so these remarks (6:9–15) are attached to the eighth and at the same time furnish a fitting climax to the whole group of visions. For especially toward the close the thought of judgment upon Israel and upon the world had stood out prominently. In pointing prominently to the Messiah as a personage who is furnished with unique and unheard-of authority as King our portion indicates that it shall in reality be He who achieves these mighty works, both in building His kingdom and in judging sinners.

This section may be divided as follows:

1) The symbolic act as such. v. 9–11;
2) The meaning of the placing of the crown on Joshua's head, v. 12, 13;
3) The meaning of the fact that the materials for the crown are taken from the men of the captivity, v. 14, 15.

✠

vs. 9–15 ⁹ The word of the Lord came to me saying: ¹⁰ Take the offerings presented by the people in captivity, namely, by Heldai, by Tobijah, and by Jedaiah; and go on the same day and come into the house of Josiah, the son of Zephaniah; ¹¹ where those from Babel have come; yes, take some of the silver and the gold and make a crown and set it on the head of Joshua, the son of Jehozadak, the high priest. ¹² And you shall speak to him, saying: Thus says the Lord of hosts: Behold, there is a man whose name is Branch, and He shall branch forth out of His place, and He shall build the Temple of the Lord; ¹³ Yes, He Himself shall build the Temple of the Lord, and He Himself shall carry off the royal honors and shall sit and rule upon His throne; and there shall be peaceful understanding between them both. ¹⁴ And the crowns shall be a memorial in the Temple of the Lord for Helem and for Tobijah and for Jedaiah and for Hen, the son of Zephaniah. ¹⁵ And people from far off shall come and help build the Temple of the Lord, that you may know that the Lord of hosts has sent me to you. And this shall come to pass if you diligently obey the voice of the Lord your God.

There is a grain of truth in the heading that *Fausset* gives this section, v. 9–15, "the ninth vision," but the expression, "the word of the Lord came to me" (*wayhî dhebhar Yahweh*) is that of the *word*-revelations that came to other prophets apart from specific "visions," for which an entirely different word is employed.

There is a certain ambiguity in v. 10, 11, because of our lack of familiarity with the situation as it then prevailed in the land, and also because of a certain compactness of style, which has marked also the preceding visions. All that seems to be

needed is the knowledge of an occurrence that may at the time
have been clearly known to all that dwelt at Jerusalem,
namely, the fact that certain "exiles" (the collective noun
gôlah, also translated "the captivity") that is, here, persons who
had continued to have their home in the land of exile—"exiles," we say—had arrived from Babylon with a contribution
for the work of building the Temple. See also Ezek. 8:25ff and
Neh. 7:69ff for kindred instances. These men were Heldai,
Tobijah, and Jedaiah. They were lodged at the home of one
Josiah, the son of Zephaniah. They had not as yet delivered
their sacred trust to its proper destination. There is a remote
possibility (*Sellin*) that Zechariah, after the analogy of Ezek.
8:33, was one of the priests who were charged with receiving
such gifts; but such an assumption contributes little to the understanding of these verses.

To these three men Zechariah betakes himself. That it is
"the house of Josiah" which the clause, "where those from
Babel have come," modifies becomes plain as soon as it is
clearly understood that *'asher,* the relative, can mean "where"
or "whither." The same use of this particle is found in I Kings
12:2. The *A.V.* preserves the correct sense in part by misplac-
ing the relative clause and having it modify the three men but
assigns no motive for the prophet's going to Josiah's house.
We cannot agree that the emphatic infinitive absolute
lagô(a)ch, which begins the direct discourse and is used as an
imperative (*G.K.* 113, 4(b)a), is a "dragging construction," as
even *Keil* admits, not to speak of more outspoken criticisms
on the part of others. We feel that the unusual construction is
clear and stresses just what needs to be said. For if a gift is
destined to be a contribution to so sacred a project as that of
building the Lord's Temple, and if a committee of three have
made a lengthy trip to bring this gift, surely, if any *man* were
to make bold to receive it, this would seem to border on the
sacrilegious. It is, therefore, quite proper for *God* to bid the
prophet: "Take . . . yes, take some . . . ," and so to overcome
all scruples regarding the seeming irregularity. The unusual
word order is quite effective and much to the point. Of course,

"Take of them of the captivity" cannot mean, "Take some of their number" with you, for the preposition used is not *min,* "from," but *me'eth,* "from with."

It so happens that all the men involved have names whose meaning can readily be deciphered, like Tobijah, "Good-is-Jahweh." But to try to work these names into the scene is unsatisfactory, for all combinations that are made turn out to be more or less artificial. Besides, practically all Hebrew names had a definite meaning and were for the most part compounded with the name of Jahweh or of God.

Verse 11. The gold and the silver that Zechariah received from these exiles were to be worked into a crown, *'aṭarôth.* Though this word appears in the plural it does not signify "crowns" (*A.V.*), or "two crowns" (*Luther*), but only "crown," as appears from the fact that it is set upon *one* man's head, and more particularly from v. 14 where the noun is construed with a singular verb (*tihyeh*). The plural form is readily explained. Various circlets were fashioned out of the precious metals obtained and were combined into one precious piece of workmanship. See *Koenig* (S) 260i, *plural, als eine mehrteilige Groesse.* The same usage is found in Job 31:36. The singular would have been appropriate in reference to a less elaborate type of crown. *Barnes* arrives at the same conclusion: "As the crowns, whether two (or more) were both (or all) fixed onto the same mitre, they might be indifferently regarded as one crown or several."

This crown is to be placed upon Joshua's head for reasons which "the word of the Lord" will now set forth (v. 12, 13).

In regard to v. 11 the critical approach has asserted that "Joshua" should be deleted and "Zerubbabel" substituted. Although none of the canons of textual criticism give warrant to such a change, yet, because (4:7) Zerubbabel's success was guaranteed, it is claimed that Zechariah must be listed as an exclusive supporter of Zerubbabel. Then to make such an assumption reasonable, various other alterations of the text are assumed, namely, when this prophecy of royal honors for Zerubbabel failed to materialize, later copyists altered parts of the text and substituted the name of Joshua for Zerubbabel.

We shall not trouble to refute this view. Time and a more re-
flective exegesis will correct it.

There follows the explanation of what was done, for it was
in reality an act of symbolic significance.

Joshua is being addressed in this statement (v. 12, 13).
Joshua's attention is directed to a man to whom this symbolic
act pointed. But even as Joshua is to give attention to this person, so should, of course, all who hear or read this statement.
That man on whom men shall fix their gaze is called "Branch"
or "Shoot," Hebrew *tsémach*. In thought this term is parallel
to the names found in Isa. 11:1, "shoot" and "branch." Besides, it has already been employed by Jeremiah as an un-
mistakable designation of the Messiah to come (25:3; 35:15).
So there could be no question in Joshua's mind that the
prophet was telling him that this symbolic act pointed forward
to the Coming One. The chief characteristic to be observed
when He comes will be that He will be what His name *tsémach*
implies, one who shoots up as a strong and vigorous plant.
There is, of course, an allusion to humble origin, for all plants
come from humble beginnings. But the emphasis lies on the
thought of a vigorous, fruitful plant. We might, therefore,
translate: "His name is *Shoot* because He *shoots up*."

The same thought is implied in "out of His place" (*mit-
tachtaw*); for though this compound preposition means literally "from under him," yet the meaning "out of His place" is
guaranteed by Exod. 10:23. This implies: wherever His place
may be, and wherever He may be planted, there, by virtue of
the abundance of life and strength resident in Him, He will
grow up successfully and bear fruit or develop a fruitful activity (*K(S)* 323c). *Horst* construes the clause "and he shall
branch forth out of his place" differently by regarding the verb
yitsmach as a neuter: *wo er steht, da sprosst es*. This seems less
natural.

The whole of the Messiah's activity is presented as being
successful. Certain parts of this activity are also described as
successful undertakings before the "word" goes on to show
what connection this has with the symbolic act which is our
starting point. First, "He shall build the Temple of Jehovah."

Since *Zerubbabel* is pointed to as the man who is to complete the material structure (4:7), something more than the material structure is under consideration. Since the Messiah's activity is in every case regarded as the spiritual completion of all outward symbols, therefore, "the Temple" must be the true spiritual Temple of which passages like I Pet. 2:5; Eph. 2:21f.; Heb. 3:6; Hos. 8:1 speak. That work of building for His people a true church in all its glory and with the perfections that He has promised is the work of which Zechariah's age could discern but little, but its successful achievement is here set forth.

Verse 13a is not an idle repetition of this thought but indicates that it shall be His work exclusively: "even *He Himself* shall build," etc., for we have the emphatic subject (*hû' yibhneh*).

There follows the explanation as to how this shall be possible, and why He must succeed, and this portion of the "word" furnishes also the exposition of the initial symbolic act. We remember that it was the *high priest* Joshua, whom Zechariah crowned. Since in the Jewish commonwealth there was a clearly marked distinction of offices—the royal, the priestly, the prophetic—it surely marked an unexpected departure to hear it said of the high priest: "He shall bear the [royal] glory" even though this thought had in a prophetic way been indicated in the days of David (Ps. 110:4). For *hôdh* regularly refers to the glory of a *king*. There does not follow a particular unfolding of His achievements as a priest, for priest Joshua is, and what his priestly functions were was clearly understood. The emphasis is laid chiefly on the new function that the priest shall also acquire. Therefore, "He shall sit and rule upon His throne." "Sit" (*yashabh*) refers to the new dignity that shall be His in occupying the royal throne, (*kis'o*) "rule," implying the successful administration of His office. But the two capacities are expressed as being united in the words: "He shall be a priest upon His throne." Here is the focus of the explanation of the symbolic act that Zechariah performed.

The achievements of this new union of offices are in a summary manner indicated in the closing statement of this sec-

tion: "and there shall be a peaceful understanding between
them both." This implies more than that, when these two
personages, ruler and priest, begin to function in one man,
they shall collaborate harmoniously. That thought is virtually
expressed by the words, "and He shall be a priest upon His
throne." "Counsel of peace" should, therefore, be understood
in such a way as to regard "of peace" as an *objective* genitive;
it shall be a plan or counsel (*'atsath*) that has peace (*shalôm*)
as its goal, or whatever *Tsemach* in His double capacity devises
shall tend toward the true peace of man. These last thoughts—
priestly mediation, successful rule, true peace—are in reality
the substance of all the achievements that the Angel of the
Lord promised to His people as being achieved by Himself.
With good reason this closing statement can be said to draw
all the visions to a focus on the Christ.

There follows the explanation as to why the materials for
the crown were taken from the men of the captivity (v. 14,
15).

The variation in the names must be considered. "Helem"
was "Heldai" above. In days of old men frequently had two
names: Simon and Peter; Saul and Paul; Uzziah and Azariah,
king of Judah. The two names usually had about the same
meaning. Helem means "strength," Heldai means "continuance." Somewhat different is the case of Josiah and Hen. Their
identity is vouched for by the fact that the father's name remains the same. Hen is, perhaps, not a proper name, for *chen*
signifies "favor," "grace"; because of his gracious act Josiah
is called "grace." The crown is to be deposited in the Temple
for a "memorial" (*zikkarôn*—root *zakhar,* to remember) to
what the deputation of three men had done and to the "favor"
that Josiah showed by graciously lodging these men as his
guests.

Verse 15. There was in all this a deeper significance, which
pointed forward to things that would transpire when the Messiah in His great double office should begin His mighty
achievements. For then would men come from afar, and their
object would be to aid in the building of the Temple, and
they, too, would be graciously received by those who were

already God's people and builders of the Temple. This does not refer to other exiles who shall also return and help to build Zerubbabel's Temple but to those of other nations, who are in every sense "far" from God, who shall draw near in faith and bring their resources for the upbuilding of the spiritual temple unto the Lord (Hag. 2:7). Zechariah would have been placing unseemly emphasis on the externals of religion had he here penetrated no farther than to the thought of more exiles coming to share in the blessings of the present Temple. Besides, v. 12 clearly defined how the phrase "build the Temple" was to be understood from that point onward.

When these things begin to transpire they will give evidence of the fact that the Angel of the Lord was divinely commissioned. Many of the people who lived in the prophet's day will scarcely have believed what was promised; or that He who promised it was divinely commissioned. He, therefore, here claims that the proof of His divine commission will be forthcoming. One might suppose that it is the prophet himself who advances this claim because he has been speaking since v. 9. Yet the analogy of the kindred passages that advance the claim, "Ye shall know that the Lord of hosts has sent Me to you," (2:9, 11; 4:9), suggests that here, too, as in each of these passages, the Angel of the Lord is the speaker. What has happened is this: as is so often the case elsewhere in prophecy, the prophet has so fully identified himself with the Lord for whom he speaks that he finally speaks in the very person of the Lord, identifying himself with Him.

The last clause, "And this shall come to pass if you diligently obey the voice of the Lord, your God," should be translated just as we have given it, with an explanatory "this" inserted as the subject of *hayah*. This clause is not an aposiopesis that ends in sudden silence, thus: "And it shall come to pass if you diligently obey the voice of the Lord . . ." For, in the first place, a weaker close of this part of the prophecy could scarcely be imagined. In the second place, this aposiopesis would be meaningless. Construed as we have indicated above, the statement means: the conviction of the divine commission of the Angel of the Lord and all the assurance of faith that goes with such a conviction will be the lot of those only who are very diligent about obeying (*shamôa' tishme'ûn* —verb plus absolute infinitive) the voice of the Lord. Spiritual blessings do not fall to the lot of those that despise the Word. The similarity of this statement with Deut. 28:1 is to be explained as being due to quotation. It is less to the point to indicate that Zech. 6 happened to be a lesson that was read in conjunction with Deut. 28, and thus the phrase came to be accidentally inserted here from Deut. 28.

Whether Zechariah ever attempted to carry out the letter of this command and actually made or had others make a crown and then set it upon Joshua's head must remain an open question. The Jewish tradition to the effect that such crowns were to be seen in the sanctuary is a bit vague and may have grown out of this passage. The truth symbolized by the passage is the all-important issue. This symbolized truth remains whether Zechariah literally did as he was bidden or not. We feel that the more natural assumption is that the divine command which was so specifically given was just as exactly carried out.

Criticism again resorts to its favorite claim of "corrupt text." In its attempt to be very literal criticism first points to the fact that Zechariah has announced that Zerubbabel will build the Temple (4:7, 9). When he here says *Joshua* (v. 11) is to be crowned and will build the Temple (v. 12), this is a contradiction that is to be attributed to a "clumsy attempt by an anxious scribe to bring the prophet into harmony with history" (*Mitchell*). Yet is the thought so farfetched when we assume that the work of completing the Temple may be ascribed *jointly* to Zerubbabel and Joshua?

Chapter VII

The Answer to the Question concerning Fasting

Barnes offers a good summary of the chapter by giving it the heading: "The Word of Jehovah. Mercy and Judgment are preferred by Him above Fasting."

It disturbs us little that a lapse of two years has occurred since revelation last came to Zechariah (cf., 7:1 with 1:1). No one has the courage to contend that prophets must have continuously received revelation. Nor does it greatly disturb us that we now leave the field of visions and enter upon the field of plain historical narrative. If a series of visions is at one time given to the prophet to set before the people, that does not *ipso facto* argue for the fact that it will be impossible for the prophet ever to receive any other form of revelation as, for example, a word from God in answer to a practical question that has arisen on the part of the people. We should consider these men as being capable of conveying God's truth to others in diverse forms and under widely varying circumstances. It is also very evident that every part of Zechariah's message agrees well with the times in which he lived. How necessary for such sorry, depressed times to have words like the visions (chapters 1–6) to emphasize the invincible character and the glorious future of God's people as well as the Messianic hope! But how equally necessary to curb the trend toward formalism in religion on the part of a people that had just been cured of its proclivities for idolatrous worship and knows the worship of Jahweh to be the only true worship and is now on the verge of debasing such worship in a new way— by self-elected worship such as became only too evident by the time Christ had appeared on earth (chapters 7–9)!

a. *The incident as such, v. 1–3*

This incident is carefully dated even as is the series of visions, chapters 1–6 (see 1:1). It appears also that the incident came to pass approximately two years after these visions as well as two years after the resumption of building activities at the Temple (see Hag. 1:12–15) and also two years before the building of the Temple was brought to a conclusion (see Ezra 6:14, 15). The month Chislev agrees approximately with our December. The fourth year of Darius was 518 B.C.

Among those who had returned from the captivity to their former homes were inhabitants of Bethel (Ezra 2:28; Neh. 7:32). The word "Bethel," *beth-'el,* though here the name of the town, stands by way of a common metonomy for the inhabitants of the town.

✣

vs. 1–3   ¹ And it came to pass in the fourth year of Darius the king that the word of the Lord came to Zechariah in the fourth day of the ninth month, in [the month] Chislev. ² Now the people of Bethel sent Sharezer and Regemmelech and their men to entreat the favor of the Lord, ³ saying to the priests which belong to the house of the Lord of hosts and to the prophets: Should I weep in the fifth month and fast as I have done now for so many years?

The *A.R.V.* translates correctly, "they of Bethel." It will not do to make "Bethel" an accusative of place to which, viz., "to Bethel." That translation would call for some preposition to avoid ambiguity in a construction such as the one before us. Nor is the translation of *A.V.* and *Luther,* "unto the house of God," appropriate as a translation of Bethel. For though *beth-'el* as such means "house of God," yet this expression is never used for *the* Temple or for *a* temple; the expressions "house of *the* Lord" and "house of *Elohim*" alone are used. Nor do we need to translate *wayyishlech* as a pluperfect, "had sent." It is doubtful, as *K.S.* 142c points out, whether the imperfect with *waw conversive* was ever to be translated as a pluperfect. A simple past meets all requirements, namely, "they sent." The men who were sent as this special delegation are "Sharezer and Regem-melech" together with "their men."

"Sharezer" is regarded as an Assyrian name and was, therefore, no doubt, one that was given to this man in the land of
exile.

The first statement of the purpose of this delegation is
found in the words: "to entreat the favor of the Lord"—
lechallôth 'eth peney Yahweh; lit., "to stroke the countenance
of the Lord" with the purpose, of course, of allaying any displeasure that may have arisen. Up to this point there is good
in the purpose of these men. But not all is apparently good,
for a sharp rebuke is the prophet's answer (v. 4). So it appears
that the good that lay behind their coming secures an answer
to them from the Lord. The evil that was mixed in their request as a motive makes a word of correction necessary.

On the whole, there is something epochal about this episode, something that would scarcely escape the eye of the
prophet. Bethel had been a center of the calf worship that had
been instituted by Jeroboam. It had had its own sanctuary
and its own priests. As long as this rival sanctuary continued
in opposition to the divinely appointed Zion, Bethel was a
symbol of schism and idolatry and of a divided nation.
Though many warnings had been spoken that testified to the
divine displeasure at this sinful worship, yet they had fallen
on deaf ears until the severe corrections of the Assyrian Exile
had done their work. Israel was now cured of seeking God
after its own devices, at least, cured in so far as to send to
Jerusalem and its priests for divine guidance. From this point
of view Zechariah must have regarded the event as a very good
omen. Besides, the fact that these representatives are intent
upon securing the Lord's good will ("stroke the countenance")
augured well. Both of these were hopeful signs.—*Albright*
points out that "Bethel . . . was occupied through this period
[captivity and restoration] and down probably unto the late
sixth century." [1]

It is not well to regard this question as emanating from
those who later came to be known as Samaritans as *Sellin* does
by disregarding the evidence adduced above that the people

[1] Albright, William Foxwell, *The Biblical Period* (Pittsburgh, for private distribution, 1950) p. 48.

of Bethel had returned from exile, and that "people of the land" (v. 5) does not refer to the mixed postexilic population as it does in Ezra 4:4.

Verse 3. The manner in which the divine favor these men sought was to express itself was to countenance the discontinuance of a certain fast day. As v. 5 will indicate and the eighth chapter as well, at least four fast days were under consideration. One, which may have been the most prominent, the fast of the fifth month, is made a test case. As the decision is rendered in the case of the one, so will it be in regard to the others. This explains why only the one case is at times mentioned; why, again, one or several of the others are also mentioned.

For a proper approach to the problem it is essential to note that nothing that is *divinely* ordained is involved. When a fast of the seventh month is mentioned, it is not the fast that is mentioned in Lev. 23 in connection with the Day of Atonement that is under consideration. In Lev. 23:27 we have the only Old Testament instance of a fast ("afflicting the soul" is the expression used there) of God's appointment. The fasts concerning which this seventh chapter deals are commemorative of the events there were connected with the tragic capture of the Holy City under Nebuchadnezzar. In the *fifth* month, on the tenth day, the Temple and the city had been burned, Jer. 52:12, 13; II Kings 25:8ff. (on the tenth day, perhaps the beginning of the conflagration). In the seventh month the governor Gedaliah had been murdered, II Kings 25:25ff; Jer. 41:1ff. Self-imposed fast days are the issue.

These days are, however, described as days of "weeping" and "separating one's self." "Weeping" is one form of expressing grief. A further modification of the expressions employed is "separating one's self," i.e., fasting, as v. 5 interprets the term. Thus the use of the infinitive absolute after the finite verb is to be explained (*K.S.* 402b). However, *hinnazer* implies self-restraint, in this case the withholding of self from food, therefore fasting. Nor is it difficult to understand that "wishes express themselves as questions" (*K.S.* 354d). Therefore: "should I weep, restraining myself?" is equal to saying:

"O that I might desist from these practices!" The same thought is suggested by the expression: as I have done "these so many years" (*zeh kammeh shanîm*). This expression implies, first, that a goodly number of years have passed. In fact, on closer computation, since the fourth year of Darius was 518 B.C., and the city had been destroyed in 587 B.C., sixty-nine of the seventy years spoken of in Jer. 25:11 had passed. By the time the next fifth-month fast day came around, the seventy years would be practically completed.

Though the fast was of their own choosing, the people of Bethel had no desire to act even in such a matter without divine sanction and so address "the priests" and "the prophets." According to Deut. 17:9 (Matt. 2:4) the priests had been appointed as interpreters of the law. They are described as "belonging to the house of the Lord of hosts" by a phrase which makes emphatic the thought that they are not priests by man's appointment. In fact, in place of the regular construct state relationship which the *A.R.V.* suggests, "priests of the house," we find a different connective, *'asher le,* which is expressive of a "more intimate connection" (*K.S.* 282g).

Though the priests were addressed first and the prophets second, it is the prophet who is bidden to return an answer because the matter under consideration has a wider scope than even the correct interpretation of the priests could supply.

b. *What God required: Obedience to the Word, v. 4–7*

✠

vs. 4–7   ⁴ Then came the word of the Lord of hosts unto me, saying: ⁵ Speak to all the people of the land and the priests, saying: When you fasted and mourned in the fifth and in the seventh month these past seventy years, was it to Me that your fasting was directed? ⁶ Or when you eat and drink do you not eat for yourselves and drink for yourselves? ⁷ Should you not hear the words which the Lord proclaimed by the former prophets when Jerusalem was inhabited and prosperous with her towns round about her and the Southland and the Low-hills were inhabited?

There follows the merited rebuke. It involves not only the questioners from Bethel but is also to be spoken "unto all the people of the land and unto the priests." Therefore the priests could not be ready to give an answer though the question (v. 3) was addressed primarily to them. "The people of the land" (*'am ha'arets*) is an expression that must be construed according to its usage in a passage. Although it later came to mean the common rabble, who were ignorant of the law, it here means the rank and file of the people over against the priests. "The people of the land" and "the priests" comprise the entire nation. This division is used because the priests had been one of the parties from whom counsel had been sought. The prophet's reply is: Yes, these priests plus all the people of the land stand in need of a correcting word; so do you people at Bethel.

A new evil was apparently creeping in upon the nation. This matter of the fast and the desire to be relieved of it were indications of what the evil was. Note that the inquiry put by the Bethel committee is not being answered directly. In fact, throughout chapters 7 and 8 no direct answer is offered. The reason is: the question is not an important issue. However, the attitude revealed by that question is of sufficient moment to receive exhaustive treatment.

What attitude had their fasting revealed? It was not done unto God (v. 5); it was done unto self (v. 6). Any religious act that is not actually done unto God is formalistic and externalistic. But that does not fully cover the case. True, the evil had been going on "these seventy years" (cf., v. 3 on "these many years"). God could ask: "Did you indeed fast unto *Me?*" *hatsôm tsamtûnî 'anî, fasting, did you fast to Me, Me?* Fasting unto God would be a fasting that is practiced to facilitate approach unto God and the reattainment of His favor—not in a spirit of work-righteousness but as a matter of removing physical handicaps and rendering the body subject to the higher impulses. Such fasting would be self-inflicted asceticism, practiced to remind one's self of the deserved affliction at the hands of the Lord. Such fasting could have been profitable. The Lord finds fault with Israel; this type of fasting was not in evidence. This is the negative side of the indictment.—*Tsamtuni* has a suffix that is to be construed as a dative (*K.S.* 21), it is reinforced by the personal pronoun.

Now the positive side. Just as the neglect just indicated ran back to the time when they began fasting—therefore the perfect (*tsamtûnî*); so the eating and the drinking, whether usually done, or done as they would have been practiced in place of the suspended fasts, run to the very present—therefore the imperfects (*to'khelû—tishtû*). The trouble is, therefore, that both what they do and what they omit to do are done for self. In just how far that was the case is not defined. Any possibility may be posited. It may have been practiced unto self merely to fill their bellies (*Mitchell*). It may have been practiced unto self as a self-chosen mode of religious exercise in which one expects to find satisfaction (*Luther*). It might even be that they pitied themselves because of the stern asceticism that they were practicing. Literally: "Are not *you* the eaters and *you* the drinkers?" The selfish objective is criticized. The unreligious motive is the faulty thing.

Saphôdh, absolute infinitive, representing the action absolutely, is used in vivid style to continue what was begun by the finite verb (*K.S.* 218b).

Verse 7. By a very strong ellipsis which it is difficult for us to render since we have no equivalent for the Hebrew sign of the accusative (*'eth*) the expression, "the words which, etc.," is placed into an emphatic position, literally: "Not the words which, etc." This covers the case and explains why no direct answer is given to the original inquiry. The matter that counts is *"the words."* These words have long ago given an answer; they speak now. Nothing more is needed. Let men consult what God spoke through "the former prophets" in the days before the present desolation was upon the nation. There was the answer to Israel's problems; there is the answer now. The picture is drawn in terms of what Israel felt most acutely at the time of Zechariah. For these were days when Jerusalem was *not* yet fully inhabited (*yoshébheth,* here used intransitively) and *not* "in prosperity"; and she lacked that cluster of "towns round about her" that a city of her rank always enjoyed. These were days when the Negeb (*hannéghebh,* the Southland) running down to the southern boundary line and the Shephelah, the low hills between the maritime plain and the central plateau, were not inhabited (*yoshebh,* as above).

Those critical commentators who do not have the first answer stop here, with this fine emphasis upon the *words* which God spoke by the former prophets, lose a very emphatic and important climax (*Mitchell, Sellin,* etc.). By removing v. 8 and 9 because they regard them as additions of a later redactor they mar the fine effect of the abrupt conclusion. It seems rather blunt to treat Bethelites thus when they first venture to return to the old sanctuary, but this is just what they need. They want *new* directions. They need the *old,* i.e., the words of the former prophets. Zechariah would be doing a grave injustice to all "the former prophets" if he were to answer as though they had never spoken. Therefore, in substance, Zechariah's answer is: You have an answer, "the words."

How long the pause lasted before he defined these "words" we cannot tell. In any case, we feel how rhetorically effective his answer was, and how, after having stressed one side of the matter which they had entirely overlooked, he could thereafter recapitulate the answers of the former prophets with greater emphasis. For after some thought honest questioners would say: "Now just what did these 'former prophets' tell us?" When men have come to that point they are ready to hear more.

c. *The dispersion due to failure to obey the Word, v. 8–14*

This section is not merely a recapitulation of the words of earlier prophets. In a very emphatic manner it links up the whole past situation with the troubled present that weighed so heavily upon the prophet's contemporaries. He had just said: Your chief mistake is failure to obey the Word (v. 4–7). He now says: *The dispersion* was due to failure to obey the Word. In other words: You are now again as people back in the same sin that brought your fathers so low, for everything in a nation's life centers about its attitude to the Word.

✞

vs. 8–14   ⁸ And the word of the Lord came to Zechariah, saying: ⁹ Thus did the Lord of hosts speak, saying: Execute true judgment and show kindness and compassion everyone to his brother; ¹⁰ and do not oppress the widow and the orphan, the sojourner, and the poor; and let none of you devise evil in your heart against his brother. ¹¹ But they refused to give heed and presented a stubborn shoulder and made their ears deaf that they might not hear. ¹² They made their mind as hard as a diamond so as not to hear the law and the words which the Lord of hosts had sent by His Spirit through the former prophets. So there came great wrath from the Lord of hosts. ¹³ And it came to pass that as He cried and they would not listen, so they shall cry and I will not listen, said the Lord of hosts. ¹⁴ But I will scatter them among all the nations which they have not known; and the land shall be desolate after them so that no man passed through or returned; and they made the pleasant place desolate.

Statements such as v. 8 should not be classed as interpolations as the critics do. If redactors shifted about phrases such as these in a rather arbitrary manner, the current Old Testament text would have lost all right to serious consideration. Then the current text could never have been treated as reverently as it was by the Lord and His disciples.

The change in person from "me" to "Zechariah" is a mere variation in form which is permissible from every point of view. From the wording of the verse one cannot judge that there is a great lapse of time between v. 4–7 and v. 8–14.

What God said is now introduced (v. 9) by a perfect, *'amar, he did speak.* Had the prophet desired to emphasize the validity of these words for his time he would, no doubt, have used an imperfect. By the tense he uses he indicates that he is referring to a speaking of God in the past, namely, prior to the Exile, as a comparison with verses 11, 12 shows.

Certain homely, practical virtues according to the second table of the law are stressed. They are the most ordinary tests of obedience to God and lie so near the surface that no particular spiritual discernment is necessary to form a correct estimate of them or to understand that failure to perform them is proof positive of disobedience to God's Word. Besides, they are words of the former prophets, among whom we may justly class all holy writers from Moses' time to the days of the prophets.

"True judgment" (*mishpat 'emeth,* judgment of truth) is judgment that is exercised with utter impartiality, with unbiased weighing of all evidence, and reaching a decision that is not influenced by subjective considerations (Ezek. 18:8). "Kindness and compassion" were advocated by Hosea (2:19–21). "Therefore the two great demands of righteousness and love were made upon the people constantly by the old prophets" (*Orelli*).

To these positive demands Zechariah appends (v. 10) certain prohibitions that aim to check injustice of the flagrant type that is practiced on the poor and the helpless. In this case he lists "the widow, the orphan, the sojourner, the poor," grouping them into two classes by the omission of the *waw connective* after the first two; "Widow and orphan" have much in common, likewise "the stranger and the poor." Exod. 20:20–22 covers the case; also Exod. 23:6–9; Lev. 19:15–18; Deut. 10:18ff; 24:14; Jer. 7:6. But the prophet probes deeper. After mentioning manifest outward wrongdoing he cites the evil that lies at the root of such wrong but cannot so readily be discerned: "let none of you devise evil in your heart against his brother." For the prophet, like all the other prophets, is an exponent of the true morality which measures deeds according to the motives of the heart. The secret wishes of the heart must be pure (Mic. 2:1).

Though *'ish 'achîw* is used reciprocally for *one another,* such a meaning appears far less simple than the other which regards the second noun as an apposition, "a man, his brother." The expression then contains a good motive for not devising evil against a "man"; he is "his brother."—Lexicographers have generalized a bit hastily on this passage and on Gen. 9:5.

Statements of earlier prophets are a good parallel to this verse, cf., Amos 5:14ff; Hos. 4:1; Isa. 1:17, 23; 10:2; Mic. 6:8; Jer. 22:3; Ezek. 22:7.

In v. 9, 10 God's demands made through the former prophets were presented. There follows a summary, v. 11, 12, of the attitude of the fathers toward these words in times past. The three actions mentioned in v. 11 together with the first referred to in v. 12 present a progression in evil. The first action is "being unwilling or refusing to hearken" (yema'anû); when they were bidden to do something they simply refused obedience. But there are higher degrees of refusal. In spite of a first refusal, men sometimes submit when an issue is made of the case. The figure now used is that of a man stepping up to an ox to lay the yoke on its shoulders. The beast rears up and writhes about in an effort to evade the unwelcome yoke, or as is stated here it: "presents a stubborn shoulder." God's law is the yoke to be imposed; wayyittenû khateph soráreth, literally, "they gave a shoulder rebellions." The third action is: to render the ears heavy, i.e., to close them so that the word spoken no longer reaches them. That pictures individuals as manifesting a high degree of distaste for, if not hatred of, the divine words, Mishshemoa', the infinitive with a min of separation, G.K. 119.3. (d) (1), a negative clause of purpose. The same construction is found in v. 12.

There is more than a rhetorical progression from the third item of v. 11 to the first of v. 12, which also, of course, marks a rhetorical climax. Such persistent refusal of God's words as v. 11 depicted must produce a hardened state of heart as here described, when it becomes so utterly immune to influences of the Word as to warrant its being likened to a "diamond" (shamîr) which was from days of old recognized as the hardest substance. Though such an effect can in one sense be regarded as the outgrowth of certain causes, yet Israel's participation in the process was so pronounced as to make it proper to say that they themselves made their hearts as an adamant stone. They are morally responsible for their state.

Since the entire unfortunate experience of Israel's past is being outlined, it is essential that an indication be given of the measure of iniquity involved in their past disobedience. That is done by describing more carefully what it was that Israel refused. It is first termed "the law," *hattôrah,* the honorary title from days of old given to the Word of God as it came primarily through Moses. As "law" or "instruction" the Word steps before Israel as being invested with the authority of the divine Legislator. It is also described as "the words which the Lord of hosts had sent by His Spirit through the former prophets." Though "the former prophets" were the human agents, there was a divine agent, God's "Spirit," (*rûach*), who was active in the giving of this Word. There was, therefore, from days of old a correct and an adequate conception of inspiration as the work of God's Spirit. A Word, worthy of all the honorable claims made in its behalf, cannot be disobeyed with impunity. "Therefore," we read, "there came great wrath from the Lord of hosts." This wrath is defined in v. 13.

Looking back upon these verses, we see clearly that v. 9 and 10 show how godliness was to express itself outwardly; v. 11 and 12 reveal the heart defects that were, of course, the chief cause of "the wrath" that came upon them. We feel that *Mitchell* has an inadequate understanding of the situation when he claims: "The neglect of these latter [the social virtues] was the cause of the banishment of his people from their country." When the social gospel receives undue attention, strained interpretations must furnish the necessary support.

We are still in the narrative as to how the Exile came to pass as a result of the failure to hear the Word. The "great wrath of God," v. 12, is merely being more fully described in v. 13. It was a just retaliation according to the *ius talionis:* as the crime, so the punishment (Jer. 11:11). God kept calling to them, they refused Him audience; they shall keep calling, said God, and I will not hear. That was the irremediable situation for seventy bitter, bitter years. Then they felt the "great wrath."

Toward the close of this verse there is a transition from the third person to the first, which lets the Lord Himself utter the closing statement: "I will not hear." This flexibility of style of the Biblical writers has many parallels, most of which are the outgrowth of one's putting himself very realistically into the position of another.

Verse 14. Since the verb *sa'ar* means *storm* it could be rendered, "I will storm them away." (On *'esa'arem* see *G.K.* 52.2 (c) R. 2.) God is still speaking, is telling how His wrath will express itself. Nothing describes what happened to Israel better than does what He here threatens to do: they were scattered among the nations with as reckless abandon as a whirlwind might display in scattering objects in its fury. What makes the Exile doubly hard to endure is to be thrown out among nations who are utter strangers, "nations which they have not known" (Deut. 28:36; Jer. 16:13). For the less known a threatening danger is, the more it disturbs. This is still an account of how the Exile came to pass. It summarizes what God had threatened before it came.

The picture is rounded out by a description of how desolate the forsaken land was left: "no man passed through or returned"—there were none left therein. "These opposites mark the entire extent of a concept" (*K.S.* 92c.) "and so are the equivalent of the indefinite pronoun 'whole' or 'all.'" The concluding sentence lays the whole desolate state of the pleasant land "to the blame of the fathers themselves," for they are the subject of "they made" (*yasîmû*). On "pleasant land" see Jer. 3:19; Ps. 106:24.

Min in *me'over* and *mishshabh,* "so that there was not left one who," etc. (*K.S.* 406p.).

So the questioners from Bethel have had their attention diverted from a comparatively insignificant point to a very vital matter without having had their original question answered. The matter to fear, however, was: being indifferent to the Word which was already available in their midst. Such indifference it was that brought the fathers to grief.

Chapter VIII

The Renewal and the Completion of God's Covenant (v. 1–17)

It will be well to recall the substance of chapter VII in order to note how chapters 7 and 8 form a well-rounded and balanced whole. The subject of these two chapters is, of course, the answer to the question concerning fasting. The incident itself is first reported. Zechariah then draws attention to the fact that the issue is not a trivial matter but a case of *obedience to the Word* and emphasizes the point by looking back into the past and demonstrating that the dire calamity, the Exile, was due to failure to obey the Word. As 7:8–14 looked back into the past, the entire eighth chapter looks forward into the future and holds up before Israel's vision the glorious program which God has just inaugurated for His people.

The chapter contains a *decalogue* of divine words, which by their very number (10) aim to demonstrate the completeness of God's program. The frequency with which the words; "Thus saith the Lord of hosts" (*koh 'amar Yahweh tsebha-'ôth*) recur, plus the words "utterance of the Lord" (*ne'um Yahweh*), cf., v. 6, 11, 17, serves to set forth emphatically, as Jerome already discerned, that the prophet was not promising these great facts of the future upon his own authority, but that every last one of them was separately guaranteed by the omnipotence of the Lord, and so faith in these divine promises was to be stimulated.

The grouping of these ten utterances is again plainly indicated by the still weightier introductory formula which appears in v. 1 and v. 18: "And the word of the Lord of hosts came [unto me] saying," which statement is not to be removed, as *Sellin* thinks, but is to be recognized as a clear indication of the two groups into which these ten words are divided, putting seven words into the first and three into the second group.

The most appropriate heading for the first group (1–17) is, "The Renewal and the Completion of God's Covenant"

(*Keil*), for when the seven words are grouped thus, it appears that God's return unto His people (v. 3) together with the assurance that the people will in truth and verity be His own even as He shall in every sense be their God is nothing other than a re-establishment of the old covenant relationship that was implied in the Sinai contract (see especially Exod. 19:5, 6). All that had hitherto been realized of this relationship was at the same time to be surpassed and perfected according to the other words spoken in this connection, that is to say, the "Completion of the Covenant" was also guaranteed.

These ten words are not ten previous prophetic utterances by postexilic prophets, some, perhaps, by Zechariah himself, which are here repeated or quoted by Zechariah. *Sellin* arrives at this result only by first drawing this conclusion, then removing the evidence to the contrary, that is, by deleting v. 1— an unwarranted procedure, to say the least.

It will also be observed that in the second group of these words, viz., v. 18–23, words no. 8 and no. 10 deal with a subject that is akin to that considered in the first group. It speaks of the altered state of the people, especially in so far as the attitude of Israel on the question of fasting shall be reversed, and also in so far as the bitter antagonism of the Gentiles round about shall be reversed into an eager appeal to Israel to share in its spiritual prerogatives.

In the course of the words the original question has not been lost sight of as appears from v. 19. In fact, the almost trivial question, asked, however, under significant circumstances, gives occasion to a very far-reaching prophetic utterance, and only in passing an answer is given (v. 19), which answer is, in fact, not even a direct reply to the question that was asked. The reason for this neglect is not oversight but, as we can readily detect, the fact that the question was one of those that did not merit a specific reply. Such worship of man's choosing as fasting does not deserve divine sanction, yet since some few may have practiced it rightly, it calls for no express divine disapproval. It belongs entirely in the sphere of the *adiaphora,* and the prophet's magnificent reply leaves it there. Jewish tradition on the action taken by the nation on the question of abrogating the fasts is conflicting and contributes nothing of moment to an interpretation of our passage.

✠

vs. 1-8

¹ And the word of the Lord of hosts came to me, saying: ² Thus says the Lord of hosts: I will be jealous for Zion with great jealousy, and I will be jealous for her with great wrath. ³ Thus says the Lord: I am returned to Zion and will dwell in the midst of Jerusalem; and Jerusalem shall be called, The Faithful City, and the mountain of the Lord of hosts, The Holy Mountain. ⁴ Thus says the Lord of hosts: Old men and old women shall again sit in the streets of Jerusalem, everyone with a staff in his hand by reason of old age. ⁵ And the streets of the city shall be full of boys and girls playing in the streets. ⁶ Thus says the Lord of hosts: If it seems unbelievable in the eyes of the remnant of this people in those days, should it also be unbelievable in My eyes?—oracle of the Lord of hosts. ⁷ Thus says the Lord of hosts: Lo, I will save My people from the east country and from the west country; ⁸ and I will bring them, and they shall be My people, and I will be their God in truth and righteousness.

After the familiar formula introducing the divine utterance (v. 1) we have the first statement (v. 2). This is the basic statement for the entire group of ten. Since they all distinctly refer to things and graces to be realized in the future, this one will doubtlessly refer to the future as well. The perfect *qinne'thî* is, therefore, a prophetic perfect or a future, as we have rendered it above, although the rendering, "I am jealous" (*A.R.V.*) is not inappropriate. "I was jealous" (*A.V.*) is incorrect. *Qin'ah* is a kind of cognate or related object (*G.K.* 117, 2R (a)). The basic assurance given for the comfort of Israel is this: There is on the Lord's part a strong zeal of love for Israel's welfare ("jealousy"), a zeal which leads Him to come to her rescue when enemies afflict her. *Chemah*, "wrath," from *yacham, to be hot*. This verse describes excellently the intensity of the interest of love which God manifests for His own. All the marvelous achievements that follow in the chapter grow out of this common root. God's kingdom is built primarily by the zealous and jealous God according to the consistent doctrine of both Testaments. "Zion," of course, signifies God's true people. On the relation of the two words to one another we may well follow *Barnes:* "Zeal for the good of Zion . . . fury to defend Zion against her foes; cf., 1:14."

The second statement (v. 3) gives assurance of God's dwelling in Zion and among His people. This is best understood when it is borne in mind that God had before the destruction of Jerusalem by Nebuchadnezzar actually withdrawn His holy presence from the sanctuary where it appeared over the ark, where He had since the time of the Tabernacle in the wilderness deigned to dwell among His people. This was His only dwelling place on earth, the only spot where He had vouchsafed to be found by men. Ezekiel had in visions seen "the glory of God," that is, the visible manifestation of His presence, rise up and depart from the sanctuary; see Ezek. 9:3; 10:4–18; 11:22, 23. That vision had portrayed an actual occurrence. By its sins Israel had made itself unworthy of this, the greatest of all blessings.

This withdrawal meant a suspension of the covenant relation. Here is the distinct promise given by divine mercy: "I shall return" or, "I am returned to Zion." Zion refers to the place where the Temple stood. There never was, nor is there here, a trace of a narrow conception which limits God's omnipresence after the manner of the heathen conceptions of the deity, for we at once read, and "I will dwell in the midst of Jerusalem." Equally possible would have been the statement, "in the midst of My people." These prophecies center attention upon Jerusalem's future because at the present it was still largely devastated, and its future seemed hopeless. The result of God's dwelling among His people is described as actually being what God had always intended it to be: a moral transformation of the people resulting from their actual dwelling with Him. This result is described as being, first: "Jerusalem shall be called, The Faithful City." "The city of faithfulness" is most readily understood as meaning that true faithfulness on the part of God and of man is at home there. For according to Scriptural usage *'emeth* is an attribute of God and of men; and here the emphasis lies on what *Jerusalem* shall become. Parallel is the thought: "The mountain of the Lord of hosts, The Holy Mountain." "Holy mountain" because God's presence separates it from all other mountains, sets it apart, and also because true holiness shall be learned there by men. We grant that in both these names the greater emphasis lies on the divine causality, but they prepare for the human reaction which is to be more fully described (v. 8).

These two statements illustrate beautifully how prophetic messages are adapted to the specific needs of the time. The first statement gives assurance of God's zealous interest in His people at a time when the sorry state of the nation seemed to indicate His abandonment of His people. This second statement brings the same truth still more nearly home to them by promising God's indwelling and holding up the prospect of a transformation of the people as a result of such indwelling.

Strange to say, v. 3 is the only instance in this chapter where the introductory words omit the words "of hosts" after "the Lord." This is, perhaps, done so that "Lord" stands alone and thus stresses the faithfulness which this name connotes, as it is manifested by this undeserved return to Israel.

The third statement, v. 4, 5, is to meet a specific problem of the time. Men were viewing the future with alarm. On the one hand, the dangers of these troubled times seemed to indicate that most men would come to an untimely end, and in the second place, it seemed ill-advised for young men to marry because of the uncertain state of all things. This third statement meets such gloomy prospects head-on with definite assurance.

This promise is given to Jerusalem because its future seemed most doubtful. Surely, if it, the capital city, experiences such good fortune, the rest of the land and its cities shall have their future assured. To understand the prophet's statement it is helpful to recall that "for the most part people

who were in the prime of life had returned from the Exile"
(*Nowack*). The city is pictured as having thrived to the point
where old folks and children are again on the scene.

A most delightful picture is painted by the prophet. In the
"broad open places" or plazas (*rechobhôth*) where the narrow Oriental streets widen out as they do near the gate or in
other parts of the city, there, not in the streets proper, shall
be a concourse of old folks and children. This implies that
they shall be plentifully in evidence and also, first, that under
God's protection men shall live to a ripe old age. The Scriptures rightly, as here, regard it as a favor of God when a man
is allowed to round out to a ripe age the measure of his days,
Exod. 20:12; Deut. 4:10; Isa. 65:20; Prov. 3:2, etc. The hard
and troubled days will not have brought an untimely end and
a fruitless life. After the manner of old folks these, unable to
engage in the tasks of their earlier years, delight in congregat-
ing where people are wont to meet and in sitting here and
there with others of their kind or in walking about supported
by their staffs.

In the second place, this scene implies that men have mar-
ried and begotten children, a blessing that God, too, will have
bestowed with a generous hand, for the broad places are
"filled" (*yimmale'û*) with them. This natural, inborn aspira-
tion, good in itself and approved by the Scriptures from Gen.
1:28 onward, will be fulfilled, and the nation will thus by
natural growth attain a strong and new life. The "boys and
girls" have gravitated to the broad places because these afford
more room for play and are naturally the scene of activities
that attract children. Besides, the picture drawn allows for
the deduction that a time of peace is upon the city. In time
of war men of war and preparations for war would have been
the outstanding features that would be noticeable in the broad
places.

Note the fine sequence of these words of the prophet which
were spoken as God's Spirit gave him utterance. After the
first three statements have in a logical progression held up the
prospect of a number of magnificent gifts for the future, the

very wretched present in which the people lived may have made the realization of such promises seem impossible and unattainable. It is that subject that engages our attention in the fourth statement (v. 6), which, as *Horst* suggests, "is directed against littleness of faith *(Kleinglaube)* and doubt."

As soon as we understand that *yippale'* means not so much "marvelous" as "beyond one's power," "difficult to do" (BDB), we comprehend this statement. "The remnant" *(she'erîth)*, being that small band that had returned and now constituted practically all that was "left" (root meaning of *sha'ar)* of the nation, could scarcely understand how the marvelous things just promised could become reality. God's answer is: Because they seem difficult to you, must they also seem difficult to Me?

Gam, "also," is here used like the interrogative *ha,* as it is in I Sam. 22:7. The inflection of the voice would indicate the interrogation. It does not seem that *Mitchell* fully established his contention: "When the particle *(ha)* is intentionally omitted, the clause which it would introduce is generally not a simple question, but contains an element of incredulity, irony, sarcasm or repugnance, which it would not so much denote as conceal." None of these emotions could appropriately be attributed to God in this case.

For this brief statement a double guarantee is given: the introductory formula and the closing "utterance *(ne'um)* of the Lord," always terse and emphatic.

That which was the chief defect of the previous days in regard to God's people is now also to be overcome: in times past Israel was not in reality what God had destined it to be; this destiny was now to become a reality. This truth is made clear in the fifth statement (v. 7, 8).

This statement, too, can be understood only if the times and the conditions prevailing in Jerusalem are kept in mind. The returned exiles could not help but contrast their small band with the far greater number of those who had not returned and then ask, "What shall become of those who have not returned?" God seems to promise that He will gather them, too, no matter how profusely they are scattered. But a closer inspection of the statement indicates that a people will, indeed, be gathered unto God, but they must neither of necessity be of the race of the Jews, nor will they all dwell in Jerusalem. For at none of these times could all Jews have dwelt in that one city. The word Jerusalem represents the true church of God. His people are in v. 8 described as those who are to God truly a people so that He is to them truly their God. Besides, the expression "from the east country and from the west country," according to the analogies of Ps. 50:1, 113:3; Isa. 59:19; Mal. 1:11, signifies from all quarters of the earth. A good exposition of this statement is found in John 10:16: "Other sheep I have which are not of this fold; them also I must bring, and they shall hear My voice; and they shall become one flock and one shepherd."

Apart from those who will make up for Israel's defection from God the chief issue is that the relation of this people to God will be as it ought to be. This mutual relation is described as existing "in truth and righteousness," which signifies that it is a reality (*be'emeth*), being a pretense no longer, and also that Israel shall actually do what is right and proper in such a relationship; that is what *tsedhaqah*, "righteousness," signifies, cf., Isa. 48:1; I Kings 3:6. On "I will be their God," etc., cf., Hos. 1:10; 2:25, 23; Jer. 11:4; 30:22; Ezek. 11:20.

To round out the picture of the future happy state of God's people, the prophet discusses another problem that had pressed rather painfully upon the people during these very years, especially to within two years ago—the problem, namely, of failing to secure divine blessing in their efforts at making an honest living. That such had been the situation, and that the failure of the nation in this respect had been rather marked appear from the prophecy of Haggai, cf., Hag. 1:6, 9, 11; 2:15–17, 19. Though the picture here painted of the times of the renewal of the covenant might have drawn upon many other features, it limits itself almost exclusively to items that have stood in the forefront of the people's attention and sketches the future in relation to these. Therefore the prophet now adds also the sixth statement, v. 9–13, the longest by far of the ten.

✢

vs. 9-13   **9** Thus says the Lord of hosts: Let your hands work sturdily, you who in these days hear these words from the mouth of the prophets who arose at the time when the foundation of the house of the Lord of hosts, the Temple, was laid that it might be built. **10** For before those days there was no income for man, and there was no income for the beast; neither he that came in nor he that went out was safe from the enemy, for I stirred up every man against his neighbor. **11** But now I will not be as in former days to the remnant of this people, oracle of the Lord of host. **12** For the seed of peace, the vine, shall yield its fruit, and the ground shall yield its increase, and the heavens shall yield their dew, and I will cause the remnant of the people to inherit all these things. **13** And it shall come to pass that as you were a curse among the nations, O house of Judah and house of Israel, so will I save you, and you shall be a blessing. Fear not, let your hands work sturdily.

Bearing in mind the description of the former days as given above (v. 10), the memory of which must have been like a nightmare upon men, we at once catch the force of the words: "let your hands work sturdily" (*techezáqnah yedhekhem*). For at that time, according to Haggai, men had sown much and had reaped little, had eaten and had not had enough; if the Lord had blown upon the little that they had brought home; if a drought had afflicted them; in a word, if failure had dogged their very steps, then, surely, those were days of such heavy failure and black despair as to require divine assurance that they would not recur. Such assurance is offered in "let your hands work sturdily." This clause is a summons to be about one's task vigorously and diligently. It only causes us to lose sight of the clear issues if we insert questions such as: Does this summons refer a) to the work of building the Temple, or b) to all undertakings that men were engaging in in those days, or c) to the matter of working on their part as a people to help to realize the program that God had inaugurated? As our introduction to v. 9 and as v. 10–12 especially show, Israel is exhorted to be strong and courageous about working at those tasks, the doing of which had recently brought such sad discouragements—planting, sowing, reaping, and all work of their daily calling.

They were to base their assurance that all would be well in their work, not upon some chance or fate that might prove propitious; not upon their courage or initiative; but, in conformity with 7:7, upon "these words from the mouth of the prophets who arose at the time when the foundation of the house of the Lord of hosts was laid." These prophets were, of course, according to Biblical evidence, Ezekiel, cf., 5:1; 6:14, and, as we should conclude from Haggai's and Zechariah's books, none other than these two prophets themselves. Attempts to rule out Zechariah because he refers to himself rather objectively, as well as attempts to refer to certain other unknown prophets of the day are unsatisfactory efforts. The words "even the Temple, that it might be built" are not a clumsy or useless interpolation but a distinct expression of certainty that the present program of building was going to prove successful and not be an abortive work that would come to an end with the "laying of the foundation" (*yussadh*). It was rather to be a founding "unto being built" (*hibbanôth*), i.e., a successful, promising, and hopeful founding.

The explanation offered in v. 10, beginning "for before those days," aims, not at supplying an explanation of what was not known, but is merely a recounting of a well-remembered fact and shows its connection with the present hopeful prospects. For previously "there was no income for man"—so we prefer to translate the passive *nihyeh* (from *hayah*). "Income" means as much as "the fruit of a man's labors" or "earnings," *Verdienst* (*Buhl*). No man, whether employer or employee, was producing anything. Even the beasts were not earning their keep—here expressed: "there was no income for the beast." On *'eninnah* see *K(S)* 349i.

To the picture of the depressed and evil days that had just passed belonged a statement of the enmity and the antagonism which were encountered by Israel at the hand of its adversaries, the people of the land, the non-Israelites, who sought to thwart all Israel's constructive designs. This antagonism was continually experienced when men "went out or came in," i.e., when they took a task in hand or when they had completed one—"a description of all those who are busily engaged in their regular pursuits" (*Nowack*). No one "was safe from the enemy" (*tsar*, the enemy). There was not only opposition that came from without but also that which came from within, for God had incited (*shillach*, literally, *sent forth*), II Kings 24:2, all men, everyone against his neighbor. The "for" introducing the clause is (*wă*), here not lengthened to (*wā*) as *waw conversive* usually is before weak laryngeals, for this last clause is not explanatory of the one preceding but adds an additional item that disturbed Israel's peace: Israelite opposing Israelite. Surely, those must have been evil and discouraging days!

"The remnant of this people" (cf. v. 6 on this phrase) shall now experience it (v. 11) that God Himself has terminated this evil state and has set afoot a different and new program for their welfare. This statement of the case sets strongly into the forefront the fact that the divine attitude toward a people is the primary cause that makes for success or failure. This promise of a favorable attitude is strongly backed by an emphatic "utterance of the Lord of hosts." In v. 12, 13, there follows the picture of the blessed state that will result.

The matter presented in this picture is determined by the previous situation; what was then lacking shall now be at hand. First, the choicest of plants, "the vine," is considered. It is designated "the seed," i.e., "the growth of peace," because, being the choicest of plants, it needs that culture which only peaceful times can make possible. But if it yields its fruit, then a season of peace is upon the land, and neither "the adversary" nor "the neighbor" (v. 10) are disturbing the husbandman. Other translations such as, "they shall be seed of peace" (*Luther*), or "the seed shall be prosperous" (*A.V.*), or "there shall be the seed of peace" (*A.R.V.*), or "I will show peace," after the example of the *Septuagint* (δείξω εἰρήνην), make necessary the insertion of words or, for the most part, textual emendations—all of which are far more difficult expedients than to consider the word "seed" as having the broader meaning "growth" and having "the vine" in apposition to it. A number of things could, however, be said in defense of the Greek translation.

Other elements are added to the picture. Even as the choicest plant thrives, so does "the ground yield its increase," that is, all those products which make up the mainstay of a man's life, grains and fruits. Furthermore, in order that these as well as all other vegetation may truly thrive, "the heavens shall yield their dew." Again it is not human endeavor or even these products of nature that make for man's prosperity. Such success and such fruits are the gracious gift of God to this small body of Israelites: "I will cause the remnant of this people to inherit all these things." The idea of undeserved, unearned goodness underlies, as regularly, the verb "inherit" (*nachal*).

This new prosperity will be so outstanding that the nations shall be made aware of it (v. 13). For as, on the one hand, the Jews had been so manifestly and heavily cursed both by the Exile and by their more recent failure in all enterprises as to become an example of how heavily a curse may rest upon a nation; so on the other hand, will the salvation that God brings to pass in their new prosperity serve as an example of how richly blessed a people may be. "Curse" and "blessing," therefore, mean *example of curse* and *example of blessing* (*Buhl: Vorbild des Fluches*); cf., Jer. 24:9; 25:9; 42:18; II Kings 22:19; Gen. 48:20; Jer. 29:22.

The recipients of this blessing will be the "house of Judah and the house of Israel." Both Judah and Israel are mentioned because there were some persons of Israel who had aligned themselves with Judah in the Return, and they stood in need of like comfort with Judah.

In order entirely to remove the thought of a cursed failure that had fallen to their lot, the prophet closes his words of comfort with the cheering statement: "Fear not, let your hands work sturdily." The absence of a conjunction between these two summonses gives the words a kind of ring of military curtness. A vigorous summons to courageous action is the purpose of the entire statement, v. 9–13.

The seventh statement (v. 14, 15) deals with God's firm determination to do Israel good. This statement is a good conclusion to this section of the address, viz., v. 1–17, for it ties the conclusion back with the beginning, v. 1, 2. For as at the beginning God's zealous interest in Israel was the root from which all the blessings enumerated sprang, so at the end the same truth, regarded from another viewpoint, is pointed out as the prime cause. The emphasis, therefore, rests as strongly as it can be stated upon the divine causality of prosperity.

✠

vs. 14,15   **14** For thus says the Lord of hosts: Just as I purposed to do evil to you, when your fathers provoked Me to wrath, says the Lord of hosts, and I relented not; **15** So again have I purposed to do good to Jerusalem and to the house of Judah: fear not.

"I devised" (*zamam*) means "I considered, purposed, devised" (*BDB*) and therefore manifests God's work both for evil in the past and for good in the future as the result of a deliberate, purposive planning. In either case nothing was a chance outcome. It was all according to the divine purpose. As the past proved that, when God purposed evil, it came, resistless like an avalanche; so for the future the conclusion is valid: The intended good must come irresistibly. God's people must have been sadly disheartened, for here again God speaks the comforting word: "fear not." *Shabhti,* v. 15, is used adverbially (G.K. 120, 2b).

It may be well to remark in this connection that "the prophets do not hesitate to trace physical evil to the hand of God; cf., Isa. 45:7; Amos 3:6 . . . ." (*Barnes*). Of course, "physical evil" refers to calamities that God allows to befall men according to His just judgment.

An appendix to this statement and practically to the whole section (v. 1–17) follows. It stresses the fact that there are conditions that Israel must meet if God is to bestow a blessing.

Since the moral duties of Israel as here outlined have appeared
previously in this book, their being added at this point gives
the impression that the prophet hopes to induce men more
readily to obedience, especially now that they have been made
aware of the good things God is about to bring to pass. Prophets are not in the habit of offering false comfort to men who
are careless about doing the will of God.

This appendix runs thus (v. 16, 17):

✞

vs. 16,17   **16** These are the things which you shall do: Speak the
truth every man to his neighbor; give true and fair verdicts
in your courts; **17** and let none of you devise evil in your
minds against your neighbor; and do not love false oaths:
for all these are things that I hate—oracle of the Lord.

In Hebrew the statement cannot be made to appear as
though it conveyed the thought: "These are the things which
you shall do," contrasting "you shall do" with "I shall do."
Rather, since "these are the things" are the words that stand in
the emphatic position, the implied contrast is: There are, so
Israel feels, certain things that ought to be done if God works
so generously for Jerusalem. "These things" are listed.

"Speak ye the truth" is implied in v. 3. "Execute the judgment of truth" is spoken in 7:9. To this is added the idea
"judgment *of peace*," which points to judicial decisions that
make for peace and cannot be gainsaid because they are de-
cidedly fair. We have let the translation express this thought:
"give true and fair verdicts." "Let none of you devise evil in
your minds against your neighbor" is to be read also in 7:10
and stresses beautifully the necessity of harboring thoughts
that are uncontaminated by evil against our neighbor. The
"love of false oaths" was alluded to in 5:4. To make these mis-
deeds abhorrent to man, Zechariah describes them as being
hated by God.

Kol 'elleh is the object of "I hate." It is placed forward in
an emphatic position and made to stand out still more by the
practically redundant *'asher*. By this device the sentence gets a

turn, however, that is well rendered: "For all these are things that I hate, utterance of the Lord." Cf. also Hos. 9:15; Amos 5:21; Isa. 1:14.

The Altered Joyous State of God's People (v. 18–23)

Now that the fullness of the glorious salvation that the Lord will bestow upon His people has been adequately outlined, an answer may be given to the original question regarding fast days (7:1–3). By postponing this answer the question is removed to its proper place. Worthier problems should have engaged the attention of the people. Yet there were some important features connected with the question that could profitably be considered. The change that these days would undergo as the covenant relationship between God and the people perfects itself more and more would show itself also in regard to fast days and serve as a good illustration of God's rich grace. It is this thought which occupies our attention in the eighth statement (v. 18, 19).

✠

vs. 18,19
18 And the word of the Lord of hosts came to me, saying: **19** Thus says the Lord of hosts: The fast of the fourth month, and the fast of the fifth, and the fast of the seventh, and the fast of the tenth shall become for the house of Judah days of joy and gladness and happy feasts; only love truth and peace!

The fast of the fourth month, Tammuz, was observed to commemorate the fact that in that month a breach had been made in the walls of Jerusalem during the final siege as we read in II Kings 25:3 and Jer. 39:24. The fasts observed in connection with the fifth and the seventh months were explained in our interpretation of 7:3, 5. The fast of the tenth month, Tebeth, recalled the arrival of the forces of Nebuchadnezzar and the beginning of the siege of Jerusalem. See II Kings 25:1; Jer. 39:1.

This group of fasts had been self-imposed in order to express the nation's grief because of these great calamities. When

God, however, brings His mighty benefits to pass for the house of Judah, such passing episodes, that were once regarded as the greatest calamities, shall be so entirely forgotten as days of sorrow that they will even be seen to be a part of God's wise and gracious dealings with His people, and shall thus be converted into days of "joy and gladness" and shall be "good feasts" (mo'adhîm tôbhîm), i.e., cheerful feasts, because they are feasts commemorating good things. This statement might also be interpreted to the effect that God will have given new blessings and so many of them that enough will be found worthy of commemoration to assign one to each of these former days of sorrow.

On yihyeh, singular after a plural subject, see G.K. 146, 2(a); also 107, 4, 3f.

There is no warrant for Wellhausen's deduction made on the basis of this passage that the law for fasting on the Day of Atonement (Lev. 16:29) cannot as yet have been in force since no mention is made of that particular fast. Failure to make specific reference to it is just as readily accounted for by the evident fact that the fast of The Atonement Day was the only divinely appointed fast whereas the four under consideration were of human choice and of comparatively very recent date. It could not have occurred to Israel to ask for an abrogation of the fast on the Day of Atonement. Sellin's supposition that the words "and to the house of Israel" have been removed from their original place after the word "the house of Judah" is also fanciful because it is founded on the desire to furnish support for his peculiar view as to who those men were that originally asked the question mentioned in 7:3.

The closing words, "and love truth and peace," are rendered "only love," etc., by Luther, and "therefore love," etc. (A.V.). By rendering the simple Hebrew waw (and) "only" the emphasis is laid on the terms that man must meet if God is to fulfil His promises; yet not necessarily in the sense that man can merit God's blessings. By rendering it "therefore" we would stress the thought that God's mercies should produce willing obedience to His precepts. Both points of view are permissible although we hold that in this chapter (cf., v. 16, 17) the former approach deserves the preference without ruling out the latter.

The promise stated in v. 18, 19 is not to be regarded as a separate and distinct matter. There are other great works of God that precede and lie in the background, because of which, as they produce their normal fruits, fast days become days of gladness. The next two statements are also only further results of the mighty works of God that have been described in the earlier part of the chapter. This ninth statement (v. 20–22) is at the same time built up on the preceding, and the thought sequence could be stated as follows: when the nations observe how Israel's singular blessings have converted their fast days into feast days they, too, will turn to the same source and seek God's mercy. In other words, the substance of this ninth statement is that *nations shall seek their salvation at Jerusalem.*

✠

vs. 20–22   **20** Thus says the Lord of hosts: It shall yet come to pass that whole nations shall come and the inhabitants of many cities; **21** and the inhabitants of one city shall go to another, saying: Let us go at once to entreat the favor of the Lord and to seek the Lord of hosts! I myself am going. **22** So then many peoples and strong nations shall come to seek the Lord of hosts in Jerusalem and to entreat the favor of the Lord.

We are set into the midst of an intense movement which is strongly affecting large groups—"peoples," nations as a whole, and "the inhabitants of many cities," emphasizing great numbers. Before the more external motive that animates them is revealed, viz., their going to Jerusalem, we find their deep spiritual purpose touched upon: entreating the favor of the Lord and to seek the Lord of hosts. They recognize, first, that His favor must be gained, or, as they state it, they must "entreat the favor of the Lord." For this phrase see 7:2. This expression is particularly appropriate here, for it gives admirable expression to the primitive feelings of those who are just beginning to seek the Lord. Before they have recognized that there is in reality nothing they can do to win God's favor they will think in terms that sound almost work-righteous. Again, since they have not as yet found Him they will very aptly speak of "seeking" (*baqqesh*) Him. Very aptly also they designate Him whom they seek by the favorite honored title employed by Israel in referring to Him, "the Lord of hosts."

An inimitable, realistic touch, revealing how eagerly individuals who are exhorting others to share in the movement, do themselves crave the salvation of Israel, is found in the words that are added without a conjunction: "I myself am going." That no one might minimize the greatness of these results and think that the number of seekers cannot be so great, v. 22 adds emphatically: "So then many peoples and strong nations," etc. In the light of what preceded we now realize that the seeking *"in Jerusalem"* is purely a bit of local coloring that states the case in the thought forms of the Old Covenant, where all seeking of the Lord was by divine ordinance to center in Jerusalem. Millennialistic misinterpretation still fails to see the force of John 4:21.

The following items in this sketch suggest a powerful mass movement at the highest point of its strength: a) the great numbers spoken of; b) the fact that large groups appeal to large groups—"inhabitants of one city going to another"; c) their eager self-exhortation—"let us go at once," lit., "let us *go going*" (*nelekhah halokh*), the strongest possible expression, (on the imperfect with *ah* hortative and infinitive absolute see K(S) 329p; and d) the individual assertion, "I will go also," very emphatic in the original: *"let me go, me also."*

The tenth statement (v. 23), though it individualizes what v. 20–23 represent, at the same time marks a distinct advance in thought, for it shows that *the favored lot of the Jew will be recognized.*

✠

vs. 23

[23] Thus says the Lord of hosts: In those days it shall come to pass that ten men from nations of every language shall take hold of a Jew by the skirt of his coat, saying: We will go with you, for we have heard that God is with you.

The number *ten* is frequently used as "the number of a strong, numerous group" (*Keil*); cf., Gen. 31:7; Lev. 26:26; Num. 14:22; I Sam. 1:8. As large a number as could be found appealing to any one man is represented as appealing to the Jew, whose lot it had hitherto been to be derided and scorned rather freely. The expression, "from nations of every language," makes the picture given in v. 20–22 more colorful by depicting the great variety of languages spoken by those who seek after the Lord. Zechariah seems to have derived it from Isa. 66:18. Taking hold of the skirt of a man is a gesture of suppliant entreaty; they hold him back by it as he seems to be leaving. It is very significant that they employ the general name God (*'elohîm*) and not Lord. The use of the latter might have suggested the thought of the Lord overagainst their particular tribal or national gods, in whose existence they might still believe. But God implies that God as such, the deity, is found only among the Jews. So they have heard, they claim; this implies that they have thus far sought Him in vain.

With the old animosity removed, the animosity which the Jews continually experienced at the hands of other nations, the ten statements of our chapter are rounded out into a harmonious whole.

In regard to this last statement *Mitchell* has the author of Isa. 45:14 appear as being more extravagant and more marked by "racial pride and resentment" than was Zechariah. Why make such contrasts when prophets do not agree to the letter!

A word as to the time to which these ten words point. Their scope would be sadly limited if their application were restricted to the time when they were spoken and the immediate future. As usual, they are prophetic words without limitation of time. They refer particularly to the Messianic age. Some very practical aspects are intended for the immediate present, for the prophet's contemporaries. A fuller realization is accomplished in the coming of Christ. Their fullest import is realized at the consummation of all things. The prophet blends all of these into one marvelous picture.

A word as to the abrogation of the fast days. It is not true, as *Sellin* argues, that "in any event according to Zechariah fasting is to be discontinued at once." Zechariah gives no explicit orders. He speaks of things that will come to pass. It is left to his hearers as to whether they will take action or not. Had their faith been sufficiently strong, they would have refrained from all fasts at once. Just because, however, the issue is one which must ultimately adjust itself for the true children of God, the prophet does not aim to make an issue of it. Whether there was ever an abrogation of these days and a later re-establishment of them we are unable to determine. They are still observed by the Jews.

Chapter IX

The Burden upon the Land of Hadrach and the Coming of Zion's King (9:1–10)

That a new section of the book is beginning is clear from the new subject matter presented and from the very distinct and prominent heading, 9:1. On the question of authorship of this part of the book (chapters 9–14) see the Introduction.

We submit a summary of the contents of these six chapters. We feel that *Keil* has the most effective treatment of these chapters, and so our outline will bear marks of having followed him. As a title for the whole section we might choose *The Future Development of the Kingdoms of This World and of the Church.*

The headings that the book itself gives are more indicative of what follows than is usually supposed. They read thus: "the burden of the word of Yahweh upon the land of Hadrach" (9:1) and "the burden of the word of Yahweh concerning Israel" (12:1). If "Hadrach," as we shall show later, refers to the world-power, then obviously world-power and Israel are the two forces under consideration, and this helps to explain the general heading we have set down above.

Unfortunately, the debate is still going on as to the force of the word we have translated "burden," *massa'*. Even *Koehler's New Lexicon* lists as first meaning "load, burden, judgment" and as second meaning "utterance." It seems to us that both meanings play into one another. In both instances a divine "utterance" is intended, but it seems equally clear that a "judgment" is obviously in the picture. In the case of the first burden, on Hadrach, the thought is certainly involved that the world-power is going to be judged by God and is to suffer defeat in spite of her seeming victories. That judgment the world-power continually experiences. In the case of the burden concerning Israel it is equally clear that Israel, or Judah, is thought of as victorious, but a judgment of God is to befall also her lest she grow overweening and proud.

161

This correspondence between the two "burdens" reaches farther. Both have the same grammatical structure. Both speak first of Israel's, or Judah's, victory. In a somewhat sharp break of the thought there follows a statement that seems more like a negation of the thought of victory in that Israel is viewed in the first instance as being ready for judgment and, therefore, to be entrusted first to a good shepherd, then to a foolish shepherd (11:1–7). In the second instance victorious Judah suddenly appears as a nation that is about to be purged for her sin and to be assaulted by her foes (13:7—14:5).

It may be remarked already at this point that much more is under consideration than a superficial reading might suggest. Though the prophet seems to speak in terms of the contemporary situation in Israel and in Judah, it is obvious that the days of the Messiah have come (cf., 9:9, 10; 12:10; 13:7), and "Judah" obviously refers to the Christian Church in those various experiences that are hers in the course of her history. The future developments and victories of the church are related in terms of Old Testament experience.

We submit the outline of these chapters:

THEME: The Future Development of the Kingdoms of This World and of the Church.

I. The Burden upon Hadrach (chapters 9–11)
  A. The Victory of Israel (chapters 9, 10)
    1. The coming of Zion's victorious King (9:1–10)
    2. Zion's victory over the Greeks (9:11–17)
    3. Israel's prosperity and perfect redemption (10:1–12)
  B. Israel, ready for judgment, committed to a good shepherd, then to a foolish shepherd (11:1–17)

II. The Burden upon Israel (chapters 12–14)
  A. Judah's Victory (12:1–13:6)
    1. The confusion of Judah's enemies (12:1–4)
    2. Judah's strength in the Lord (12:5–9)
    3. Judah's true penitence (12:10–14)
    4. Her true sanctification (13:1–6)

B. The Lord's Victory (13:7–14: 21)

   1. The purging of God's people occasioned by the shepherd's death (13:7–9)

   2. The deliverance of Jerusalem occasioned by the assault of her foes (14:1–5)

   3. The new state of affairs after the Lord's day (14:6–11)

   4. The confusion visited upon all enemies (14:12–15)

   5. The submission of the nations (14:16–19)

   6. The new state of holiness (14:20, 21)

We are ready to take up the first section, which proclaims primarily the coming of Zion's King (9:1–10).

✠

vs. 1-10   [1] This is the burden of the word of the Lord against the land of Hadrach, and it shall come to rest upon Damascus. For the Lord hath an eye upon men and upon all the tribes of Israel; [2] and also Hamath, which borders on it; Tyre and Sidon, because it is very wise. [3] And Tyre did build herself a stronghold and heaped up silver like dust and fine gold as the mire of the streets. [4] Lo, the Lord will make her poor and dash her power into the sea; and she shall be consumed by fire. [5] Ashkelon shall see it and be afraid; Gaza also, and shall be in bitter anguish; Ekron also, for her expectation shall be put to shame; and the king shall perish from Gaza, and Ashkelon shall become uninhabited. [6] And trash shall settle in Ashdod, and I will break the pride of the Philistines. [7] And I will take away their blood out of their mouth, and their abominations from between their teeth. And they, too, shall be left for our God. And they shall be like chieftains in Judah, and the people of Ekron like the Jebusites. [8] Then I will encamp about My house as a guard against all that come and go, and no oppressor shall pass through them any more; for now I have seen with My eyes. [9] Rejoice greatly, O daughter of Zion; shout for joy, O daughter of Jerusalem. Lo, your King comes to you. He is just and saved; lowly and riding upon an ass, that is, upon a colt, the foal of an ass. [10] And I will exterminate the chariots from Ephraim and the horses from Jerusalem; and battle bows shall be cut off. And He shall speak peace to the nations; and His dominion shall be from sea to sea, and from the River to the ends of the earth.

We have here a statement that threatens doom—"a burden."
This "burden," at the carrying of which the nation over whom
it is spoken shall assist, is not to be regarded as an idle threat.
It is "the burden of the *word of the Lord.*" Though this combination of terms is not found elsewhere, that fact does not
stamp it as unreliable. Divine inspiration has greater resources
of expression than criticism would allow.

This burden is laid upon "the land of Hadrach." A surprisingly large number of conjectures as to the possible meaning
of this word *Hadrach (chadhrakh)* has arisen. To sum up and
pass upon the merits of all would be a very tedious undertaking. Let the following suffice, in which we touch upon the
outstanding suggestions. All interpretations that necessitate
some changes of the text are to be rejected, for they do not
meet the facts of the case but trim down the evidence to conform to their theories. The view of the Targums that the land
of the South is meant is devoid of all support. Those commentators who make Hadrach a person have no evidence of
the existence of such a person and ignore the fact that the
Scriptures usually give some clue when unusual proper names
occur; besides, these critics need several textual emendations
before their view seems to accord with the thoughts of the text.

The most commonly accepted view is that Hadrach is identical with the land Hatarikka, mentioned in cuneiform inscriptions, as pointed out first by *Schrader* and accepted by
Delitzsch (Das Paradies, p. 279). The case is, however, far from
closed, and *Sellin* is letting a kind of consensus of opinion influence him when he claims the identity is "definitely established" *(sicher nachgewiessen). Barnes* says, more correctly,
"Assyriologists place it conjecturally south of Hamath." It is
concluded that this otherwise unknown land lies somewhere
north of Lebanon, at least the other lands mentioned in the
inscriptions are to be sought there. But why this land with
which Israel never had contact should be mentioned here has
not yet been satisfactorily explained.

The old traditional Jewish view advanced by *Jarchi* and
Kimchi still deserves the preference. It makes this a figurative
compound name: *Chad* = sharp; *rach* = soft. The compound

THE BURDEN UPON THE LAND OF HADRACH

is the land *Sharp-soft* although these Jews took this to be a name of the Messiah, "who was severe toward the Gentiles and gentle toward Israel." We take it to be a designation of the dual Medo-Persian Empire, which had in it the sturdy material which made the Persians conquerors and produced men like Cyrus. Persia was at the same time characterized by an effeminate softness that later made Persian debauchery and effiminacy a byword and the source of the moral contamination of Greece and Rome. The reason for a *hidden* reference to this world-power lay in the dangers that might have resulted from open criticism at a time when neighbors were trying to prove Israel traitorous.

Similar notable cases of words with mystic meaning are Dumah (Silence) for Edom (Isa. 21:11), Sheshach (Humiliation) for Babylon (Jer. 25:26; 51:41), Ariel (Hearth of God) for Jerusalem (Isa. 29:1, 2, 7). So this use of Hadrach is supported also by the analogy of the Scriptures.

With this as a starting point, we notice that the chapter proceeds logically. It gives the burden upon the Medo-Persian Empire but touches only upon the lands that are contiguous to Israel, allowing us to infer that the lot that befalls the one set of subject nations will be the same for all the rest. The same manner of argument runs through the first seven verses: what, for example, is set forth as befalling one Philistine town is mentioned merely as an example of what befalls all alike. Then, too, the enigma that was troubling Israel in these days was the apparent success of the world-powers overagainst the almost certain failure of God's people; cf., Mal. 2:17; 3:13. The prophecy aims primarily to meet this difficulty.

This prophecy was, no doubt, so designed by divine providence as to cover the victorious progress of Alexander the Great, for the order of the towns mentioned is identical with Alexander's line of march after the battle of Issus. Yet we dare not conclude that verses 1–7 are a prophecy of this hero's success, for v. 7 marks a result that did not follow upon his conquest. The prophecy is, however, a word portraying in colors taken largely from Alexander's conquest the downfall of the Gentile power and the conquests achieved by Israel's King,

the Messiah. All the towns mentioned after Hadrach are portions of this "land."

Though almost all lexicons are agreed that the word rendered "burden" (*massa'*) should be translated "oracle," yet in
one sense or another the idea of burden is connected with
every instance of its use; cf., *Hengstenberg, Christology,* on
this verse, who has effectually established this claim. Or as
Barnes has effectively put it, "The reference is in each case to
an utterance of an important kind, either a threat or a warning."

Of the lands adjacent to Israel Damascus is mentioned first,
then Hamath farther to the north. The reason for this seems
to be that Alexander actually proceeded from Damascus to
Hamath. The "and" before "all" (*wekhol*) is rightly defined
as a *waw augmentativum* and is translated "especially" (*K(S),*
375d). He made Damascus his objective after the victory at
Issus, sending another commander to attend to Hamath. So
the first place upon which "the burden of the word of the
Lord" lights is Damascus; or Damascus shall be its (the word's)
resting place (not "rest" *A.V.*). The parenthetical conclusion
of the verse emphasizes what we stressed above, the fact that
God has a watchful eye over both those who afflict Israel and
especially upon Israel itself. Though, indeed, the words of 1b
could be rendered "for the eye of man," etc., is toward the
Lord, that translation fails to fit into the connection. Our
rendering is just as permissible. "Men" (*'adham*) in the sense
of *mankind* is the meaning of the word when it is set overagainst Israel as similarly Jer. 32:20. *'Eyn 'adham,* "eye *upon*
man," the preposition lying in the idea of the word "eye"; see
K(S) 336t.

Verse 2. "And also Hamath" means also Hamath shall be
the resting place of this "burden." The reason for its being
involved next is that "it borders on it," i.e., on Damascus.
There is no relative expressed in the subordinate clause, however. On *chamath tighbal,* see *G.K.* 155, 2, b, 1.

"Tyre and Sidon" follow next in order, being the next
towns encountered on an expedition going south as Alexander's did.

It will be observed that four towns are mentioned in this group. The symmetrical arrangement is maintained also, v. 5 and 6, when the Philistine towns are listed, but only four of the well-known five are listed. The symbolism of the number apparently governs this arrangement, four being the number of the world, and these towns being overthrown because they are dominated by the spirit of the world which is hostile to the nature of Jahweh. That thought finds expression in 2b, "because it is very wise." Its wisdom is the wisdom of this world (I Cor. 1:20) which is hostile to God. Destruction does not come in spite of ("though"—*A.V.*) its great wisdom but more directly because of it ("because"—*A.R.V.*); see Ezek. 28:2. The singular (*wattibhen*) is used, referring directly only to Tyre though Sidon is also mentioned, because Tyre so completely outranked its mother city, Sidon, as to dominate the situation. Tyre's wisdom consisted in the ability to acquire great treasures, Ezek. 28:2–6, as well as in knowing how to secure for herself an almost invincible stronghold, New Tyre, the island. This is referred to in v. 3.

Verses 3, 4. Before, v. 1 and 2, the account of how the burden of the word of the Lord was fulfilled was very general; Damascus and Hamath are mentioned as having been afflicted. As the circle is drawn closer, and those countries come into consideration that are under Israel's immediate observation, the account becomes more detailed. This is especially true in the case of the four Philistine cities mentioned. Verse 3 is naturally attached very closely to v. 2b. In fact, "they are very wise" (v. 2) finds its explanation in v. 3. We see our estimate of the character of this wisdom justified, for this wisdom found expression in the building of a superbly strong "stronghold." *Matsôr,* which may also be rendered "rampart for defence," is rather "late" because the word usually means "siege enclosure." Such indications of late Hebrew usage confirm indirectly the authorship of this part of the book of Zechariah. This stronghold resisted siege on the part of Shalmaneser for five years and on the part of Nebuchadnezzar for thirteen years. See *Delitzsch's* remarks on its strength, on Isaiah 23. Isaiah 23:4 uses an expression that is rendered "stronghold of the sea" in reference to this island fortress. Incidentally, there is a clever paronomasia in the Hebrew which might very inaccurately be rendered: *Tyre* did build herself a *tower*.

A further instance of Tyre's "wisdom" is given: She "heaped up silver as dust and fine gold as mire." The word for "dust" is *'aphar,* which here refers not so much to dry dust as to materials that are easily acquired in abundance. Again, "gold" (*charûts*—from a root signifying "to be yellow") is said to have been heaped up as "the mire of the streets." Strictly, the simile does not quite denote contempt, but it does suggest that this precious metal became so common that no more note was taken of it than would be taken of the garbage-cluttered mire of the streets.

When it is said (v. 4), "Lo, the Lord will make her poor," this refers primarily to the successful siege of Alexander when the city capitulated after several months of beleaguerment. The verb *yarash* usually means "possess" or "dispossess," but the contrast with her former riches here as in I Sam. 2:7 gives it the meaning "impoverish" (*BDB* and *K.W.*). Besides, God's activities through mighty agents of His are described as "dashing her power into the sea." This is a drastic figure. God delivers one mighty blow, and the city, lying as an island in the sea, is swept into the sea. The preposition *be* is better taken in the sense of "into" than "in," for the latter meaning presents a rather weak picture. The ultimate fate of the fortress is described as: "she shall be consumed by fire." Only a literalistic criticism would seek to establish a conflict with the preceding figure according to which Tyre was swept into the sea. For, in the first place, the preceding figure was hyperbolic in character. In the second place, one blow would scarcely be conceived as being so sweeping that every remnant of the city would be removed by it. What remains after the disastrous blow will be consumed by fire. Each of the three clauses describes complete downfall and overthrow. All three together spell total ruin. The article in "with the fire" refers to the fire that is customary when conflagrations occur (*KS* 299c).

The rendering of the second clause, "He will smite the sea which is her rampart" (*ARVm*) appears a bit fantastic and fails to yield an unforced meaning.

Verses 5 and 6. Four of the famous Pentapolis are mentioned—Gath being omitted—to emphasize the ecumenical character of this punitive work of God. The same four are mentioned elsewhere in the Scriptures, cf., Amos 1:6–8; Zeph. 2:4; Jer. 25:20. The order in which they are mentioned is: first Ashkelon, the second last to the south; then Gaza, the southernmost; then Ekron, the northernmost; then Gaza, in the extreme south, again to be followed by Ashkelon, the first mentioned; Ashdod is last. Ashkelon is apparently mentioned first because it lay on the sea and would thus have been the first to hear the news of Tyre's fall, perhaps from escaped Tyrian ships. The news is then pictured as flying to the adjacent Gaza; soon to the extreme north; and presently as having covered the land. Another reason advanced for the silence in reference to Gath is that "it may be that it no longer existed."

We have here what is called an "individualizing account," that is to say, what is ascribed specifically or individually to one of the towns is not restricted to it alone. All the subjects, i.e., all the Philistine towns mentioned, may be construed with all the verbs; what the inhabitants of one town experienced was really common to all. They all "fear" (*tîra'*, singular, referring to Ashkelon); all are "sore pained" (*tachîl*—refers to the "writhing" of a woman in labor); they are all put to shame in reference to "the object of their expectation" (*mebbatah*, lit., *the thing looked for*, from the root *nabhat*). These are only the evils that are dreaded in anticipation of their certain arrival. Thereafter the verse foretells directly the things that will actually befall the cities though apparently only Gaza loses its king, and Ashkelon becomes uninhabited.

The picture becomes complete when all the elements are assembled, including those mentioned in v. 6, where it is finally indicated that only a "mongrel" population (*mamzer*) shall be found in towns like Ashdod. The term *mamzer* presents difficulties. It must refer to one to whose birth some defect is attached, like a "bastard." *Hengstenberg* therefore renders it *Gesindel,* i.e., ragtag population. The *Septuagint* renders ἀλλογενεῖς, "mixed population." It apparently thought of the mixture resulting from the intermarriage of Philistine remnants and the conquerors. When such a population is all that a city can boast of, she certainly has been brought very low, in fact, is on the verge of passing off the scene. As the last clause indicates, this signifies a "cutting off of the pride of the Philistines." The last vestige of what Philistaea might have had to be proud of will utterly disappear. If in nothing else, nations usually take pride in their nationality. Even that shall have been corrupted. So pride can cling to nothing: Philistines are no more. As the picture is completed, it becomes apparent that nothing less than the utter and final destruction of the nation is being predicted. Yet in reality not only this one nation is meant. It has been mentioned only as a type of what shall befall all such who are enemies of God's people.

All attempts to find an individual to whom the term might apply are unsatisfactory. The connection in which the word appears proves this.

But, as usual, the chief objective in the subduing of the enemies of God's people is not so much their discomfiture as their conversion. Therefore v. 7.

It is primarily this verse that indicates that the preceding account cannot be a prophecy. For a conversion of the Philistines or of a remnant of them to the true God never occurred. What is meant by the verse is that God's corrective work upon inveterate enemies of His people such as the Philistines will often bring about a conversion of at least a portion of them.

The tenacity with which all such will, however, cling to their traditional idolatrous practices is forcefully indicated by the figures employed. These idolaters are pictured as still drinking the offering of the blood mingled with wine and as still devouring the meat of their abominable sacrifices, here called abominations (*shiqqûts*). So stubbornly do they cling to these wretched practices that the blood has to be removed from their mouth and the very idol meat torn from between their teeth. But when God thus forcibly deprives them of these things, the heathen will submit, and even as there was a remnant of Israel that was left for God, so "also he" (*gam hû'*) shall be a remnant for the God of Israel. In a parallel statement this remnant, taken collectively, is in a simile likened to an outstanding chieftan in Judah, i.e., a man of some influence among God's people. In old Edomite history the word *'allûph* signified a "tribal chief." The term somehow came into use in later prophecy; cf. also Zech. 12:5, 6. Coming from the root *'eleph, thousand,* it may signify a *chiliarch.*

The parallel statement of the case indicates the same idea of sympathetic association in the interest of God's people: "Ekron like the Jebusites." "The reason for which Ekron is singled out for incorporation in Judah lies in its geographical position." It lay nearer Judah than did any other Philistine town. There were outstanding Jebusites like Araunah (II Sam. 24:16; I Chron. 21:15) who were glad to acknowledge Jahweh as their God and serve Him. Ekron shall follow his example. On the whole a pleasing picture which rounds off in a pleasant conclusion the story as to how the nations shall be subdued before God's agents when He lays His burden on them. In fact, what befalls all these shall befall mighty Persia as the "burden" of v. 1 began to indicate.

When God's judgment is let loose and comes sweeping down through the lands, what will Israel's fate be? Will she not also be caught by the nameless terror that is being described? The answer is furnished by v. 8.

Against any powers of hostile and raging troops One shall encamp who alone is sufficient defence against them all. His "house," for whose good He encamps (*báyith* with *le*), is in this case His land or His people Israel among whom He has taken up His dwelling; this use of "house" is found also in Hos. 8:1; 9:15; Jer. 12:7. The translation "as an outpost" or "as a guard" is based on the form that appears in the text and disregards the marginal reading. The word *matstsabhah* has the meaning "outpost" also in I Sam. 14:12. Equally strong is the description which assures them that the Lord will guard them against those hazards of war that arise when troops surge back and forth through the land in the course of a campaign. As the Lord guards against the entire army, so He guards also against such smaller yet dangerous troops, here described as "those that pass through and return," "that come and go." The completeness of God's protection is thus described. The ultimate result of God's protection of His own shall be that there shall be no "oppressors" passing through any more. The nations, bent on making a prey of Israel, shall cease from all such efforts only when all wars are dispensed with.

So this prophecy is seen to point to the fulfillment of all prophecy. All such gracious protection of God's people is to be attributed to a state of watchful care over His own which is in contrast with a time in the past when He could be said not to have taken note of the distress of His people, as during the Exile. With a strongly anthropomorphic expression He now describes Himself: "for now have I seen with My eyes." He likens Himself to One who had previously not regarded but now has discovered a sad plight which requires His attention, and this attention He will give. So God gives His people assurance of His watchful care. This statement of the case covers also what happened in the days of Alexander when he approached Jerusalem intending to assault the city but was moved to spare it when the elders, headed by the high priest, came forth in solemn procession to implore his mercy (cf., *Josephus, The Antiquities of the Jews* (trans. by Whiston) XI, 8, 3–5).

In strongest contrast to the warriors and avengers that have been sweeping through the lands the prophet new sees a figure appearing, drawing nigh unto His people, One whose entire appearance is as different from that of the ordinary run of conquerors as His peaceful achievements are from theirs, and yet the utmost reach must be ascribed to His realm. For Israel in particular His arrival will be a matter of such supreme joy that she is introduced to Him with the summons to exult greatly at His appearing, for He is described as her King. In fact, He is the One by whom the protection and the deliverance described in v. 8 are to be wrought. By this sequence of thought we understand how v. 9 follows upon v. 8.

Whence this King comes is not mentioned, for all understand that He is sent by the Lord on high. To impress strongly upon His people the truth that the supremest joys shall be theirs through Him, the prophet summons them to begin rejoicing at His mere approach. The double summons expresses this strongly: "rejoice" (from *gîl, to go around* or *about*) coupled with *me'odh*, "exceedingly"; and *harî'î*, from *rû'a, to shout* in applause or even in worship—the same verb is used in Ps. 100:1. The very one who profits by this deliverance and who was (v. 8) seen to be the whole land or people is here described as "daughter of Zion." When the word "daughter" (*bath*) is used in such connections it is a "poetic personification" (*BDB*) of the inhabitants of that city. Therefore *K.W.* translates this word *Bewohnerschaft* and *Koehler, Bevoelkerung*. Zion, of course, stands for Jerusalem, rather the spiritually-minded dwellers of Jerusalem. To *her* the summons to rejoice is addressed, again in the individualizing manner described above (v. 5), because she is the most prominent city in the Land. That these terms are not to be restricted to a purely literal meaning appears also from the fact that "Zion" and "Jerusalem" are used in strict parallelism.

The vigorous summons to rejoice, however, precedes the statement of the cause for such rejoicing. Such a word order is naturally preferred when the speaker is deeply agitated and impressed with the fact that the cause for rejoicing is supremely great. Special attention is drawn to the great cause itself by a "behold" (*hinneh*). The cause is: "your King comes to you." *Malkekh*, "your King," implies a full kingly relationship: He has claims upon His subjects; they have claims upon Him. Yet he does not come merely as a helper but as their supreme ruler. It is strictly translated not "unto you," but *lakh, for you*, dative of advantage: He comes for your good. This preposition precludes the thought of mere approach and indicates strongly that deliverance is involved in this coming.

At this point the description of the King takes a sudden

and most unusual turn: it sets forth qualities and attributes that one would least expect to find mentioned. Other prophets have in similar connections emphasized the heroic attributes (cf., Isa. 9:6; 11:1-5; Mic. 5:1-5). Zechariah draws attention to lowliness and apparent infirmity, much in the spirit of Isa. 53. There is reason for such an approach. There are in the Messiah two contrasting sets of attributes. It is the class of lowly attributes that needs emphasis the nearer the time of His coming draws because His extreme lowliness proves a stumbling block to natural human pride.

True, the first attribute scarcely belongs in the one or the other of the classes mentioned. *Tsaddiq* means "just," "righteous." This quality is placed first because it is the prime requisite in any ruler, no matter in what guise or for what work he appears. All ruling functions become distorted when this fine regulative is absent, cf., Isa. 11:4 and especially II Sam. 23:3, where this quality is for the first time stressed in reference to the King that is to come as a Messiah from David's line. But the second quality, conveyed by the word *nôsha'*, presents quite a different facet of the Messiah's character. It is correctly and naturally translated "saved." *Keil* and *Hengstenberg* have established the passive meaning of this word. They have it signify "salvation having been granted," *mit Heil begabt*. The passage aims to stress the supreme lowliness of this King as the next three terms or phrases indicate. The fact that, in spite of this lowliness and apparent weakness, He, nevertheless, attains success is to be emphasized later, namely in v. 10.

A very reasonable and acceptable meaning is conveyed by the simple passive *nôsha'*, saved. In His great work this God-man, as a man, requires help. He seeks it in prayer. When He is performing His individual miracles He appeals to God for aid; in the work of redemption proper He prevails in answer to prayer made in bloody sweat. The help He needs He receives. There is nothing unworthy of Him or unacceptable about regarding His work from this angle. We reject as being contrary to the context all such meanings as "having salvation" (*A.V.*) or "saving Himself" (*A.V.m.*) or "victorious"

(*BDB*). *Koenig* (*Messianische Weissagungen*) summarizes excellently: in his "conflicts with the enemies of the true kingdom of God he will be sustained by the heavenly ruler of Israel and so will be led to victory."

The next attribute of the Messiah is along the same line, *'anî—lowly, afflicted*. This was in truth a prominent feature of His life. The opposition of His enemies, the burden of man's sin afflicted Him and pressed Him down. His lowliness was very noticeable; in fact, it was an offence and a stumbling block to haughty minds. Further to emphasize this lowliness, the author presents this King as "riding upon an ass." This is not an allusion to the King's peaceful character, to the fact that He is an exponent of peace, as is so frequently contended. That characteristic appears in v. 10. A careful consideration of the history of the use of the ass (*chamôr*) reveals quite a different thought. It appears from passages such as Gen. 49:11; Jud. 5:10; 10:4; 12:14; II Sam. 17:23; 19:27 that in the earlier days of Israel's history even the nobility used no other beasts for riding than asses. In Solomon's time there came a change: horses became the distinctive riding beast of the nobility (I Kings 10:25, 28, 29; II Kings 9:18, 19, etc.). From this time onward the use of asses was characteristic of persons without rank. If the Messiah appears riding thus He must be of a humble rank and station. *Horst* overlooks these later passages and describes the ass as the "beast used by the nobility," *fürstliches Reittier*. In fact, the thought of humble rank appears with still stronger emphasis in the parallel phrase, "upon a colt, the foal of an ass." The conjunction "and" introducing the phrase (*we'al-'ayir*) is the *waw* epexegetic and means "namely." Not only does the King appear upon an ass; in fact the beast upon which He rides is a mere "foal of an ass." The plural "asses" in *ben-'athonôth* has the meaning: such a colt as "asses" are wont to have (*K(S)* 264a).

We have throughout the exposition above regarded the strictly Messianic character of v. 9 as being unassailable, as being established by Matt. 21:5 and John 12:15. There is, however, another aspect of the case that deserves consideration. This namely: does the fulfilment of the passage actually require that the Messiah in reality come riding to His people on a colt, the foal of an ass? We do not believe so. The fact that requires fulfilment is the fact that is symbolized by His riding, that is to say, His lowliness of station. If that is in evidence (and it is throughout Christ's life) then we have a complete fulfilment. What Christ, however, did on the occasion of the first Palm Sunday was to add to His usual mode of approach such outward signs as might serve to draw the attention of His people with unusual emphasis to the fact that He was this lowly One.

Mitchell fails properly to evaluate the spirit of the passage when he contrasts it with others: "The person here described, though still a King, is not the proud and confident figure of the earlier prophecies." "Proud" is an ill-chosen adjective with reference to the Messiah. *Sellin* classes the riding upon an ass as one of "the constant factors in the earliest expectations concerning the coming King." He refers especially to Gen. 49:11. But in that passage the one riding upon an ass is Judah. Such an approach is somewhat mechanical. *Nowack* misreads the passage by arriving at the conclusion that the Messiah is here "a rather idle figure, which could be omitted without any appreciable loss."

Verse 10. Verse 9 had not given the reasons that great joy and glad shouts should be manifested on Israel's part over its King; it had merely described His unusual appearance and His character. His achievements are now listed. The momentary change of the person—"*I* will exterminate"—disturbs the reader at first but is readily understood on the basis of the close relationship—practical identity—between the Savior and God. God speaks in the person of the Messiah, but the discourse almost at once reverts to the former mode of speech: "He shall speak peace," etc.

The fact that Ephraim and Jerusalem are mentioned separately is not an indication of an early date of composition, when both kingdoms existed side by side, but rather an indication of the fact that the former harmful division of the nation is to be removed. Again we have what we have termed *individualizing narrative*. Several prominent warlike implements are by synecdoche referred to for the sum total of them. They as well as the wars in which they are employed shall be done away with. Again, not only Ephraim shall see chariots disappear, but all parts of His domain shall see all implements of war disappear through the activity of the Messiah. This state will, as we know, be achieved in perfection only when the new heavens and the new earth shall have come into existence.

The removal of arms does not describe as *Hengstenberg* suggests: being reduced to a state of defencelessness (*Wehrlosigkeit*); but rather the removal of warlike implements because they are no longer needed. And they are not needed because, as the words immediately following suggest, the Prince of peace has "spoken peace unto the nations." In other words, Israel's King will not make conquest by force of arms. All misconceptions of this truth are ruled out by this statement.

All former achievements in the direction of banishing implements of war are summed up in the comprehensive statement: "He shall speak peace unto the nations." This implies an effective speaking on His part when by His omnipotent word He shall effect what the nations so eagerly desire, "peace." What others desire and discuss He shall make a reality. The "peace" (*shalôm*) here referred to includes more than the cessation of warfare though that is primarily under consideration in a passage such as this. "Peace" is in itself a much broader concept. It includes that wealth of spiritual treasures which He alone is able to bestow, and which is referred to in the statement: "Peace I leave unto you."

Nor shall it be only one nation that is thus blessed. All "nations" (*goyim*), who were once characterized by their hostility to Israel, shall share in this treasure. This prophecy is very broad in scope. He shall be able to extend His beneficent efforts so far because His rule extends so far, for "His dominion shall be from sea to sea." Since the next expression in the parallelism is a similar statement that covers world-wide dominion ("from the River to the ends of the earth"), this one must apparently mean more than from the Dead Sea or the

Red Sea unto the Mediterranean. It includes all domain that lies between the bounds where sea ends and sea begins, i.e., the wide world. The River (*nahar*), when not specifically referred by the context to Egypt as the Nile, always signifies the Euphrates; the absence of the article is poetic usage (*KW*, *sub verbo*). Since the Euphrates was the northern boundary of the promised Kingdom of Israel, this expression begins at the utmost limits and goes thence "to the ends of the earth." Such expressions can mean nothing other than world-wide dominion, and, as Ps. 72 indicates, can be referred only to the Messiah (Ps. 72:8–12 should not be called "a later and more extravagant form of this propecy" [*Mitchell*]; such criticism fails to evaluate rightly the glories of the kingdom that are promised.)

So our chapter has shown us Israel safe (v. 8) against the background of the overthrow of the nations (v. 1–7); but it has also shown us Him to whom Israel's safety as well as the conversion of inveterate foes (v. 7) is due, the King (v. 9) and His glorious world-wide achievement (v. 10) of peace.

Though we have in this section moved up into Messianic times, even up to the consummation of all things in v. 10, yet the conclusion should not be drawn that the prophets must remain at this point of time. As is often done in other instances, the prophets, in touching upon the Messianic fulfillment, depart from their immediate purpose but presently return to the immediate needs of their own time and to situations that lie in the less remote future, so Zechariah does in this instance. If v. 1–7 were particularly adapted to the situation as it prevailed in the days of the conquests of Alexander the Great, so after the interlude of v. 8–10 the section, v. 11–17, concerns itself particularly with the situation in Israel during the next period, more especially with the days of the Maccabees, ca. 168–104 B.C. Only when it is first decided that another sequence of thought would be more natural can the sequence of the chapter seem unnatural and seem to call for readjustments or for the claim that this passage (v. 11–17) is written after a "borrowed passage," v. 1–10 (*Mitchell*). It is true that the warlike scene, v. 11–17, is in strong contrast with the scene of perfect peace described in v. 9, 10. But no statement of the prophet indicated that the line of thought running through the chapter would be a strict temporal progression. G. A. *Smith* has indicated that the "result" is given first in this chapter, then "the process by which it is achieved." More correct is the view which labels the description given in v. 11–17 as one of the "stages" through which the history of God's people must pass rather than the "process" of the achievement of peace.

Zion's Victory over the Greeks (v. 11–17)

The key word of this passage is 13b: "I will stir up your sons, O Zion, against your sons, O Greece." The preceding section of the passage is preparatory to this; that which follows outlines Zion's subsequent prosperity.

✠

vs. 11–17   **11** And as far as you are concerned, because of the blood of your covenant, I will set your prisoners free from the pit wherein no water is. **12** Turn to the stronghold, you prisoners of hope. Even today I declare that I will amply repay you. **13** For I have bent Judah as My bow. I have filled it with Ephraim. And I will stir up your sons, O Zion, against your sons, O Greece; and I will make you as a hero's sword. **14** And the Lord will appear over them, and His arrow shall go forth like lightning, and the Lord Lord shall blow the trumpet, and He shall advance as with the storms that come from the South. **15** The Lord of hosts will shield them; and they shall devour and tread down the sling-stones; and they shall drink; they shall make a noise as through wine; and they shall be filled like the sacrificial bowls, bespattered like the corners of the altar. **16** And the Lord their God will save them in that day as the flock of His people; for they shall be as crown jewels glittering all over His land. **17** For how great is His goodness and His beauty! Grain shall make the young men flourish, and new wine the maidens.

The situation as it still obtained in the prophet's time is first, v. 11, reckoned with. Israel's lot was quite discouraging in spite of the return of a minority from the Captivity. There

were many who had not deemed it worth the trouble to return. Besides, those who had returned were far removed from
having achieved anything outstanding by way of rehabilitating
Israel as her prophesied future seemed to warrant. In several
senses the nation was still like a prisoner, as hopelessly caught
in its misery as if it were cast into a pit as was Joseph in days
of old (Gen. 37:14) or Jeremiah at a later date (Jer. 38:6),
for these pits or "cisterns" (*bôr*) were commonly so constructed as to be bottle-shaped, with narrow openings at the
top so that persons enclosed therein would be safely im-
prisoned unless others assisted them to escape.

The term "prisoners," *'asîrîm*, from the root *'asar*, means
literally *bound ones*. To be cast into a pit besides being bound
made the case of such unfortunates doubly hopeless. The
clause, "wherein is no water," (*'ên mayim bô*="there is no
water in it") is necessary to complete the accurate and correct
description: if men were thrown into a pit that had water in
it, there could be no other result than immediate drowning.
Critics, however, chiefly for metrical reasons, reject this clause
as a gloss—"the last three words have long been recognized as
a gloss," *Sellin*. The idea of prisoners in a pit refers not only
to unreturned captives; they were not actually prisoners—
Cyrus' decree had given them leave to return. Nor does it
refer to them merely as a "figurative description of the deepest
need and most extreme misery" (*Hengstenberg*). It is descriptive of the full measure of circumstances in which Israel as
a nation seemed hopelessly caught. From this situation the
Lord promises, "I will set free," *shillâchti*, a prophetic perfect
as so often in prophetic descriptions of the future (*KS* 132).
The fact that, in spite of the seemingly hopeless state, Israel
still had a future is expressed by the opening words, "even
thou" (*gam 'at*) which imply: "as far as you are concerned,
brought low as you are." *Luther's* translation cannot be accepted: "Thou deliverest Thy prisoners," for *'at* is feminine,
and *shillâchti* is the first person.

No cause of worthiness inherent in Israel can be established
for this deliverance. Israel cannot be said to have merited it.
The reason God helps her is "because of the blood of your

covenant" (*bedham berîthekh*), a phrase which could be adequately paraphrased: "because of the covenant made with you by blood." The covenant is God's, made with Israel at Sinai (Exod. 24:8) and previously made with Abraham and sealed by sacrifice (Gen. 15:9–12, 17, 18). The blood of the sacrifice it was that had covered Israel's sins and so made the nation acceptable to God, and if it was acceptable, then there was no reason for God's withholding help (on the need and the efficacy of blood cf. Lev. 17:11; also Heb. 9:18–22).

As this verse presents Israel on the lowest level of its fortunes, the next (v. 12) reckons with a more acceptable situation.

Those who were as a nation regarded as prisoners are still being regarded from that point of view, but now as prisoners who have a definite hope of being liberated. This is what the expression *'asîrê hattiqwah*, "prisoners of hope," means. *Luther* comes near to an understanding of the phrase with his translation: *die ihr auf Hoffnung gefangen liegt.* So far has the deliverance of these unfortunates progressed that no more is required than obedience to the divine summons, and they will be out of prison. This summons says *shûbhû*, "turn you," and indicates the need of a definite turning from their miserable state and an entering upon the new and hopeful situation. Unless they personally do this they will not share in the deliverance. The verb used is the same as that which in other instances implies a turning to the Lord in repentance. The perfect safety of the new lot they are to experience is stated by the term *lebhitstsarôn*, from *batsar*, "to cut off," therefore "the inaccessible stronghold." They are not merely to exchange a most miserable and forlorn state for one that is perfectly neutral but for one that is entirely strong and safe, where thoughts of future dangers are excluded. This means: Return from captivity; turn to the Lord.

"Even today" (*gam hayyôm*), when the situation still seems so hopeless, the Lord declares as a kind of glorious proclamation: "Double (*mishneh,* placed first for emphasis) will I render unto you," or more freely: "I will amply repay you." According to Isa. 61:7b this term "double" includes the thought of a double measure of glory in comparison with the glory formerly enjoyed. All this double measure includes is about to be unfolded in the following verses.

The progression of thought in vv. 11–13 is as follows: v. 11—deliverance; v. 12—safety; v. 13—victory—an ascending climax, which is lost, as well as the purpose of the passage if such key terms as "Greece" are deleted (*Mitchell*) for metrical considerations—a very insecure criterion since the metrical structure is still a very mooted problem. There is not even adequate reason for altering "thy sons," *banáyikh*, to *benê*, "sons of" (*LXX*). Since when can there be but a single personification in one sentence? Such arbitrary canons furnish the basis for the attempted but very unsatisfactory reconstructions made of the Masoretic text.

We have construed *qésheth*, "bow" (v. 13), as the object of "bend," *darákhtî*, contrary to the accents which require an object for the first verb and render the word "bow" to "fill." Our reason for doing thus: *darakh* never occurs in the sense of bending the bow except when the object is expressed.

The thought that nations are instruments or weapons in the Lord's hand is not so uncommon. Here one nation functions as a bow, the other as an arrow. So completely are nations under God's control. In this case these two function as weapons of conquest. The fact that both are mentioned is not by any means an argument for the separate existence of each of the two kingdoms of the divided nation and so an argument for an early date of the passage. Just as reasonable and far more conformable to the context is the thought that this statement of the case indicates that the once tragic division of the nation is a thing of the past. The nation is restored to a harmony that is as close as is that of bow and arrow. But the thought already arises, if it is the Lord who wields the bow, how formidable a weapon!

God furthermore promises that it will be He Himself who will arouse Israel or Zion's sons against the Greeks—not for aggressive warfare, for Israel and Judah never waged that kind of war; but for the purpose of deliverance of self from oppression. This apparently refers to the days of the Maccabees when they bestirred themselves to rise against the Seleucids, who expedited Greek domination in Syria and were regarded as exponents of Greek culture. A reading of the books of Maccabees leaves one under the impression that the courage that animated these heroes had an element of divine inspiration in it. Of course, this "stirring up" involves victory for Zion as the outcome. *'Orarti* does not here mean "shake the lance," for in that case the object would have to be expressed.

From this point onward a series of bold pictures presented in quick succession depicts the success that Zion's God-inspired sons will have in the conflict. Israel is first likened to the "hero's sword." God Himself will make it to be such. As heroes' swords were renowned for what mighty men had wrought by them, so this Excalibur, as it were, shall achieve like renown. Rather a startling prospect for little and rejected Zion! Almost unbelievable, yet divinely promised.

This would be the place to notice that the passage is not to be limited to a purely literal interpretation. That, indeed, is its first and most natural sense. But, without advocating a dual sense, we cannot help but point out that the marvelous pictures which follow in quick succession are too rich and glorious to be limited to the Maccabean days. One would scarcely venture to assert that that brief effulgence of national glory merits so extravagant a description—for in that case it would be extravagant—as now follows. One is rather forcibly reminded of the whole series of glorious victories that attended Zion's warfare through the ages. What Zechariah does is this: he regards the conquest of the Greeks as a type—as in physical warfare Zion threw off the Greek yoke, so she will be successful in all her warfare through the ages and achieve unbelievable success. The picture given in v. 16 and 17 practically arrives at the consummation of all things. Therefore care should be taken lest the picture be forced within too narrow limits. It is this safeguard against too narrow an interpretation which gave rise to our introductory remark: "that which follows (namely, v. 14 onward) outlines *her subsequent prosperity*." Yet such a definite application also to the Maccabean era by no means gives warrant to the conclusion that this prophecy was first *made and written* in the Maccabean age, as criticism so strongly maintains.

Verse 14. This verse, like v. 13, is still an unfolding of the "double" (v. 12) rendered unto Zion. It at the same time depicts what happens when the Lord stirs up Zion against Greece, or, leaving the narrower concept, when the Lord gives Zion the victory over all her foes. For not in only one certain age are the Lord's manifestations in behalf of His church as rich and as glorious as they are here set forth.

The first manifestation is: "The Lord will appear over them." As in the days in the wilderness, which are a figure of the entire history of the *ecclesia pressa,* the Lord hovered over His people, the cloud being the visible symbol of His presence (Exod. 13:21, 22, etc.), so He will still be giving shade by day and light by night. Yet the verb used here is "shall be seen" (*yera'eh*), which implies that there will be some who can discern His presence; they will be those whose eyes are opened by faith. If certain Assyrian or Persian reliefs showed "in the air above the human combatants the figure of a god [Asshur] or a goddess [Ishtar] who is giving supernatural help" (*Barnes*), Israel shall enjoy the full truth of such a conception.

This figure is quickly replaced by another: The Lord is doing battle for His people as a bowman, His arrows are flashing forth, but not with the slow-winged flight of the arrows of battle, for they shall flash forth as swiftly and as dangerously as lightning. There is no "mythological concept" (*Sellin*) in this figure. Scriptures stand on a higher level than does mythology, nor do they often borrow their materials from such sources. This is merely a natural simile that anyone might use even if he had never heard of mythology.

Again the figure changes. The Lord Himself appears as a trumpeter who is sounding the signal for battle, calling His embattled host together: "The Lord shall blow the trumpet," cf., Job 39:25. All these activities of the Lord will, of course, serve to "stir up Zion's sons" (v. 13). They see that they are not alone; the Lord has appeared over them; He incites them to battle by letting His terrible arrows go forth; He summons them by trumpet calls. As any army would be mightily heartened in courage by seeing a valiant champion on its side, much more is Zion encouraged by the presence and the activity of the Lord.

Again the figure changes: "He shall advance as with the storms that come from the South." These tempests are the fiercest of all, cf., Job 37:9. They come with excessively hot winds and cause all vegetation and all mankind to wilt. In such blasts the Lord swoops down upon the foes. This great variety of figures serves to depict the infinite resources that the Lord has at His command when it comes to the matter of helping His own. This figure is again a purely natural one, such as anyone might use, since the Southland (*Teman*) breeds the worst storms. To find the thought suggested here that "the original abode of Yahweh was in the South" (*Mitchell*) means to read something into the figure; it is the *storms* that come from the South (lit., "storms of the South-country") not the *Lord*. Besides, the passages adduced as proof for the South as the "original abode of Yahweh" fail to support this view; viz., Judg. 5:4; Deut. 33:2; Hab. 3:3. "The whirlwind is the Lord's weapon against His foes," cf., Ps. 18:15.

The bold, almost daring, figures concerning the Lord are brought to a close by the first statement of v. 15: "The Lord of hosts will shield them." *Yaghen* (from *ganan*) means "to cover as with a roof or a shield," the word for "shield" being derived from the same root. As the nation goes forth, the Lord's shield is continually over her to cover her when she is in danger. The name "Lord of hosts" is particularly suitable here, His hosts are His protecting agents.

The picture changes, and in a series of strong and picturesque metaphors and similes *Israel's* activity in this stirring warfare is described. The hues of this scene are rather dark and the colors very striking, but nothing unseemly or cruel is involved in them.

It is first asserted that Israel "shall devour." The conception that Israel figuratively devours the flesh of its enemies is relieved by the fact that an allusion to Num. 23:24 is apparently embodied in the passage, where Israel is likened to a lion. The Oriental mind delights in such more colorful scenes. There is a deeper truth involved. When God's people triumph they not only subdue their enemies but actually acquire their strength and utilize it for their own purposes. Nor do the sling-stones that, as it were, the enemy is hurling against them deter them, for since the Lord is holding His shield over them, the sling-stones are deflected to the earth before them, and as the people of Zion advance they "tread down the sling-stones."

From this point onward the figures become even more powerful, almost violent, in aiming to depict how triumphantly God's people march on unhampered to complete victory. "They shall drink" again alludes to Num. 23:24, and, therefore, the object "blood" will have to be supplied. The figure loses its offensiveness if it is borne in mind that we have a metaphor, Israel being thought of as a lion. It may even be possible that the *weapons* should be thought of as drinking blood, as some interpreters suggest, offering as parallel passages Deut. 34:42 and Isa. 34:5.

By a bold change in the figure Israel is now conceived as a man. The blood is thought of as a potent wine that he has drunk; therefore: "they shall make a noise as through wine." As a drink of strong wine might move one under the further impulse of strong excitement to bold and challenging shouts and cries, so shall Israel, confident in the Lord, deport herself.

The last change in this rapid succession of forceful figures likens the gory, blood-stained conqueror to a "bowl," *mizraq*, the type of bowl used to catch up the sacrificial blood that it might then be dashed against the altar. This dashing of blood against the corners of the altar was done in such a way that the blood bespattered two sides. Red as such bowls or as the corners of the altar might be, so covered or "filled" (*mal^e'û*) with blood shall victorious Israel emerge from the hard-fought field.

It must be admitted that the more fastidious taste of our day would scarcely picture victory in such colors, but, surely, the intent of the writer is rather to draw a figure that shows victory in a fierce struggle than to create the impression of gloating over the enemies' downfall. The emendations of the critics are largely in the direction of removing what might of-fend the more delicate taste of our day, for several sections are removed as "glosses"; for instance, *we'akhelû*, "they shall devour," etc.

The picture is rounded out and brought to a close at this point, v. 16. All the Lord's activities for His people are summed up in "He will save them," which stands first for the sake of emphasis. The reason for His care of them is: they are "the flock of His people," lit., "the flock that is His people"— appositional genitive. Such being their relation to Him, He as Shepherd owes it to them to do this.

Practically parallel with this statement is the next statement as to why He delivers them: "they shall be as crown jewels glittering all over His land." This difficult statement is variously translated and variously interpreted. We take its meaning to be the following: As previously (v. 15) the enemies were practically regarded as "sling-stones," so here God's people are as precious as "crown jewels" (*'abhney nézer*, stones of a diadem). As the enemies are merely to be "trodden down," so these precious stones are visualized as lying on the dark soil of the Lord's land (*'adhamah*) and glittering there. As such fields of diamonds would be highly valued, so is Israel in the Lord's sight, and, therefore, will He deliver them.

Since an account is being given of how previous God's people are in His sight, and the closing half of v. 17 speaks of the flourishing state of God's own people after He begins to shower blessings upon them, it would seem that the intervening section, 17a, also has reference to this blessed state of Israel and not to God, all the more so since the bestowal of blessings may well occasion the exclamation: "How great is His goodness!" but scarcely: "How great is His beauty!" Besides, the similarity with Jer. 31:12 is not so close as to allow labelling v. 17 a direct quotation as *Hengstenberg* does.

"Goodness" is, therefore, taken in the sense of "prosperity" (*A.R.V.m*), and "beauty" is a further indication of a flourishing state. In a kind of vision the prophet foresees a degree of prosperity that rouses him to exclamation. The picture is completed by another of those "individualizing accounts" in which "grain," thought of as being available in profuse abundance, makes "young men" to flourish, and "new wine" as giving the glow of health to "virgins." Both products are naturally available for both these classes and all others besides. Grain is associated with sturdy young men because it is a major article of diet for sustaining strength, and wine is associated with virgins because they stand in the full glow of their maidenly beauty, which wine might more appropriately seem to indicate.

Chapter X

The Perfect Redemption of Israel (10:1–12)

The heading (9:1) includes everything stated in chapters 9, 10, and 11 until a similar new heading appears in chapter 12 (12:1). As in chapter 9 we found that "the land of Hadrach" represents the world-power, and yet not only the one individual world-power of that time, Persia, but everything that goes under the name of world-power, so also in this chapter. Similarly, the victories granted to the people of God were not victories for that time only but for all times, for all those who constitute the true people of God. Yet there is a difference between chapter 9 and chapter 10. Chapter 9 presents the victory of God's people from the positive side for the most part, showing how the true Israel shall be made strong by the Lord and shall prevail. Without abandoning this point of view, chapter 10 brings greater emphasis to bear upon the negative side of the victory, namely, how the enemies shall be brought low. Yet particular stress is at the same time laid upon the gathering of the scattered Israelites.

The first two verses of this chapter are in the nature of transitional verses. They surely continue very positively along the line of thought of the preceding chapter. Verses 3–6 treat of the visiting of God's wrath upon Israel's oppressors. Verses 7–12 confirm the thought of the salvation of Ephraim which was touched upon in v. 6. The whole chapter may be brought under the caption, "The Perfect Redemption of Israel."

✠

vs. 1, 2   ¹ Ask the Lord for rain in the time of the spring rain. The Lord it is who makes lightnings, and copious rains He will give them, to every man herbage in the field. ² For the teraphim have spoken empty words, and the soothsayers have had lying visions; dreams yield empty counsel, vain comfort do they give. Therefore the people have gone away as sheep; they are in trouble, for there is no shepherd.

This is not primarily a summons to the people to pray for rain as in a season of drought they had, perhaps, failed to do hitherto. Nothing points to drought, nothing to a failure on the part of the people to seek help from God as they ought to have done. The preceding chapter had referred to the goodness of God which would grant "grain" and "new wine." Continuing the line of thought of that chapter, the prophet emphasizes the fact that God will be very gracious in bestowing this blessing so that all Israel needs to do is to ask, and God will give. The imperative is, therefore, practically an emphatic "rhetorical device" (*Mitchell*) for conveying the thought: *If you ask,* God will bestow. The "spring rains," commonly termed "latter rains" (*A.V.*), were essential for the proper filling out of the ears of grain and so were the condition of a copious harvest. But surely, this one divine gift, rain, is mentioned in lieu of all others by way of example, the thought being: Whatsoever you shall ask of the Lord, you shall receive.

It is somewhat more emphatic to translate as we have done by beginning a new sentence with: "The Lord it is," etc., rather than to make the second *Yahweh* an apposition to the first: "even of Jehovah that," etc. (*ARV*), or "so the Lord," etc. (*A.V.*). The thought thus gains strong emphasis that the *Lord* is the one who alone maketh these things. He is said to give "lightnings," which are here regarded, not as dread and marvelous workings of the Almighty, but merely as the precursors of rain, as in Jer. 10:13 and Ps. 135:7. In fact, there is the distinct purpose of setting forth the thought that God gives above "what we ask or think," for He gives "copious rains" (*metar géshem, rain of showers*) whereas only the latter rains have been asked for. In the word *to them* the discourse veers from the second person to the third, cf., *K.S.* 344L.

The "herbage" spoken of (*'ésebh*) refers not only to pasturage, as some interpreters contend, but, as Gen. 1:29 distinctly shows, includes all manner of herbs that man can consume. So the *le'îsh* has the distributive idea, "to every man" (*K.S.* 76), and not the less distinctive thought, "every herb." But to get the full reach of the idea it must be remembered that this one blessing stands for all temporal or spiritual blessings that it may please the redeemed of God who according to chapter 9 stand under God's favor to ask for. In each case they shall receive more than they sought if they ask as God's redeemed should ask.

For a moment the prophet glances back and aside at those who did not in faith seek all their help from God and shows by contrast how they were left destitute, yes, were even plunged into the miseries of the Exile. The contrast set forth in verse 2 thus strengthens the force of the preceding verse.

This verse is referred to in support of a particular theory of the time of composition. It is pointed to to prove the pre-exilic date of this section (*v. Orelli*). Its integrity is questioned (*Mitchell*). It is carried down to Maccabean times, yet is thought to betray the author's ignorance of the methods previously used in divining (*Sellin*) etc. If the tenses of the verbs are observed and given the simplest possible construction, all difficulties vanish, and the verse harmonizes with the theory of authorship by the postexilic Zechariah.

First, two perfects, "spoke" (*dibberû*) and "saw" (*chazû*), refer to a procedure different from that followed in v. 1, that was followed in the past, that is to say, in the not very remote pre-exilic days. At that time such idolatrous practices as consulting "teraphim" to find a safe course for the future were in vogue, cf., teraphim thus used, Ezek. 22:26–31. These small household divinities never gave a substantial, truthful answer. *'Awen, vanity, emptiness,* was the sum of their prognostications, and poor souls were deceived. See other instances of the use of these household gods in Gen. 31:19, 34, 35; I Sam. 19:13, 16; 15:23; and especially II Kings 23:24. Furthermore, whenever in times past men had consulted the diviners (*qosemîm*), these diviners had, indeed, pretended to gaze into the future (*chazû*), but what they had seen was a downright lie (*shéqer*). Since these practices lay in the not very remote past they may well be referred to in order to demonstrate how unhappy was the lot of those who did not consult the Lord in prayer.

Such vicious practices are not easily eradicated. The coarser forms of sin, teraphim and diviners, may have been abandoned, but more subtle forms may still be found, such as "dreams." No article is used before this word as it is before "teraphim" and "diviners" because they are not so definite a quantity. But when men were not seeking their guidance from the Lord but were superstitiously letting themselves be guided by dreams even after all the warnings of the past—note the present tense of the verb (*yedabberû*)—they needed to be told that "dreams yield empty counsel, vain comfort do they give." The better element in Israel realized that it was for reasons such as these sins that the people "have gone away as sheep" into captivity; that they "are in trouble" (*ya'anû*) with the very grievous afflictions they and their fathers so clearly remembered. For God had withdrawn Himself and refused to care for them: "there is no shepherd."

This brief reference to this wretched experience sets off the blessed state of v. 1 by strong contrast and so helps to complete the picture of the marvelous things God does for His redeemed, which picture had been developed in such brilliant colors since 9:13.

It is an instance of misconstruction in favor of preferred theories when *Sellin* claims that these two verses have no connection with what precedes or what follows, thereby making prophetic discourse lacking in all logical sequence—disjointed fragments.

Of course, as chapter 9 indicated at various points, this prophecy was not to be confined to the particular situation of Israel but enunciates several principles that are applicable to the situation of God's true Israel at all times. The promises given in v. 1 still hold true, and the warning given in v. 2 is still most appropriate: all who seek help apart from God shall be visited with sad confusion.

The next verses, 3–6, set forth *the visiting of God's wrath upon the oppressors of Israel.*

✠

vs. 3–6   ³ Against the shepherds is My wrath kindled, and upon the bellwethers will I bring punishment. For the Lord of hosts will visit His flock, the house of Judah, and will make them like His majestic steed in battle. **4** From Him shall come the cornerstone, from Him the tent peg, from Him the battle bow, from Him all the rulers. **5** And they shall be like heroes treading down enemies in the mire of the streets in the battle. And they shall fight boldly, because the Lord is with them. The enemy cavalry shall be confounded. **6** And I will make strong the house of Judah, and I will save the house of Joseph, and I will make them to dwell safely, for I will have mercy upon them. And they shall be as though I had not cast them off, for I am the Lord their God, and I will hear them.

Again and again the prophet must meet up with the burning question: how about the mighty nations that oppress Israel and seem to thrive so splendidly whereas Israel's lot seems to be very dubious? Here in particular the mighty *rulers* and their oppressions are under consideration. Note how the order of the words indicates this by putting first the words *'la haro'im,* "against the shepherds." The Masoretes clearly recognized that a new turn of thought sets in at this point as their paragraph division indicates. The term shepherds, however, here as very commonly (cf., Jer. 23; Ezek. 34, etc.), indicates primarily rulers. *Barnes,* who suggests that the term means "priests and prophets," scarcely goes far enough. The contrast found in the second half of the verse indicates that Gentile rulers are under consideration. They are likewise designated as "he-goats" (*'attûdhîm*), a term that is used elsewhere for rulers; cf., Isa. 14:9 and Ezek. 34:17. Perhaps, as *Barnes* suggests, they are "subordinate leaders of the people," a thought our translation—"bellwethers"—includes.

The works these rulers wrought against Israel have called forth His wrath, which now "burns" (*charah*) and has waxed hot to the point where God feels it to be requisite to visit it upon these rulers. The verb used is *paqadh,* which, having the meaning "visit," connotes the idea: visit for punishment when it is as here construed with the preposition *'al,* "upon." A strong contrast in the original, indicated by our translation as also in the German version, now follows. It uses the same verb in a good sense by asserting that this grievous punishment is caused by His having visited (with favor) "His flock, the house of Judah." Though all Israel is under consideration, yet "Judah" is here mentioned specifically, for Judah constituted the major part of restored Israel, the very kernel of the nation.

By another of those pregnant comparisons the author indicates how great God's deliverance will be when He begins to show favor unto His flock. When it comes to a battle, as it were, (*milchamah*) between the timid flock and the oppressors, the flock shall receive such a measure of courage as to necessitate its being likened to a "splendid steed," literally, "the horse of his majesty" (*sûs hôdhô*="His majestic steed"; *Lange: Prachtross*). Here, as so often, criticism exercises liberty in emending the text. "In the battle" is called a useless gloss whereas it is an essential feature in the picture employed.

Whereas the opinion was beginning to prevail that Judah was devoid of all essential resources in its conflict with surrounding nations, v. 4 shows that Judah has a great abundance of resources.

"From him" (*mimmennû*) must refer to Judah because it would be most inappropriate to assert that a taskmaster goes out from the Lord whereas not even as much, as *Keil* points out, was ever asserted concerning the Messiah, namely, that, He goes out from God, though Mic. 5:2 comes near to being such a statement. By standing first this phrase indicates that such resources will yet be granted to Judah that he will in the future be able to produce all that he needs by way of leadership and control. The passage rests on Jer. 30:21.

It is first claimed that the "cornerstone" shall originate from him. It is better to supply the verb *yihyeh*, "shall be," rather than *yetse'*, "go forth," from the last clause, because "cornerstones" do not go forth, neither do "pegs and bows." *Pinnah*, "cornerstone," however, in the Scriptures repeatedly refers to outstanding leaders, who head up the nation as a cornerstone on a hillside supports a structure; cf., Judg. 20:2; I Sam. 14:38; Isa. 19:13; see also Ps. 118:22. In like manner *yathedh*, "peg," refers to rulers upon whom much depends; cf. the reference to Eliakim, Isa. 22:23, 24. For such "pegs," not *nails*, are said to be characteristic of Oriental homes, being firmly fixed in the wall and used for hanging up in an orderly fashion all manner of household implements. These two subjects are used figuratively. The figure is now abandoned, and it is asserted that "the battle bow" will be produced by Judah as well as all "taskmasters" or exactors (*noghesh*) that may be required to keep hostile nations in check. To the idea of necessary leaders there is added that of necessary armaments and ability to restrain hostile people. For *noghesh*, from *nagash*, *to drive*, is never used in the good sense of *ruler* but always suggests one who employs force to keep another in check.

Zechariah thus teaches the nation to regard itself as having through God's grace received all resources that future exigencies may require. Now, by another figure, their future success as well as the suppression of the enemy is guaranteed in v. 5.

As was the case in the second half of chapter 9, the successive figures employed keep growing bolder. Judah now appears as a nation of "heroes" (*gibborîm*), every man, as it were, an outstanding heroic personage; as they engage in conflict, their foes shall be so powerless before Israel's mighty men that the latter shall trample them under foot in the mire of the streets. The enemy is likened to insignificant worms or creatures that may thus be trodden down; cf., 9:15. Though "the enemies" are not mentioned as the object of the verb "treading down," this thought is suggested by parallel passages, Mic. 7:10; II Sam. 22:43.

Men who have been thus strengthened by the Lord and enjoy His continual support shall not hesitate to engage in battle if they must: "they shall fight boldly because the Lord is with them." In fact, when Israel, who has thus far, in conformity with the principles of the Mosaic law, Deut. 17:16, been described as infantry, engages in battle with cavalry, it will not be God's people who are worsted, but "the enemy cavalry shall be confounded (*hobhîshû* = be ashamed). So mighty does God make His own.

Here, too, more is apparently said than is applicable to Judah exclusively. The very boldness of the figures points to spiritual truths which are stated in terms of well-known situations. So completely invincible do God's people become in the

Lord, their God. A small measure of fulfillment became reality in the days of the Maccabees.

Indeed, the idea of imparting strength to the people of God pervades the passage; therefore v. 6 begins: "and I will make strong." But the new thought is, first of all, this, that the *entire* people of God shall share in the strength God will impart, "Judah" and also "the house of Joseph." Whatever is left of the old Kingdom of Israel and is found truly desiring God's salvation shall surely be saved. There follows a multiplicity of divine activities, multiplied here apparently to show how richly God can bless His own, and how divine grace can erase the effects of man's stubborn persistence in sin. The divine activities bestowed upon the whole of God's people include first that God "will make them to dwell safely," (*hoshibhóthî* —a Hifil form of the verb *yashabh,* modelled as late forms occasionally were; not a double form according to the clever view of the old rabbis who have it mean both "to cause to dwell" and "to cause to return"). Like the Kal, this verb partakes of the idea of *abiding* or *enduring.* The explanation offered for the permanence of their state is that God's mercy is turned toward them, (*richamtîm*—a kind of future perfect according to the connection, *G.K.* 129).

Besides, all the devastating effects of their dispersion shall be removed: "they shall be as though I had not cast them off." For this effect a cause is assigned which is merely another divine favor: "I am the Lord, their God, and I will hear them." This last statement, *we'e'enem,* implies God's readiness at all times and in general to hear when they call, not merely that He will hear them in this particular matter.

This, of course, in its entirety depicts God's attitude toward His church, also the New Testament church; but as to form the statement is cast in terms of conditions as Zechariah found them in the land in his day. This is a strong assurance of God's mercy in rich measure upon the whole body of His people. So closes the statement concerning the visiting of God's wrath upon Israel's oppressors. The passage does not have the physical or carnal cast that might appear at first glance.

The Confirmation of Ephraim's Redemption (v. 7-12)

Since v. 6 made mention of the fact that Ephraim or "the house of Joseph" would share in the Lord's redemption, it was felt that this thought required particular development, for that any of the kingdom of the North should associate themselves with Judah and wait for the Coming One seemed out of the question. Particular assurance is, therefore, given that Ephraim shall be restored. The beginning of the fulfillment of this prophecy came about when, after prophecy had ceased, greater numbers of scattered Jews began to repopulate Galilee, being made up mostly, it seems, of stock of both the Northern and the Southern Kingdom, but of necessity containing a goodly percentage of Ephraim, i.e., the Northern. This statement at the same time becomes a prophecy for all times of the bringing back unto God's people of elements that had strayed rather far from God, and whose redemption, therefore, seemed quite hopeless.

Luther recognized clearly the drift of v. 7-12 when he says: "Having come to speak of the house of Joseph in addition to the house of Judah, he continues the discourse concerning the house of Joseph unto the end of the chapter."

The wealth of detail employed in unfolding this one thought is due to conditions of the times in which any future good for any inhabitants of the Northern Kingdom seemed quite impossible.

✠

vs. 7-12   7 And Ephraim shall be as a hero, and their hearts shall be glad as through wine; also their children shall see it and be glad. Their heart shall exult in the Lord. 8 I will whistle for them and gather them, for I will redeem them; and they shall be as numerous as they once were. 9 And though I saw them among the peoples, yet they shall remember Me in distant countries, and they shall live with their children and they shall return. 10 And I will bring them again out of the land of Egypt, and gather them out of Assyria; and unto the land of Gilead and Lebanon will I bring them, and room shall not be found

for them. ¹¹ When they pass through the sea of affliction,
He will smite the waves in the sea, and all the depths
of the Nile shall dry up; and the pride of Assyria shall be
brought low, and the sceptre of Egypt shall depart. ¹² And
I will make them strong in the Lord, and in His name shall
they freely walk about—oracle of the Lord.

The particular form of the assurance given to Ephraim is
conditioned by the tenor of the chapter. Since the emphasis
in treating of the redemption of God's people has shifted more
toward the point of view of the discomfiture of the foes of
God's people, the part that God's people as such plays is that
of victors. Now Ephraim, too, shall manifest strength and be
a "hero" (*gibbôr* from *gabhar, to be strong*). And the
Ephraimites shall also taste of the joy of participation in such
victories of the people of God, i.e., "their hearts shall be
glad." Whenever the *heart* rejoices, the thought conveyed is
that the inmost personality shares in the joy: the joy has gone
as deep as it possibly can. An abbreviated comparison (see *K.S.*
319g) makes the preceding thought more picturesque. *Kemô
yáyin,* literally, "as wine," supply "makes glad." As surely as
the temperate use of wine produces a distinct feeling of uplift,
so definitely shall Ephraim experience exaltation at the victory
achieved. Nor shall the achievements be temporary or of short
duration. They shall endure long enough and be of so outstanding a character that "also their children shall see it and
be glad" because they sincerely appreciate God's dealings with
His own. To make emphatic the children's joy, to stress that
it is more than a superficial joy, the prophet describes their
joy as being an *exulting* (*yaghel* from *ghûl, to go around* or
about) *in the Lord.*

Verse 8. *Sellin* regards this *hissing* as a form of witchcraft
without having Scriptural or historical ground to stand on.
The figure of hissing in order to collect is not uncommon in
the Scriptures; cf., Isa. 5:26; 7:18, 19. It seems to refer to a
distinctive call that shepherds employ to gather their sheep.
J. M. P. Smith translates very appropriately, "I will whistle for
them." Since it is a very special kind of summons to which the
sheep respond instantly, the figure connotes the intimacy of

the relation between God and His own. Much of this still lies
in the future at the time of the prophet's writing, especially
the complete redemption. It is, therefore, best to regard the
verb "redeem" (*padhah*) as a prophetic perfect. *Mitchell's*
translation of the last two clauses is very satisfactory: "They
shall be as many as they ever have been." God's grace promises
for the future as much as it ever wrought in the past. '*Esreqah*
with the end *ah* expresses determination rather than mere
futurity.

These verses do not aim to list a sequence of the various
activities of God here mentioned. They deal with the same
situation. Verse 9 refers to the same return that is in v. 8 described as a gathering. The "and I shall sow" may, as so often
in Hebrew, therefore, be rendered concessively, "though I
sow." The dispersion is referred to in the kindest possible
terms: though Ephraim may be said to have been scattered,
the Lord here terms it a sowing among the people. For Israel
sowed among the peoples and bore fruit in spreading abroad
the saving faith of Israel. The people among whom they were
sown are also regarded from a more friendly point of view, as
"nations" (*'ammîm*) not as "hostile Gentiles" (*gôyîm*). God
will bring it about that they shall "remember" Him even in the
far countries that often erase all remembrance of their native
land and what it stood for. Their remembering will, however,
imply a penitent turning to Him and so a spiritual revival,
here termed "they shall live" (*chayû*) in the fullest sense as
found in Exod. 37:14 or else in the sense of "revive" (*Barnes*).
It shall be a return unto the Lord, the source of life, that is so
thoroughgoing in nature as to include all, old and young:
"live with their children." The words, "they shall return," are
a repetition of the thought expressed in v. 8, "I will gather
them," with this difference that v. 8 stresses the divine causa-
tion, v. 9 the human participation.

Confusion results when artificial reconstructions are attempted. This verse is offered as proof that this section was
written prior to the deportation of 722 B.C. (*v. Orelli*); on the
other hand, it is said to establish the fact that the Maccabean
period was the time of its composition, 168–104 B.C. (*G. A.*

Smith). Yet the verse agrees excellently with all that precedes and follows when it is interpreted as it was written by the postexilic Zechariah, a contemporary of Haggai.

The same scene that was described in v. 8, 9 is here being unfolded more fully. "Egypt" is referred to in a symbolic sense, as a type of the oppressors of Israel. In connection with this passage *Hengstenberg* has clearly shown that this use of the term becomes more frequent in prophecy as time goes on. There is, therefore, no need to assume that some deportation to Egypt occurred at a later date. The flight of a few people in Jeremiah's time (Jer. 43:4–7) is not regarded as being of the same importance as were the Assyrian and the Babylonian deportations. Even if Ptolemy deported many Jews, to regard "Egypt" as the type of the earlier hostility and "Assyria" as the type of the latter (see this use of "Assyria" in *B.D.B.* 2, *sub verb.*) gives a very harmonious sense to this passage. *Nowack* may be correct when he takes "Assyria" to mean "Syria" in later usage. God promises to gather together His own, no matter by whom they may have been scattered and how long ago, or whether it was from the East or from the West. If Ephraim is under consideration, a restoration would naturally be pictured as bringing her people back to the old domains. Therefore "Gilead" refers to the East Jordan country as it often does in the Scriptures (see *B.D.B.* 3, *sub verb.*) and "Lebanon" must refer to the Cis-Jordanic section. That God will not do this work in a paltry fashion is indicated by the clause: "and room shall not be found for them" (*Yimmatse* used in a sense as is found in Josh. 17:16, supplying *room* as the subject).

The scene (v. 11) grows more graphic in that a brief sketch is given of the Lord at work delivering His own. The person of the verbs shifts from the first to the third. The subject is the Lord. The deliverance of God's chosen is first regarded as another passage through the Red Sea. The scene is highly idealistic. The Lord is pictured as walking before His people through the sea. But in this case the sea is the Sea Affliction or Distress. *Tsarah* is in apposition with *yam*, which is in the absolute state. This simple construction is rejected by *Sellin* who states: "Nothing can be done with *Tsarah*" and determines it must be a textual corruption.

The scene becomes marvelous and stupendous as it unfolds. As the Lord thus leads His people He disposes of threatening waves by smiting them down as they surge in on Him. Besides, the very "depths" (*metsûlôth*) of the Nile dry up and offer uninterrupted passage. That perennially fresh stream, the Nile, (*ye'ôr*, an Egyptian loan word that is used almost exclusively with reference to this river) is represented as actually drying up at the Lord's approach to admit a free passage for Ephraim. Of course, no such occurrence ever transpired. But the bold picture conveys the impression of the ease with which God removes obstacles when He proceeds to work deliverance.

In still different terms both Assyria and Egypt are described as growing weak in their opposition. Assyria was often distinguished by her pride. *Feinberg (God Remembers,* p. 194), quoting from *Luckenbill (Ancient Records of Assyria and Babylonia),* offers the following by way of illustration: "In the records written after the sixth campaign of Sennacherib we find the following: 'Palace of Sennacherib, the great king, the mighty king, king of the universe, king of Assyria, king of the four quarters [of the world]; favorite of the great gods; the wise and crafty one; strong hero, first among all princes; the flame that consumes the insubmissive, who strikes the wicked with the thunderbolt. Assur, the great god, has intrusted to me an unrivaled kingship, and has made powerful my weapons above [all] those who dwell in palaces. From the upper sea of the setting sun to the lower sea of the rising sun, all princes of the four quarters [of the world] he has brought in submission to my feet.' " This boast, it is predicted, "shall be brought low" (*hûradh*) when it clashes with the Lord. The failure of Egypt's power is described as a "departing of her sceptre," cf., Gen. 49:10. Two outstanding mighty nations sink into nothing when they seek to oppose the delivery of God's people—an everlasting truth concerning all who oppose the Almighty.

The success that will thus fall to the lot of Ephraim is, however, by no means to be regarded as a human achievement

202 EXPOSITION OF ZECHARIAH

growing out of human merit. This is the thought that concludes the section. The Lord says: "I will make them strong"
but indicates with double emphasis that the source of strength
is in Himself exclusively by adding: "in the Lord." This implies that on the part of the Ephraimites there will be a right
relationship of the inner man, namely, the relationship of
true faith. It is somewhat unusual to find the Lord saying: He
will make the people strong *in the Lord,* thus speaking of
Himself in the third person; yet compare Hos. 1:7. Since the
verse is a description of what God does for the Israelites, the
second half of the verse is not a reference to godly conduct or
behavior but a description of the fortunate state of Israel. The
"name of the Lord" shall not be a terror to the Israelites or a
confining restriction but a realm in which they may "freely
walk about" (*yithhalakhû,* the Hithpael has this meaning, *to
walk to and fro,* with the connotation of being unrestricted).
Such freedom is possible only where the right relation to God
prevails. This concludes the statement of God's favor to
Ephraim.

Chapter XI

Israel, Ready for Judgment, Committed First to the Good
Shepherd, then to the Foolish Shepherd

The preceding chapters (9, 10) presented a picture of the
victories of Israel and of her complete redemption by the
Lord. All of the problems that might have engendered anxious
thoughts receive an answer that bespeaks Israel's success and
her glory. Such strains of prophecy, however, usually need to
be offset by words of warning and counsel, for there is no
group in this still sinful nation that is entirely ready for God's
favors and blessings, and to whom only good can be prophesied. Promises of future greatness need to be offset by words
of judgment against sin lest the gracious words breed carnal
pride and a false sense of security. Though it is true that God's
true people shall, indeed, receive at God's hands unspeakably
great blessings, it is equally true that many crudities and sins
prevailed in Israel, in fact, even a tendency to cast off the yoke
of her Lord and to refuse His guidance. Such a tendency must
be reckoned with and curbed, and so there follows a chapter
(11) which stands in the sharpest contrast with the preceding
two chapters. The land and the people suddenly appear as
being ripe for judgment, for very severe judgment. By making
no gradual transition the prophet sets forth these words of
judgment in very sharp relief.

The chapter may be divided thus:
a) v. 1—3, a picture of the impending outward devastation
   of the land
b) v. 4—14, God's last faithful endeavors to reclaim Israel
   in the face of the impending destruction; and
c) v. 15—17, the surrender of the worthless flock to a reckless shepherd.

a. *A picture of the impending outward devastation of the land, v. 1–3.*

✦

vs. 1–3   ¹ Open your doors, O Lebanon, that the fires may devour your cedars. ² Wail, O cypress, for the cedar is fallen, for thy glorious ones [trees] are destroyed; wail, O oaks of Bashan, for the impenetrable forest is cut down. ³ Hark, how the shepherds cry! for their glory is destroyed. Hark, how the young lions roar! for the Jordan thicket is laid waste.

Because of its height and its inaccessible position Lebanon is likened to a mountain citadel, which in the present instance is so positively doomed to destruction by fire that it may as well forget all thoughts of resistance and open its doors and let the fire enter and consume its beauteous cedars. In the Scriptures, when the higher are fallen, the lower are often bidden to take up a lament because with the removal of the mightier the downfall of the less mighty is assured. (cf., 9: 1–5).

Verse 2. "The cypress" is, therefore, next summoned to take up a lamentation. We have adopted the rendering "cypress" (*A.R.V.*) although this tree is now not native to the Lebanon mountains. Possibly one of the coniferous trees is meant, so the rendering "fir tree" (*A.V.*) is also permissible. Since it is a lesser tree it finds its fate sealed with that of the cedars when those "glorious trees" (*addirîm*) are destroyed. Next to the cedars "the oaks of Bashan" were regarded as mighty monarchs of the forest. Their doom, too, is sealed because "the impenetrable forest" is cut down. The "impenetrable forest" is the Lebanon, called *ya'ar habbatsîr,* the forest that is cut off or separated (on *ya'ar* without an article see *G.K.* 126.5.R.1) because its mountain slopes and its density rendered it difficult of access.

Verse 3. It will be noticed that not the entire land of Israel has thus far been described as having been touched by the grievous judgment that God sends but only Lebanon and Bashan. The reason for this appears to be that in the preceding chapter (v. 10) these same sections of the land were referred to as recipients of particular blessings from God. But the devastation will, nevertheless, affect all the land because not only the shepherds of Lebanon and Bashan wail over the loss of pasturage but shepherds generally. Furthermore, the Jordan thicket is not found in the northern section of the land so much as in the central section, along the Jordan south of the Sea of Galilee.

This dramatic presentation of the devastation of the land, having begun with an apostrophe to Lebanon, to the cypress, and to the oaks, continues by calling attention to cries that are uttered in the land as a result of the great devastation. The one cry is that of the shepherds. For the devastation, likened to a fire, has swept away all their fine pasturage, here called their "glory." The other cry is that of the lions whose lairs have been destroyed. Their lairs are called "pride of the Jordan" (cf., Jer. 12:5; 49:19; 50:44) which is nothing other than the tall growth, jungle-like in density, found in the narrow Jordan valley where tropical climate prevails (German: *Hochwuchs*). We translated this phrase "thicket." The effect produced by v. 3 is actually as dramatic as we rendered it; for in connections such as these the word *qôl*, "voice," may be regarded as an interjection, "Hark," etc.

These three verses, therefore, present in a vigorous picture a scene of complete judgment and devastation upon the land to which such fair things had been promised in chapters 9, 10. To this literal understanding of the passage we ought to adhere. Because this note of judgment upon Israel that runs through this chapter was not understood, some interpreters have regarded these three verses as a metaphor, letting the trees mentioned represent either the mighty monarchs of Syria and Egypt or the great ones of Israel. Since nothing stated in these verses compels us to draw such a conclusion, and since the literal understanding of v. 1–3 is perfectly reasonable and in harmony with the context, we contend that a nonfigurative interpretation alone is justifiable. Even if in passages like Isa. 2:13; 10:34; Ezek. 17:8; Jer. 22:6, 7, 20, mighty trees represent mighty nations, it would follow only that such an interpretation is *possible*. A literal interpretation, however, carries us far enough. For surely, if the land is so completely devastated as is here described, all greatness and great men will also have been involved in the universal ruin.

It need scarcely be mentioned that our interpretation of the passage does not imply that an actual "fire" is going to break out and sweep over the land. So much of the figurative is certainly found in the passage that fire stands as a representative of some form of grievous destruction. Nor does the passage necessarily refer to some one particular devastation. Some commentators, like *Barnes,* say that "fire" is a metaphor that denotes the destructiveness of the invader. It does, however, portray what Israel merits, and what kind of punishment she may receive if repentance does not soon become evident.

b. *God's last faithful endeavors to reclaim Israel, v. 4–14.*

This section may be described as picturing the activity of a good shepherd who takes charge of Israel, for through him God makes His faithful efforts at Israel's reclamation.

✠

vs. 4–14   4 Thus says the Lord, my God: Tend the flock destined for slaughter; 5 for their owners slay them and do not feel guilty, and those that sell them say: Blessed be the Lord, for I have become rich, and their own shepherds spare them not. 6 For I will no more spare the inhabitants of the earth—oracle of the Lord—but, lo, I myself will deliver the men, every one into his neighbor's hand, and into the hand of his king, and they shall smite the land, and I shall deliver none out of their hands. 7 So I tended the flock destined for slaughter, particularly the poor of the flock. And I took for myself two rods. The one I called Grace, and the other I called Unity, and I tended the flock. 8 And I disowned three of the shepherds in one month. And my soul grew impatient of them, and their soul also loathed me. 9 Then I said: I will not be your shepherd: that which is about to die, let it die; that which gets lost, let it get lost; and they that are left, let each one eat the flesh of the other. 10 Then I took my rod grace and broke it, to break my covenant which I had made with all the peoples. 11 So it was broken in that day; and thus the poor

> of the flock that gave heed to me knew that it was the
> word of the Lord. [12] Then I said to them: If it seem good
> to you, give me my wages; and if not, pass it by. So they
> paid me my wages—thirty shekels of silver. [13] But the
> Lord said to me: Cast it to the potter, the magnificent
> price that I was valued at by them. Then I took the thirty
> shekels of silver and cast them into the house of the Lord
> to the potter. [14] Then I broke my second staff, unity, to
> break the brotherhood between Judah and Israel.

Two major questions must be answered before it is possible
to interpret this section satisfactorily. The first is, "What is
the nature of the prophetic act here described? Did the
prophet, when he was commissioned to feed the flock of
Israel, actually assume the leadership of the nation and function as the religious and, perhaps, also as the civil head of
Israel?" Such procedure is entirely without a parallel in
Israel's history and surely not supported by any historical
facts on record even though *v. Orelli* advocates that such an
interpretation be adopted. If the event described is not to be
conceived as an actual and literal experience, is it permissible
to conceive it as an inner, visionary (in the good sense) experience? This is apparently all that remains. Even as in a
dream a man may live through strange experiences, all of
which may be far removed from reality, so the same experience
is, no doubt, possible in visions. The entire experience as such
is the essential matter. That will prove rich in instruction for
Israel. It teaches its lesson in the details that it records.

Nor is such an approach to our problem without analogy.
Prophetic acts are described in the prophetic records, acts
which certainly were not literally carried out (cf., Jer. 25:15ff
and Hos. 1) and yet their lesson for Israel is perfectly clear.
Horst's interpretation suggests this thought when he says:
"This is not a parable acted out by the prophet but an allegory
of a purely literary sort *(schriftstellerische Allegorie)*." A
quotation, offered by *Pusey*, may be added in further explanation: "The actions presented by the prophets are not always
to be understood as actions but as predictions. As when God
commanded Isaiah to make the hearts of the people dull, i.e.,
to denounce to the people their future blindness, through

which they would, with obstinate mind, reject the mercies of Christ. Or when He says that He appointed Jeremiah to destroy and to build, to root out and to plant. Or when He commanded the same prophet to cause the nations to drink the cup, whereby they should be bereft of their senses, Jeremiah did nothing of all this but asserted that it would be. So here."

The other question is, "Whom does the prophet impersonate?" Some commentators say, the prophetic office generally speaking (*der heilsmittlerische Beruf, Koehler*); other interpreters say, Jesus Christ Himself, who from the Old Testament point of view must be designated as the "angel of the Lord" (*Hengstenberg*). However, the only tenable claim apparently is: the prophet represents *the Lord Himself*, for, as *Keil* indicates, v. 8, 12, 13 refer to acts which were in reality done by no prophet, nor even, strictly speaking, by Christ, but by God through His Son.

There is an intimate connection between the first three verses of the chapter and our section. It is this: since Israel is ready for judgment, God will make a last vigorous attempt to retrieve the nation from utter loss. Yet it may be correctly said that, since the beginning of the chapter predicts God's judgment, this section shows how much of this judgment actually came to be a matter of necessity.

Verse 4. The commission: "Tend the flock destined for slaughter" is not an imaginary one; it is actually laid upon the prophet by the Lord. This name, "the flock of slaughter," *tso'n hahareghah*, used again in v. 7, implies that Israel is a flock that is being slaughtered by its proud masters as v. 5 describes it and as the parallel statement in v. 7 suggests. Feeding the flock is more accurately translated "tend the flock," for the verb is *ra'ah*=to do the work of a shepherd, *weiden*. God's reason for giving them a shepherd is that they sadly stand in need of one as v. 5 indicates.

As 10:3 has shown, the rulers of Israel were treating the nation harshly. Though this is one reason that God from this time until the coming of His Son showed particular mercy unto His people, it is seldom mentioned. The cruelty prac-

ticed by the various masters of Israel is here described. They
are called the ones "who buy them," *qonêhen,* by metonomy
this then comes to mean "their owners" or "their possessors"
(see *K.W.* on *qanah*). When a nation has passed into the rule
of another nation like a flock into the power of a shepherd, it
is not right for the ruling nation simply to slay whomsoever
of the subjugated nation it will. That, however, is what the
nations that dominated Israel did.

Nor did they in any wise feel themselves guilty, for "they
hold themselves not guilty." This is the meaning of *ye'shamû,*
as it is in Hos. 5:15. Again the figure of Israel as a flock and the
foreign ruler as a shepherd is employed in the charge although
it is not strictly carried through. Although those who possess
a flock may slay of it as much as they please and sell the slain
animals whenever they are inclined to do so, yet when the
flock represents a nation, certain moral obligations enter in
that condemn such a course. The nations are here represented
as trafficking with Israel and acquiring wealth at Israel's ex-
pense and blessing themselves with a half-pious statement as
though the Lord were looking with favor upon their unholy
endeavors, for they say: "Blessed be the Lord, for I have become rich." They half fear that the Lord, Israel's God, might
avenge the wrong done; therefore they bless Him and ascribe
their success to Him when He does not interfere. In a word,
the attitude of all these shepherds or foreign rulers can be
described as heartless; "their own shepherds spare them not"
as the prophet expresses it.

The contrast in the use of the verb "spare" (*chamah*) at
the close of v. 5 and at the beginning of v. 6 necessitates that
the expression *yoshebhê ha'arets* be translated "inhabitants of
the *earth,*" not of "the *land.*" The contrast is clearly this: since
they show no pity to God's people, God will not pity them.
The "for," *kî,* at the beginning of the verse shows why the
prophet receives his commission to "tend the flock": the nations are being judged, and thus opportunity is given for the
prophet to do his work. This judgment consists in a kind of
mutual slaughter: men are delivered into the hand of their
neighbors and into the hand of their king. There is a just

retribution in this: they slaughtered Israel, they are now themselves slaughtered. Besides, a kind of divine irony is manifested: God lets one of those who are guilty punish the other, and heartless kings take advantage of their people even as they took advantage of Israel. When the rulers establish such cruel policies as many did in days of old—witness the cruelties of the Roman emperors—God often does not interfere: "they shall smite the land, and I shall deliver none out of their hands." The punishment befalling the sufferers is justly deserved.

Verses 5 and 6 showed what made it necessary and possible to feed God's flock. The next two verses indicate the manner in which the shepherd did his work.

We must in thought attach v. 7 to v. 4; the intervening verses have removed several difficulties. God said, "Feed" (v. 4), so, "I fed" (v. 7). Those who were the particular objects of his care were the persons that required the most attention, "the poor of the flock." Already that is evidence of the spirit in which the newly appointed shepherd did his work. We may specifically think of Christ as fulfilling this statement, but it is a statement that includes everything that was done from the prophet's day onward until an outstanding fulfillment came in Christ. *Lakhen*="therefore" as *conclusio cognoscendi* in the sense of "and so." German: *somit* or "particularly" (*K.S.* 373i).

The spirit that characterizes the shepherd's activity is more definitely indicated by a symbolic act which he performs as he takes these duties upon himself. For he takes two staves— nothing suggests even remotely that a diviner's rod is meant (*Sellin*), for the prophets do not deal in such wares nor confound true religion with false. *Barnes* remarks: "The Eastern shepherd carried a rod (*shebet*) or club for repelling wild beasts and a crooked staff (*mish'eneth*) for helping the sheep and himself in difficult places." The names that the shepherd gives to the staves shows what purposes he had in mind and what objects were continually in his hand as he went about his duties. These staves serve to remind him and to show to others what motives actuate him in all his work. These two motives are "grace" and "unity." *No'am,* "grace"=*pleasantness, graciousness* (cf., Ps. 90:17). *chobhelim,* "bands" or "unity," plural to express the abstract (*G.K.* 1241.R (b)) is explained in v. 14 as referring to "the brotherhood between Judah and Israel." Israel could never thrive as long as it was a divided nation. The shepherd purposes to put an end to the harmful division that had for so long proved the bane of Israel's normal growth and development. The concluding statement of v. 7, "and I tended the flock," is not an idle repetition. Being intimately bound together with the first half of the verse, it signifies that, guided by the two motives or principles that the staves represent, he went about his shepherd duties.

A further statement regarding the fidelity with which he administered his duties as a shepherd is given in the words: "and I disowned three of the shepherds in one month" (v. 8). These three must have been undershepherds that were under his jurisdiction. Because they failed to measure up to the high standard of duty that he required of them they were summarily dismissed. That is the meaning of *'akhchîdh,* "to cut off" in the sense of "disavow" (cf., *K.W. sub verb.*), not necessarily such a thought as "put to death." Simply: men fail to work so that the flock is profited by their labors as it ought to be, and they find that their services are no longer required. If such dismissals occur three times in "one month," then, surely, the chief shepherd is intent upon fidelity in office and laboring hard to give the best of care to his flock.

By interpreting thus we arrive at the general sense of the passage as it developes in the context. This sense is simple and plain and harmonizes most beautifully with the sequence of thought in which it appears. Yet the majority of interpreters endeavor to find a specific reference to some historical event. They are for the most part influenced in their view by the words *shelo'sheth hara'îm* which they translate: "*the* three shepherds" (*A.R.V.*). *Luther* and the *A.V.* did better by translating: "Three shepherds also I cut off," a meaning which is permissible grammatically as *Keil* proves by reference to parallel cases, Exod. 26:3, 9; Josh. 17:11; I Sam. 20:20. When this meaning is preferred, too much effort is made to identify three specific individuals or three classes (*Hengstenberg*). At least forty different interpretations of the passage are offered, ranging from the effort to find three men in the days of the Exodus down to the time of Christ, where the civil, priestly, and prophetic offices are selected. Even Roman emperors are mentioned. The interpretation meeting with most favor at present is that which selects the age of the Maccabees and points to the three renegade high priests, Lysimachus, Jason, and Menelaus, and lets their successor, the good and faithful Onias IV, be the good shepherd. This is an obscure event in Jewish history that certainly does not deserve to be the subject of so outstanding a prophecy as this, nor do we have proof of the removal of these three high priests in one month.

Some interpreters regard the "one month" to be 210 years. All efforts to find a fulfillment in pre-exilic days have proven equally unsatisfactory. The outstanding feature about all of them is their failure to agree with the text on at least one important item. *Hengstenberg's* effort to identify the three shepherds with the three classes of leaders of the people—civil, prophetic, and priestly—offers an insurmountable difficulty in the fact of the discontinuance of the prophetic office with Malachi, long before Christ's time, whom (as Angel of the Lord) he regards as the one typified by the prophet's work. *Mitchell*, finding the eighth verse difficult, says it was "interpolated."

This last effort of the shepherd revealed more clearly than any had done before this time how utterly unworthy the flock was of such attention. How this impression is borne in on the shepherd as a result of this experience is now disclosed, 8b–11. This interpretation has been clouded by the failure to sense the beginning of a new thought in 8b, a failure that is apparent in the translation of *A.R.V.*, "for my soul was weary." Again the *A.V.* is better: "*and* my soul loathed them." The Hebrew uses the conjunction "and." Besides, *wattiqtsar*, cannot stand for a pluperfect as it would have to be rendered if it belonged to 8a.

Only when the shepherd is made to represent some foreign monarch like Ptolemy III (*Mitchell*) is there a possibility of supposing that 8b is a statement of the disgust of a neglectful shepherd who desired to be relieved of duties that he disliked. The chapter rather moves along with good sequence of thought and arrives at a climax of proof of the utter unworthiness of the people to receive any further care. Since the nation was suffering injustice ("flock of slaughter," v. 4) God made it an object of very particular care. The principles of "grace" and "unity" predominated in this care (v. 7). Incompetent shepherds were weeded out (8a). But the attitude of the flock was such that the shepherd who had this special commission could not endure the unresponsiveness and the ingratitude manifested and so finally grew impatient. As the sequel proves (v. 12–14), this impatience was entirely justifiable. But 8b already shows that the impatience was justified. For the flock actually loathed its good shepherd, and thus did it repay his special care. *Tiqtsar=be impatient,* from the root meaning, "to be short" (cf. *K.W.*). *Bachal=to be disgusted* (German: *überdrüssig sein*). Though these verbs, descriptive of the mutual reaction, are rather strong in themselves, the fact that both have as the subject "the soul" and not merely the personal pronoun shows how deeply the inner revulsion of feeling went. The shepherd's impatience is naturally the result of the "disgust" or "loathing" that the people felt for him. There is such a thing as righteous and merited disgust. It is this feature in the development of the situation that portrays with increasing clearness that a totally unmerited grace was being bestowed as a last expedient, both that the grace might prove its nature to the utmost, and also that the punishment predicted (v. 1–3) might be revealed as being entirely merited.

Verse 9. As a result of his experience the prophet expresses sentiments that indicate that he feels he must terminate his shepherd's commission and let Israel suffer the consequences. The burden of the resolution that he has reached is *lo' 'er'eh 'ethkhem,* "I will not be your shepherd." So that the seriousness of this attitude of his might be felt, he reveals all that this includes: "that which is about to die," etc. (to the end of v. 9). The participle feminine *methah* we translate as a future (*moritura*—see *G.K.* 116.2). Ordinarily, if a sheep was in danger of death, the shepherd would administer such care as might tend to save the sheep. But this shepherd would not act thus after the people have given final and conclusive proof of their being utterly unworthy of any care: "let it die." So that which is in danger of being cut off is likewise simply abandoned. The remnant may without interference on the shepherd's part prey on one another. At this point the figure is plainly being abandoned, for even in direst straits sheep do not act thus. Since pestilence, war, and famine are frequently represented as three agents to whom God abandons the disobedient (cf., Jer. 15:1, 2; 34:17; Exod. 6:12), these may be the forces referred to: "about to die," i.e., in pestilence; "about to be cut off," i.e., by the sword; "eating one another's flesh," i.e., due to the extremity of famine. In one word, the shepherd feels perfectly justified in taking the attitude: Let happen what will to the flock, I shall do nothing for it; it has not deserved it.

Verse 10. Such an attitude necessarily has as a result that the particular features that marked his watchful care must also be abandoned by the shepherd. Therefore, by a symbolic act, he first breaks the staff *grace*. In addition to what was said on v. 7, it is now clear that in this case grace included the favor of the friendly relations existing between "all the peoples" and Israel. In fact, these friendly relations had been guaranteed by nothing less than a "covenant" (*berîth*) which God had made with all the peoples. The term "covenant" is here used in a looser sense, not as descriptive of a formal agreement entered into by contracting parties, but to indicate that, when the peoples round about Israel did her no harm, this was due to the fact that God had put them under as strong a restraint as might be exerted upon a nation by a covenant solemnly sworn to. A similar use of the term is found in Hos. 2:18–20 and Job 5:23. *Karátti* here has the sense of a pluperfect; see *G.K.* 106–1 (c). Surely, this statement of the case clearly indicates with what ease God restrains nations and also the greatness of the favors that He bestowed on His people in a last attempt to win them. "Peoples," the plural of *'am*, which is usually used with reference to Israel, cannot here have such a meaning (*Fausset*), for the plural cannot be reasonably applied to Israel, nor is the word limited in its use to Israel (see *B.D.B.*).

Verse 11. What the symbolic act of the breaking of the staff sought to depict actually happened. To show that is the purpose of the opening statement of this verse: "So it was broken in that day." All restraining influence upon the nations was actually removed. That a change had been wrought in this respect by God was immediately apparent to "those who gave heed" (*shomerîm*, literally, *watching*) unto the Lord. Furthermore, (*yedhe'û*), since those who regard God closely have deeper spiritual discernment they "knew" that "it was the word of the Lord," i.e., the fact that the nations were beginning to afflict Israel was not a matter of chance but the result of God's word, which regulates all and in this case gave the adversaries permission or power to proceed against God's people. Those who "gave heed" unto the Lord are called "the poor of the flock," *'aniyyey*, for it is the lowly and wretched who for the most part consider diligently God's ways and His doings.

In this experience that the prophet lived in a vision the next step was a formal severing of relations between the shepherd and his flock. He wanted the people to know what he had done and also to know their exact feeling at his refusal further to function as a shepherd. This information could be secured by demanding such hire of them as he as a shepherd was entitled to. This "hire" (*sakhar*) is not one of the features of the vision that calls for particular interpretation. Even if some commentators put repentance and faith into this term they scarcely know how to use to advantage what they have thus gained. It is better to stay with the more general meaning that this represents the last step in concluding the shepherd's relations with the flock. Of course, as far as the flock is concerned, it is not even certain that, after all its scurvy treatment of the shepherd, it will consider acknowledging any obligation. Therefore the case is put hypothetically: *"If it seem good to you, give me my wages."* This truly Hebrew clause says literally: "if it be good in your eyes," *'im tobh be'ênêkhem*. However, mercenary motives so little prompt the prophet's request that he can conclude with the words: "if not, pass it by." He is more concerned about making the flock feel that he is done with it than he is about money. He trusts that this emphatic termination of his responsibilities might awaken some of the people to the seriousness of the situation.

The flock replies to his demand, but in such a manner that its act is nothing short of willful insult. The people show how utterly unworthy they are of any care by selecting a sum that expresses how shamelessly they have scorned his kindly offices. As it has been well put in German, instead of *Lohn* (hire) he receives *Hohn* (mockery). For, according to Exod. 21:32, "thirty shekels of silver" is the sum to be paid for a slave who was gored by an ox. It was not even the price of a freeman. The shepherd was, therefore, regarded by them as a common slave. The measure of their depravity is now clearly marked: God's kindliest services are very lightly esteemed by them. After the word "thirty" the term *she'qel* is omitted as being self-evident (*K.S.* 314h). On *'im lo'* in 12a, used in an elliptical statement, see *G.K.* 159 *fin.* R.2.

At this point, v. 13, the Lord Himself intervenes, for the one upon whom this very slight value has been placed is His prophet, His representative; consequently this is the measure of what *He* is worth in their estimation. Therefore, too, He calls this the price that *He* was valued at by them. God's command to the prophet is: "Cast it to the potter," *hashlîkhehû 'el-hayyotser.*

This command presents unusual difficulties. The most approved solution of the present time is the least satisfactory. It operates thus: it substitutes an *a* for a *y* in the term "potter," which yields the meaning, "into the treasure-chamber." Though it seems quite proper to put money into the treasury, yet here the Lord's treasury is involved (cf., v. 13, "in the house of the Lord") and, surely, it is the gravest impropriety to argue: It's a despicable price, but rather than lose it, let it be put into Lord's treasury. *Torrey,* writing in the *Journal of Biblical Literature* (1936, p. 247ff) says, p. 255, that this interpretation has for it "the consensus of Biblical scholarship." This solution of the problem is, however, just as unsatisfactory as is the conjecture of the *Septuagint:* χωνευτήριον, smelting furnace. It appears that the most satisfactory solution of the difficulty is that which has regard to the particular meaning that the verb *shalakh* must have in this connection. In countless cases it connotes casting an object away in disdain, therefore, *to fling aside,* expressing disgust or disapproval by the very act. Apparently, "cast it to the potter" was a proverbial expression that suggested this very thought. Farther than this our analysis of the phrase cannot go at present.

There is strong irony in the expression "the magnificent price" (*A.V.,* "a goodly price"). *'Édher hayqar,* literally, "the glory of the price"; for a more paltry sum that connoted disdain could not have been offered.

The prophet does as he is bidden and casts away the price that was paid him. This act he performs "in the house of the Lord," *beth Yahweh* (without a preposition). This added phrase serves to indicate that the act was performed publicly and before the eyes of the Lord. This was a public transaction that involved the people's standing before God. In the vision the prophet, therefore, cast down the sum involved "in the house of the Lord." Since the expression "to the potter" must be regarded as proverbial, the word "potter" no longer requires that a particular potter be thought of. Compare the parallel German expression: *"zum Henker gehen."* The preposition *'el* before persons with *hayyotser* as in I Kings 19:19.

Since all relations that had been established between the shepherd and the people are to be formally and conclusively severed, there remains the disposal of the second of the two staves. This is now presented in v. 14.

Since this staff represented unity in the nation as an object to be sought and brought about by God's favor, the breaking of the staff signifies that God will no longer labor in the direction of healing the breach caused by the division of Israel. Whatever disunion exists may be allowed to continue and bear its evil fruits. Or it might be stated thus: the prophet represents God's activity in behalf of the people, and he shall no longer advocate the blessing of unity nor strive for its maintenance. All disruption of unity that has set Israel against Israel ever since that time is the result. Outstanding instances of the fulfillment of this statement are all those cases of intestine discord that tore the Jews apart into factions before, during, and after the time of Christ as reported by *Josephus.*

The use that Matthew (27:9) makes of this passage is a problem that belongs primarily in the field of New Testament exegesis but, nevertheless, requires at least a few explanatory remarks here. Comparing Matthew's citation with the *Septuagint* and with the original, we notice that Matthew is not citing the *Septuagint,* for its manifest mistranslations are not repeated. The original Hebrew was apparently in Matthew's mind as well as the purchase of the potter's field with the "price of blood." He reproduces the original freely with a few changes such as of number and of person in the verb—all of which can readily be understood—and almost the chief variation from the original is the use of the phrase "for a potter's field" in place of the original "to the potter." But even that can be understood as an interpretative emphasis on the phrase that still causes us difficulty in the original.

The chief difficulty encountered is that Matthew attributes the passage to Jeremiah. The labored attempts to make Jeremiah 18 and 19 contain the thought that is unfolded in Zech. 11, and so to make Jeremiah the original and Zechariah a parallel but secondary statement of the thought are too artificial and fail to convince. Nor will it do simply to attribute a slip of memory to Matthew by claiming that the prophecy as such is the main issue, not its author—as *Luther* does. An error could plainly be involved, but we are not wrong in assuming that the error may be attributed to early copyists, whose efforts are to be dated earlier than any manuscripts in our possession at present. Another simple solution to which *Lightfoot* first drew attention (cf., *Horn's, Introduction*) is this: different groups of Old Testament writings were named among the Jews according to the first book of the roll. Zechariah happened to be in the Jeremiah roll or in the roll whose first book was Jeremiah.

We ought yet to seek an answer to the question: "In what sense is this passage Messianic?" There is no doubt of its strictly Messianic character according to Matthew 27. Since the statements, v. 4–14, were spoken directly to the prophet and called forth a response on the prophet's part (cf. our remarks on v. 4), these statements apply first, in point of time, to Zechariah. Since Matthew applies them to Jesus, we must conclude that the passage is Messianic by type, that is to say, in what he does the prophet becomes a type of the Messiah according to the governing influences of divine providence.

c. *The surrender of the worthless flock to a reckless shepherd, v. 15–17.*

After everything has been done that could possibly be done to reclaim the house of Israel, and after all efforts of this sort had finally to be discarded (v. 4–14), the Lord inaugurates a different type of treatment. If Israel will not appreciate a careful, conscientious shepherd, let it have a reckless fellow who has no concern for the welfare of the flock. This character, too, must be impersonated by the prophet, and the whole experience must be referred to the realm of inner experiences and does not demand a corresponding outward activity on the part of the prophet before the eyes of all the people; cf. the comments on v. 4.

The fulfillment of this passage is to be seen in all those leaders of Israel who, under the guise of shepherds, misled and harmed the poor flock, and that, by the way, is all that the misguided leaders have been doing ever since Zechariah's day, especially since the time that the nation has rejected the Christ. Every unbelieving Jewish teacher is a "foolish shepherd," a "worthless shepherd."

✢

vs. 15–17   15 Then the Lord said to me: Take to yourself again the implements of a foolish shepherd. 16 For, lo, I will raise up a shepherd in the land—that which is going to ruin, he will not visit; neither will he seek out the young, nor heal that which is broken, nor feed that which is sturdy; but he will eat the flesh of the fat ones and will tear their hoofs in pieces. 17 Woe unto the worthless shepherd that forsakes the flock! May the sword come upon his arm and

> upon his right eye! His arm shall be utterly dried up,
> and his right eye shall be utterly blind.

The same man is involved that was active in v. 4. Since in that passage Zechariah was to function, so he is to do here. This is further indicated by the use of *'odh,* "again." The expression is somewhat condensed. What it implies is this: "Again take to yourself shepherd's instruments, in this instance, however, those of a foolish shepherd." The thought is by no means that the prophet had previously taken such implements as foolish shepherds use. To be still more exact—the gear of a foolish shepherd was the same as that of a faithful one. *Kelî=* vessel, instrument, or implement, and may be used collectively as it is here. Such implements include a staff (I Sam. 17:40) and a pouch (*ibid.*) and a pipe (Judg. 5:16). But when taking these implements of a shepherd the prophet was "this time to play the part of a foolish one" (*Mitchell*). Now a foolish shepherd was such a one as the word *'ewîlî* indicates. For this word, from a root meaning *to grow thick,* denotes a person who has grown thick and insensible to higher purposes and aspirations, in this case the purposes of the Lord with His people. He is, therefore, a man who lacks what is surely the first requisite of a shepherd. There follows (v. 16) a statement as to what this act of the prophet portended.

One shepherd is mentioned as a type of those that will be the rule in Israel. Israel is to observe this strange thing which God is about to do. Note the "lo" (*hinneh*). The order of the words in the original suggests that it is the Lord Himself who is allowing such a situation to develope: the emphatic personal pronoun (*'anokhî*) stands first, *I* am the one who will raise up. Besides, the participle (*meqîm*) is used instead of the finite verb. Of course, *hinneh* with the participle almost invariably points to the future.

Several classes of those who are in need of care are listed first. The pictures are taken from the types that may be found among sheep. First "that which is going to ruin," *nikhchadhoth;* the participle here describes "an incomplete process" (*B.D.B.*). In a flock such sheep need to be "visited" or looked after. That the shepherd described will not trouble to do. Next are "the young," *na'ar*. Being weak and feeble, they are naturally the objects of special care (cf., Isa. 40:11). They will not be carefully sought out to determine whether all is well with them. *Na'ar*, usually meaning *youth*, may be taken as referring to the young among animals. Otherwise it becomes necessary to conjecture some difficult participial form. Those are next listed that have broken a limb, *nishbéreth*. If any sheep is in need of care it is such a one. This shepherd will, however, make no effort to effect a healing.

Mention is now made of one class that has no particular needs, "that which is sturdy," *nitstsabhah* (Nifal participle from *yatsabh*). An indolent shepherd might at least take care of the well and the strong among the sheep because the care of these calls for the least effort. Even they will not *be fed* or *provided for* (*yekhalkel*). After all these grievous forms of neglect, which are in themselves a climax, have been listed, more serious charges follow, which show that the shepherd's attitude is not one of mere passive neglect but one of even greedy and selfish destruction, which prompts him to feed upon the sheep rather than to feed them. He does not regard himself as a shepherd who is to care for them, but he regards them as sheep that can be put to use to satisfy his selfish appetite. If there are such among them as are "fat," their flesh will he consume. In his efforts to get every last tidbit and delicacy the appetite of this shepherd will induce him even to "tear their hoofs in pieces" after he has eaten every shred of meat, in an effort to extract even the luscious marrow (*KW*).

What a picture of a selfish shepherd! It is purposely drawn in repulsive colors in order to make the warning as strong as possible for Israel: such a leader will you have if you reject what I graciously offer. How this statement has been fulfilled to the letter in the case of Israel as well as in the case of all who refused particularly the Good Shepherd!

Though God's avenging justice may send such shepherds, that does not imply that their extreme guilt is a matter of indifference to God. Though God is, on the one hand, justified in using such a shepherd as a tool, He is, on the other hand, roused to just anger and threatens to wreak His vengeance upon the guilty offender. Both points of view mutually demand one another.

A terrible woe (v. 17) is pronounced upon all those who, like this worthless shepherd, neglect their duty and destroy the flock. His neglect is, in substance, that he "forsakes the flock." He abandons it to any harm to which it may come. *Ro'i ha'elîl*=*the shepherd of worthlessness, ro'i,* with the ending *i,* as designating the construct (cf., *G.K.* 901). According to its root meaning *'elîl* is equivalent to "to be weak" or "insufficient." "Worthless" is a good translation.

The statement following is modelled after Jer. 50:35–37. It is a severe imprecation. Since the shepherd neglected to use his arm to fend for the sheep and his eye to watch over them, the avenging sword is pictured as coming upon these members. Should it fail to do its work, they will, as it were, blighted by the curse of God, shrivel up and wither away completely. The absolute infinitive used with each of the last two verbs makes the thought of the verb very emphatic, a thought which the English seeks to reproduce by rendering: *"utterly* dried up" and *"utterly* blind." With this solemn curse the passage, v. 15–17, as well as the entire portion, chapters 9–11, comes to a dramatic and effective close. The concluding curse was naturally not pronounced upon Zechariah, the prophet; for he only impersonated the faithless shepherd as God has bidden him to do.

Chapter XII

THE BURDEN CONCERNING ISRAEL, CHAPTERS 12–14

A. *Judah's Victory (12:1–13:6)*

We come to the second half of the last section, namely, to chapters 12–14.

That this section is to be regarded as a parallel to the first section appears from the similar headings, "the burden of the word of the Lord." The similarity extends farther: both sections indicate upon whom the burden is to be laid—9:1, "upon the land of Hadrach"; 12:1, "concerning Israel." It, therefore, becomes apparent that, whereas the first section (chapters 9–11) was concerned primarily with the *hostile world-power,* our section has *Israel* as its chief concern. The parallelism extends still farther: as 9:1 showed that "the Lord hath an eye upon men and upon all the tribes of Israel" and thus was well qualified to bring judgment upon those who needed to be judged, so 12:1 shows God as the One who "spreads out the heavens and lays the foundation of the earth," etc. Still more: 9:1–7 shows the conquest and the overthrow of the surrounding nations; v. 8, Israel's safety; 12:1–4 pictures the confusion of Israel's foes; v. 5–9, Judah's strength.

We prefer to outline this section under the head of Judah's Victory.

1. It consists in the *confusion of her enemies,* v. 1–4.
2. It is possible because of Judah's strength in the Lord, v. 5–9.
3. Her *outstanding* victory consists
   a. *in her true penitence,* v. 10–14.
   b. *in her true sanctification,* 13:1–6.

The names by which God's people are addressed in this chapter should be carefully observed. Failure to do so has led some interpreters to charge the author with inconsistency or to claim that some of the names used were later and improper interpolations. In v. 1 we have the word "Israel" in the heading, this being the chief and most expressive name by which God's people were designated, and which now, after the two portions of the divided Kingdom no longer stand over against one another, again most properly refers to the entire people. However, even if Israel is truly the name for God's people, yet those who had returned from the Exile lived primarily, if not almost exclusively, in Judah and in Jerusalem. In conformity with the historical situation we, therefore, find sometimes the one, sometimes the other locality referred to, and sometimes both together, depending on the particular cast of the thought, cf., v. 2., Judah and Jerusalem; v. 3, Jerusalem; v. 5, Judah and Jerusalem; v. 6, Judah and Jerusalem; v. 7, by way of contrast to these two, the house of David; v. 8, 9, Jerusalem. When a new grouping now appears in v. 10, "the house of David and the inhabitants of Jerusalem," it becomes apparent that the new designation regards the people of God from another point of view. This different use of terms should be rightly evaluated, and only then does it serve to throw light upon the purpose of the section. The procedure of criticism here, too, confuses and casts reflections on a very good text.

The Confusion of Judah's Enemies (v. 1–4)

When the general heading that we have affixed to this section as well as the particular caption under which we have summarized these verses are considered, the very first word of the chapter, which provides the author's heading for chapters 12–14, seems quite out of harmony with the idea of Judah's victory. The word "burden," which was, no doubt, chosen to put chapters 12–14 into a parallelism with chapters 9–11 is, however, quite appropriate insofar as what ultimately results in Judah's victory at first appears as a grievous burden, when the nations storm in upon her and seek to devour her. On *massa'* as *burden* and not as *oracle* see our remarks on 9:1.

The heading of v. 1 is furthermore based upon the fullest authority when it in a threefold way emphasizes the divine origin of its message: "burden," "word of the Lord," "oracle of the Lord." These three modes of expression are standard terms to convey the idea of an authoritative divine revelation.

THE BURDEN CONCERNING ISRAEL 225

Ne'um Yahweh—seldom placed at the beginning—cf., II Sam. 23:1; Ps. 110:1 (*K.S.* 374 ff.).

✠

vs. 1-4

¹ The burden of the word of the Lord concerning Israel —oracle of the Lord, who spreads out the heavens and lays the foundation of the earth and forms the spirit of man within him: ² Behold, I will make Jerusalem a cup of reeling unto all the peoples round about, and it shall also affect Judah when Jerusalem is besieged. ³ And it shall come to pass in that day that I will make Jerusalem a stone of lifting for all the peoples: all who attempt to lift it shall be badly wounded, though all the nations of the earth shall be gathered together against it. ⁴ In that day—oracle of the Lord—I will smite every horse with terror and its rider with madness; and I will keep My eyes open upon the house of Judah and will smite every horse of the peoples with blindness.

The burden of the Lord is said to be "concerning Israel," *'al Yiṣra'el,* literally, *upon* Israel. Burdens are naturally laid *upon* others. Yet here *concerning* seems to be the more appropriate translation because in the whole passage there is less emphasis on the burdens that press Israel down.

Since promises are to be made in the passage before us, promises so rich and great as to seem beyond the possibility of realization in the case of small and unimportant Israel, the resources of the Lord who made the promises are also brought to our attention. The name *Lord* is first used twice, the divine name that is particularly reminiscent of God's faithfulness in keeping the promises made to His people. Three participles further describe the Lord, *noṭeh, yoṣedh,* and *yoṭser.* We cannot agree with *G.K.* 116.2a and *K.S.* 237b. who give a past meaning to these participles by pointing to the past tense used in v. 2 (*sam,* a prophetic perfect). For, as has rightly been pointed out by *Keil,* the last of the three terms points to an activity of God's which is continuous into the present: God still forms the spirit of man within him. If that is a form of activity which continues in the present, and since participles more naturally describe actions that continue, we do best to let the first two of this series also be regarded as participles that are descriptive of continuous acts going on progressively in the present. God's work of stretching out the heavens and laying the foundations of the earth as well as that of forming man's spirit is in the Scriptures regarded as being performed continuously. Were He for a moment to cease this creative activity, all of the visible and the invisible creation would sink back into nonexistence as *Hengstenberg* has rightly stressed.

Consider the magnitude of the works here ascribed to the Lord. The mighty heavens are "spread out" by Him, (*noteh*), a verb that is descriptive of the ease with which the work is done, as a man stretches out a tent cloth (Ps. 104:2). Again, "He founds the earth" (*yosedh*). The result: a solidity and an immobility of the old earth that have caused ceaseless wonder to those who have considered them. However, not only works of tremendous magnitude but works that require infinite pains and most delicate adjustments are the objects of His care such as "forming the spirit of man within him," *yotser,* implying careful shaping like that done by a potter. What a delicate organism—none more marvelous of all those that come under our observation! No man has seen "the spirit of man." No man can create anything like it. As long as it resides in a man's body it animates dead clay and makes a sentient human being of it. When it is withdrawn, man returns unto the dust whence he came. The whole passage is based on Isa. 42:5; cf. also, Amos 4:13; 5:8ff. *'Erets* and *shamáyim* without the article, poetic (*K.S.* 292a).

If He that makes the mighty promises to Israel that are about to be unfolded is a Lord who is capable of performing works of such magnitude, it surely becomes Israel ill to doubt that these promises will be fulfilled. By rehearsing these mighty works first God makes it clear that He is about to mention other works of His that might well challenge the small faith of man.

Verse 2. It was surely a thought passing belief that Jerusalem should be capable of working the confusion of the nations round about. Therefore the introductory *hinneh, be-*

hold, which draws attention to a most unusual situation. For in Zechariah's day Jerusalem was small. Its walls were not to be rebuilt until perhaps 60–75 years had passed. A prediction such as this, then, seemed utterly beyond the range of the possible.

This is the picture employed to portray the confusion of the foes of Jerusalem. Jerusalem is like unto a "cup," *saph*, or *bowl*, cf., Exod. 12:22, filled with wine. "All the peoples round about her" are desirous of approaching this cup and draining its contents. Such was the hostility of Israel's neighbors; they desired to dispose of Israel. It was to be to them a simple and pleasant task, like drinking wine. What a scene: a huge bowl of wine; several men, respresentative of Syria, Ammon, Moab, Edom, Philistaea, Phoenicia, crowding around the bowl and setting their lips to it! They are athirst to gulp down Israel. But, strange to say, one after another steps back, reels and staggers as a drunkard, for God has made this to be a bowl of *reeling, ra'al;* (through this expression is a ἁπὰξ λεγόμενον, its meaning is well established; from the corresponding root comes *tar'elah,* cf., Isa. 51:17, 22). They are rendered impotent by the wine of the wrath of God and stagger about like drunken fools. The bowl of wine, however—Israel—still stands. Israel's neighbors perished. The city of God stands undefeated. For similar passages of a drink that makes men reel cf. Isa. 51:17–20; Hab. 2:15ff; Jer. 25:15ff; Obad. 16.

The second half of the verse is quite regularly misunderstood, especially by those who are critically minded. It reads: "and it shall also affect Judah when Jerusalem is besieged." The subject of the verb, *shall (yihyeh)*, is to be supplied. It cannot be *matsôr, siege,* because that word refers to cities, not countries. We may, therefore, think of the general *distress* of such troubled times, which shall be upon the whole land of Judah as well as upon its capital city. This is the specific thought of this half of the verse. It should not be forgotten that a siege of a city like Jerusalem involves not only the city but the whole land as well. From this we learn further that this experience as a whole cannot result in the confusion of Israel's foes without bringing a distinct amount of suffering also upon

God's people. This is the thought of the *A.V.* and of the *German: auch Judah wird's gelten.*

Other interpretations confuse the issue by making Judah share in the assault upon Jerusalem, though under compulsion, and so run into difficulty when interpreting v. 5; or making Judah first help to assault Jerusalem, then having her swing over to help Jerusalem—a thought certainly not expressed in the text. Or the text is amended to bring it into conformity with a preconceived interpretation; cf. the deletion of *'al* before "Judah." Or the artificial translation is offered: "it shall be upon Judah [to assist] in the siege against Jerusalem." *Mitchell* simply calls this half of the verse a *gloss.*

Verse 3 parallels the preceding as to its line of thought. It represents by a different picture the idea of the confusion of Israel's foes. Jerusalem may also be likened to "a stone of lifting," *'ébhen ma'amasah* = "a stone of burden, hard to lift" (*B.D.B.*), *ein Laststein* (*Luther*). Several senses in which such a term might be used suggest themselves. It might simply be a heavy stone imbedded in the field. It might be a heavy building stone. It might be a stone that is used by youths in a weight-lifting contest. This last, which is *Jerome's* suggestion, who in his day saw the young men of the Holy Land strive to lift certain stones, a scene also witnessed by *v. Orelli* in his travels through the Holy Land, finds particular favor with those who have this passage express their particular view, viz., that it supports the theory of the Maccabean date of this section of the book. For by that time Greek gymnasia and athletic contests had been introduced into Palestine.

The simplest view is still the best, and that is the one that regards this simply as an ordinary stone that is hard to lift, half-embedded in a certain field. Whatever may have prompted anyone to attempt to lift it is immaterial. The picture seems to gain color from the assumption that a husbandman desires to remove the stone from the field he is working. For, surely, much of the stone-lifting that was done was prompted by the desire to clear the fields for purposes of husbandry. "The nations of the earth" now fit into their place in the picture. As a husbandman seeks to increase his acreage by removing a stone around which he would otherwise be obliged to plow, so the surrounding nations desire to gain territory by the dismemberment of Israel, which involves lifting Jerusalem out of the way. However, the fate of those who "attempt to lift it"—*'omes ê'ha*—"the participle here used in an inceptive sense = *would lift,* or . . . *light on*" (*Mitchell*)—is that they are "badly wounded," *sarot yissaret,* the verb with the absolute infinitive. All who tried to do away with God's people suffered as a result. The contemporaries of Zechariah, the nations thought of in this passage, have vanished and exist no longer. God's people are mightier than ever. This figure marks an advance over v. 2; there foes were rendered impotent, here foes are actually harmed.

It seems preferable, as we have done in our translation of this verse, to regard the conjunction introducing the second half of the verse as *waw concessive:* therefore not "*and* all the nations" but "*though* all the nations," etc., for the fact of their advance upon Jerusalem had already been reported in the preceding verse. This verse, then, reveals beautifully how the enemies may be harmed but not the church. *Marck* says of the stone: *damnum non sentiens, ipse magnum damnum eis affert* (suffering no hurt itself, it shall, nevertheless, inflict great hurt on them).

The same general thought offered by the two preceding verses is repeated here (v. 4) by the use of a third comparison. Israel, the little group, could not dream of such equipment as cavalry for purposes of war. Her foes could muster many a cavalry squadron. These are pictured as storming against Israel. By the omnipotence of the Almighty a wild confusion seizes these seemingly dangerous foes. Wild *terror (timmahôn)* seizes the steeds, and they become unmanageable. The riders themselves are smitten with *insanity (shigga'ôn).* Yea, in the concluding statement the climax of affliction visited upon these squadrons is reached: even the horses are smitten with *blindness ('iwwarôn).* The first two of these statements are apparently a quotation from Deut. 28:28, where the terrors were mentioned that would befall Israel because of her disobedience. In any case, a group of horsemen, themselves crazed and mounted upon terror-stricken and blind steeds, constitute a terror only to themselves. They will set their sword every man against his fellow and will exterminate each other. Such panics are mentioned in the Scriptures are coming upon Israel's foes, Exod. 14:24ff; Judg. 4:15; cf., Hag. 2:22. Similar blindness is mentioned in II Kings 6:18ff. These instances, especially the last, are, of course, mentioned chiefly as illustrations of the manner in which God can and will dispose of the foes of His people. In every case the foes are sadly put to shame. The safety of God's people lies in the benign protection which the Lord's providence affords, a thought here expressed in the words: "I will open My eyes upon the house of Judah," cf., 4:10; 9:1.

The progression of thought marked by these three illustrations should also be noted: v. 2, the enemy is thwarted; v. 3, the enemy is painfully hurt; v. 4, the enemy is destroyed. All this implies that, when they begin to oppose Judah, God will make them feel their mistake. Persistent opposition will meet with increasing severity of punishment until men destroy themselves.

Judah's Strength in the Lord (v. 5-9)

Thus far we noticed the foes of Judah and their fate. We now learn what it is that makes victory possible for Judah: her strength is in the Lord.

✠

vs. 5-9
⁵ And the chieftains of Judah shall say in their heart: The inhabitants of Judah are my strength in the Lord of hosts, their God. ⁶ In that day I will make the chieftains of Judah like a fire pot among wood and like a flaming torch among sheaves; and they shall devour all the peoples round about, on the right hand and on the left, and Jerusalem shall still abide in its own place, namely, in Jerusalem. ⁷ The Lord shall also save the tents of Judah first in order that the glory of the house of David and the glory of the inhabitants of Jerusalem be not greater than Judah's. ⁸ In that day shall the Lord shield the inhabitants of Jerusalem, and he that totters among them at that day shall be as David; and the house of David shall be as

divine beings, as the angel of the Lord before them.
⁹ And it shall come to pass in that day that I will seek to
destroy all nations that come against Jerusalem.

What outstanding men confess, namely, "the chieftains of
Judah," is mentioned in order to show us what manner of confidence it is that animates God's people and makes them victorious. For as the leaders, so the people. The word for
"chieftains," 'alluphîm, is used, apart from Zechariah, with reference to early chieftains of Edom and might, therefore, appear in a late writer who has acquired his vocabulary largely
from the study of sacred writings of the past.

The confidence of Judah was expressed thus: "The inhabitants of Jerusalem are my strength" (lit., "strength to me,"
'amtsah lî). The literal statement removes much that might
seem objectionable about their claim. They do not actually
say: "are my strength," but, "afford strength to me." Again,
they add the qualifying statement: "in the Lord of hosts, their
God." This makes the Lord Himself the ultimate source of
Jerusalem's strength and so, mediately, of Judah's chieftains.
We find the thought becoming still clearer as we notice some
subsidiary material that the book of Zechariah offers. It is not
only a harmless attitude that Judah's chieftains express; it is
the only one possible and permissible after what preceded.
This is one of the many indications that the two sections of the
book mutually require one another: 1:7 and 2:12, as well as
10:6, 12, indicate that God has chosen Jerusalem and will
strengthen her. Therefore, because of God's choice, men
should choose it also and adhere faithfully to it.

The critical treatment of 'amtsah (a perfectly normal form
though a ἅπαξ λεγόμενον from the root 'amats, like 'omets, Job
17:9; in this case a feminine noun is formed to obtain the abstract quality by the addition of ah) may be accounted for in
part by the desire to remove this indication of the unity of the
two sections of the book. The Hebrew word need not be
altered to 'ashmah, "guilt" (Sellin), for this change mars the
harmony of these verses by subjective alteration, which Sellin
introduces with the assertion: "I make bold to claim" this was

the original form. There is some merit in the proposed emendation *leyoshebhey*—implying dittography of *y;* this yields the good translation: "there is strength for the inhabitants of Jerusalem in the Lord . . . ."

Because the chieftains of Judah are minded thus and put their confidence in the object of the Lord's choice, therefore God can use them to destroy their foes as v. 6 states.

The emphasis is predominantly on the *divine* activity—how God uses men, not on what men themselves achieve. Since the fate of Judah's foes is under consideration, none of the blessed uses to which God can put His people are reflected upon. "The chieftains of Judah" are first used by God as a "fire pot" (*kiyyôr 'esh, pan of fire*) "among wood" (*'etsîm* = pieces or sticks of wood). The term "fire pot" (*B.D.B.*) refers to a vessel that is used to carry hot coals for the purpose of building a fire. A goodly mass of hot coals put under dry sticks of wood will mean the utter destruction of the wood. So shall Israel be for the people round about. Or, to make the picture more drastic, a flaming torch thrown in among sheaves makes the fate of the sheaves quite hopeless. Similar cases of burning grain may be noted in the Scriptures: Exod. 22:6; Judg. 15:4ff; II Sam. 14:30; Isa. 10:17ff. In their conquest of these foes of theirs God's people shall "devour all the peoples round about, on the right hand and on the left." Universal destruction of her foes goes out from the church. Not directly: those who oppose themselves unrelentingly to her always destroy themselves. But as for Jerusalem, she "shall abide (*yashᵉbhah*) still (*'ôdh*, yet or still) in her own place" (*tachtéhah*, lit., *beneath her*). Jerusalem is described as continuing *to sit* in her own place to show that all the efforts made toward her destruction had not even disturbed her: she still sat where she belonged—a picture of security and victory.

Everything that is stated up to v. 9 is built up on the basis of v. 5. Since men made the Lord their strength they could be used by God for the destruction of the nations round about (v. 6); therefore also shall they be delivered from threatening danger by God. When, however, they are described as dwelling in "tents" (v. 7), this term is an indication of the lowly condition in which the people of God generally found themselves in these days. The city dwellers were, of course, an exception. But even in this deliverance God shall proceed in such a manner that fine brotherly unity shall be preserved, and the old curse of tribal division shall not again be a bane to the people. This the Lord will achieve by working deliverance for "the tents of Judah first." The "house of David" naturally had intrinsic honor. "The inhabitants of Jerusalem" basked in the lustre of the fair name of their city. The general run of those people who dwelt out in the country of Judah might ultimately have felt slighted but for a bit of distinction that God allows them: they are delivered *first, bari'shonah*. It thus becomes manifest that God's blessings are bestowed with wise discretion.

This verse (8) unfolds more fully how fortunate the lot of those will be (v. 5) who make the Lord their strength or, at least, the city of His choosing after the pattern of the inhabitants of Jerusalem: they shall be defended, and they shall be made strong. The phrase "in that day" has been recurring (v. 3, 4, 6) and is found here again, its object evidently being to mark the days that are being described as very unusual. One advantage that the "inhabitants of Jerusalem" (*yoshebh,* singular used collectively) shall enjoy will be that God will "defend them" (*yaghen,* primary meaning *cover;* hence *shield* or *defend*). The Lord's defence is absolute safety.

The second advantage is that the Lord will grant them an unusual measure of strength. He that "totters" because of weakness (*nikhshal, Nifal* participle of *kashal, to stagger*) shall be made as sturdy a warrior as David, Israel's ideal hero, was, whose ankles did not slip (Ps. 18:36) so that he tottered. He, however, that is of the "house of David" shall be as a supernatural heavenly being, *'elohim*—for this is the meaning of the term here as it is in I Sam. 28:13. Though *'elohim* usually means "God," here a climax is reached in "the angel of the Lord," so the preceding term is apparently used in this other well-established sense. Of course, the word order of this verse suggests that the climax would indicate that "the angel of the Lord" is divine as the Old Testament clearly teaches elsewhere, cf., Exod. 23:20ff; Josh. 5:13ff. Since "the angel of the Lord" usually functioned as the leader of Israel both in the days of the wilderness wanderings and also during the time of the conquest of Canaan (cf. the two passages just indicated) therefore, the expression here means: "the angel of the Lord *before them*."

Days are apparently being referred to in which unusual equipment is given to true Israelites. We would remind the readers particularly of Christ's statement, where He says that he that believeth on Him shall do the works that He does and do greater works (John 14:12). In any case, a remarkable advance beyond the feebleness of former days is promised.

Verse 9. Notice again the phrase "in that day." Whereas in former days God often sought to stir up hostile nations against His people because of Israel's disloyalty, in this day He "will seek to destroy all nations that come against Jerusalem." The import of the clause "I will seek to destroy" is not that He will, indeed, *seek*, but that it will be quite problematical whether He will succeed. His continued attention will be given to the achievement of this object; it shall be a purpose that He keeps continually before His mind's eye.

In our study of the following section it will become quite apparent to what time this entire prophecy refers. It will be seen that it covers all time from that in which the prophet spoke to the end of days. What is said concerning Judah applies to the people of God of all times. The claims made for Jerusalem's future find their ultimate fulfillment in the true Zion of God—His church; in fact, they can be applied to Jerusalem only insofar as she for a time harbored the church of God. The whole passage speaks of God's sovereign care and protection of the church of the Old and the New Testaments through the ages and more particularly of the church's victory rather than the victory of Judah after the flesh.

Judah's True Penitence (v. 10–14)

We have placed this section under the head, "Judah's Victory," because it is the outstanding victory that Judah gained, namely, the victory over *self*.

The relation of v. 10–14 to the preceding verses (1–9) is not, as some interpreters have tried to establish, causal, namely, that, because Judah lamented its sin, therefore God granted her the victory just described, especially as it is depicted in v. 5–9. There is nothing in the context to indicate that such a connection of thought is to be established, true as it might otherwise be. The sequence of thought is rather as follows: to those who expect defeat of God's cause the emphatic assurance of victory is given first. But it is also shown that a spirit of true penitence will animate the hearts of God's people, and this, apparently, for the purpose of showing that the result of victory on Judah's part will not be pride. For, being aware of her grievous sins, she will sorely lament over them. Victory and a penitent spirit are, then, two characteristic marks of God's true people.

✠

vs. 10–14   10 And I will pour out upon the house of David and upon the inhabitants of Jerusalem the spirit of grace and of supplication; and they shall look unto Me whom they have pierced; and they shall mourn for Him as one mourneth for his only son, and shall bitterly lament for him as one that bitterly laments for his first-born. 11 In that day there shall be great mourning in Jerusalem like the mourning of Hadad-Rimmon in the plain of Megiddo. 12 And the land shall mourn, every clan apart by itself: the clan of the house of David apart, and their wives apart; the clan of the house of Nathan apart, and their wives apart; 13 the clan of the house of Levi apart, and their wives apart; the clan of the Shimeites apart, and their wives apart; 14 all the families that remain by clans apart, and their wives apart.

Note the people to whom this blessing comes. They are designated as "the house of David" and "the inhabitants of Jerusalem." That would not give warrant for the conclusion that the whole Jewish nation would become penitent—a tenet taught neither here nor elsewhere in the Scriptures. "The house of David" signifies the true descendants of David's line, who, sharing the spirit of earnest longing for the Messiah's coming, shall penitently welcome Him. By metonomy the term might include the rulers of Israel, but again the term does not permit us to think of all the rulers, but only of such who have David's spirit. We might paraphrase the expression "inhabitants of Jerusalem" (*yoshebh yerûshaláyîm,* singular used collectively) as the true inhabitants of the city of God, ideal inhabitants of Jerusalem; or better, consider the capital city as representing the people (*Keil*).

Building up on earlier passages such as Isa. 44:3; Ezek. 39:29; Joel 2:28–3:1, the prophet describes a future outpouring of the Spirit, who is, however, described as "the spirit of grace and supplication." Though "grace" does also denote such qualities as "kindness" (*Mitchell*) and "tender emotion," *Rührung,* (*Sellin*), the words that follow disallow so narrow an interpretation of the term. For when men lament bitterly, that is not "kindness" or softheartedness but in this case the deep sorrow of penitence. What, then, is "the spirit of grace and of supplication"? Beginning with the second term "supplication," we readily discern that "the spirit of supplication" is the spirit that brings about or induces "supplication" (*tachanûnîm*—intensive plural, *G.K.* 124.1(b) fin.). The parallel conclusion does not require that we find some appropriate *human* quality like "kindness" for the word "grace" (*chen*), for the Spirit may operate in two directions after He is imparted to man. He may work in man so as to cause earnest entreaty to arise in him; He may do His work because He is motivated or sent by the grace of God. Therefore, as *Koenig* (*Messianische Weissagung,* p. 214) very clearly points out, "grace" indicates the *motive* that prompts the outpouring of the divine Spirit, "supplication" indicates the *result* that will follow it. There is, however, a connection between these two qualities: *chen* and *tachanûnîm* are derived from the same root *chanan* and, therefore, signify "grace" and "pleadings for grace," a fact which indicates that the former must be imparted before the latter can be heard. These two nouns are in construct relation to a double prepositional object—unusual.

It is on the whole now apparent that, when such a movement as the turning of many unto God to seek grace actually transpires, that is one of the operations of the divine Spirit. Exactly that it is that God promises to the house of David and the dwellers of Jerusalem.

The result of the imparting of the Spirit is that those who have received Him look to Him whom they have pierced and mourn. The question very naturally arises, "Whom did they pierce?" The second member of the verse says very directly that it is He who will pour out His Spirit upon them. This clear statement must be retained. But if God is pierced, it is very obvious that the verb "they pierced" must be used in a figurative sense and not literally, for God cannot be literally pierced. A good parallel is Lev. 24:11, 16, where also a verb "pierced" is used (not *daqar* as here but *naqab*), and its object is the "name of God." But "to pierce God's name" must mean something like "profane His name." The same meaning may, therefore, be assumed for the expression under consideration. At one time they insulted and blasphemed the Holy One. They shall now reverently and penitently "look to Him" and "mourn" deeply over Him or over what they once did to Him.

We believe it is more satisfactory to interpret this passage in this way than to introduce the Messiah already at this place in an unmotivated way that is difficult to account for. The Messianic sense of the passage, therefore, lies in this that it pleased God to let the message of the prophet be cast into terms and words that later find their new fulfillment in the life of the Messiah, who, too, is first insulted and rejected (figuratively "pierced") but sees the attitude toward Him undergo a change on the part of those that were guilty of it and later come to regard Him with reverent esteem.

The change of attitude on the part of the people of Israel is the significant feature of this prophecy. And the rejection of God in Zechariah's time becomes a type of the rejection of the Christ. In this sense the passage is Messianic, that is to say, by type rather than by direct prophecy. This approach in no sense, however, denies the obvious fact that some passages of the Old Testament are Messianic by direct prophecy and not by type.

This raises the further question, "Does John (19:37) not indicate that this passage *refers directly to Christ?*" We answer: "He does not. He merely indicates that Christ's death in some way *fulfilled* this passage." John does not indicate in what sense our passage is to be regarded as Messianic; he merely indicates that it is Messianic in some sense. We, therefore, believe that those commentators are correct who say that our passage would have been fulfilled in the rejection and the later acceptance of Christ even if His side had never been pierced. The piercing of Christ's side by the spear was merely an additional element in the fulfillment that happened to offer a literal parallel for what was originally not to be construed in a literal sense.

It should be noted in this connection that the expression "they shall look *unto Me*" (*'elay*) has caused some difficulty. The *'elay* is firmly supported by the evidence of textual criticism although a very small minority of manuscripts substituted "to him" for "to Me," thereby demonstrating that they did not grasp the situation or thought the expression too bold that God should say men had pierced Him.

It should also be noted that this passage and the literal interpretation of the verb "pierced" led the Jews to a somewhat eccentric view concerning the Messiah, in fact, to the notion of a dual Messiah. One was to come from the tribe of Judah, the other from Ephraim or Manasseh. It was this second one who would have to be put to death, suffer a death which for some mysterious reason was associated with chapter 38 of Ezekiel, that is to say, this one would perish in conflict with Gog and Magog. The name associated with him was "Messiah, the son of Joseph."

There is a strange reversal in the attitude of these persons: first they pierce in enmity; then they look with deep grief at Him whom they pierced, for He is their only hope. This reversal of attitude is the thought that receives the strongest emphasis in the text, for the resultant mourning is stressed from this point foreward to the end of the chapter. That is, of course, the mourning of penitence, for the prophecy at once goes on to say: they "shall mourn for Him as one mourneth for his only son." Even if it were not the mourning for an only son it would be penitent mourning, for if you yourself are guilty of slaying him who alone could help, it would involve deep regret even from an earthly point of view. But when it is their only helper who was treated so insultingly, the grief becomes actual penitence. Its depth is attested by the fact that it is like the mourning for an "only son," *yachîdh* (cf., Amos 8:10), a grief which has a singular poignancy. The parallel statement dwells on the bitterness of soul that marks this grief: "as one that bitterly laments for his first-born." To sum it up: the whole statement of the case is calculated to emphasize the fact that a sincere and actual repentance on the part of God's people is involved.

When we ask concerning the fulfillment of the passage as a whole we dare not limit such fulfillment unduly in point of time, for no one individual event is referred to. This mourning may include the penitence of Israel in the day of Zechariah as well as the smiting of the breast on the part of the onlookers at the crucifixion (Luke 23:48); it includes the reaction of the hearers to Peter's Pentecost sermon who "were pricked in their heart" (Acts 2:37) as well as that of those who were added later (Acts 4:4; 5:14). In fact, whenever through the ages one of the people of Israel turns to Christ penitently, recognizing his and his people's share in the "piercing" of Him, then is this word fulfilled until thus, after the fulness of the Gentiles has come in, all Israel shall be saved (Rom. 11:25ff).

In the text there follows an extended description of the mourning of which v. 10 speaks—a description that brings out a few essential features of it somewhat more clearly, v. 11–14.

There is about these verses a certain monotony of form such as is found in litanies for the dead.

First of all, the greatness of the "mourning" (*mispedh* also, *wailing*) is made evident by likening it to the greatest display of grief that the history of Israel records, at least in later times, namely, the lamentation that was made over the pious King Josiah, whose tragic death occurred near Megiddo in 609 B.C. when he was slain by Pharaoh Necho (II Chron. 35:20–24). The extent of the lamentation made at that time is indicated in II Chron. 35:25, and since he was the last godly king of Judah, men might well wail over him, for with his death Judah's fate was practically sealed.

The only difficulty is the use of the word *Hadad-Rimmon*. According to *Jerome's* identification, this was a small village near the city of Megiddo itself. It is apparently to be identified with the village Rummaneh (cf. Rimmon) which lies quite near Taanach and perhaps four miles southeast of Megiddo. It is true that the brief historical record of Josiah's defeat does not mention this locality, but tradition may well have kept in mind the exact place where Josiah was wounded even though the description names the most prominent near-by town, and though the death of the king actually occurred in Jerusalem. Those who lamented the king's death in Jerusalem, lamented in thought what had happened in Hadad-Rimmon. So this may be called "the mourning of Hadad-Rimmon."

Since all known facts tend to make this interpretation acceptable, the alternative interpretation, which meets with so much favor at the present, is improbable. It claims that Hadad-Rimmon is another name for a Syrian divinity (Hadad was a Syrian idol, but the name Hadad-Rimmon has never been known to have been applied to him) who is, by roundabout reasoning, identified with Tammuz, i.e., Adonis, for whom Greeks and Syrians are known to have lamented (Ezek. 8:14, 15). But all finer proprieties are violated when the weeping over sin is likened to sentimental grief over an idol. *Sellin* recognizes that a Babylonian-Aramaic *weather*-god may be referred to but then promptly charges the prophet with having accidentally cited the wrong name; even so, *Sellin* incidentally explodes the Tammuz legend.

When it is indicated in the remaining verses (12–14) that "every family apart" shall mourn, this is an emphatic way of saying that individual groups will feel their personal responsibility as well as—since the mourning idea prevails—that they will mourn as do those who have suffered a personal loss. By way of example, two royal families are mentioned. David's and Nathan's families mourn David's son (II Sam. 5:14; Luke 3:31), one being more important, the other less so. Two priestly families are also mentioned, Levi's and Shimei's, Levi's son's (Num. 3:13), again, one being more important, the other less so. Attempts to make *Nathan* refer to the outstanding prophet of David's time and *Shimei* either to the tribe of Simeon or to the Shimei who cursed David (II Sam. 16:5) are less satisfactory than is this one explanation, which was advocated already by *Luther*. The *wives* are spoken of as mourning apart because in public lamentations the custom prevailed of separating into groups, also according to sex. After v. 13 modern style would have inserted an "etc.," as *Sellin* suggests, because the mention of royalty and of priests merely suggested a few names by way of example. The expression "all the families" (v. 14) cannot be broader than what v. 10 allowed for, "the house of David and the inhabitants of Jerusalem." It means, therefore, all the families that remain of that group.

Chapter XIII

Judah's True Sanctification (v. 1–6)

This is the continuation of the subject of Judah's true victory, which, after her true repentance (12:10–14), results in her true sanctification. The fact that a close connection between this passage and the preceding is intended appears from the opening phrase "in that day." Also from the name by which the persons in question are described as "the house of David and the inhabitants of Jerusalem," the same phrase we found used in 12:10.

✠

vs. 1–6   **¹** In that day there shall be a fountain opened for the house of David and the inhabitants of Jerusalem to wash away sin and uncleanness. **²** And it shall come to pass in that day—oracle of the Lord of hosts—that I will cut off the names of the idols out of the land, and they shall no more be remembered: and I shall also remove the prophets and the spirit of uncleanness out of the land. **³** And it shall come to pass that if a man will still prophesy, then his father and his mother who bore him shall say to him: You shall not stay alive, for you are speaking lies in the name of the Lord. And his father and his mother who bore him shall stab him for his prophesying. **⁴** And it shall come to pass in that day that the prophets shall be ashamed every one for his vision in his prophesying. Neither shall they wear a hairy mantle to deceive. **⁵** But a man will say: No prophet am I, but a man who tills the soil am I; someone made me a bondsman from my youth. **⁶** And if someone says to him: What are these scars on your hands? then he will say: Thus I was wounded in the house of my lovers.

Now that the people have grieved thoroughly over their sin (12:10–14) there shall not be wanting that cleansing which they so earnestly desire. It shall be a copious and satisfactory cleansing as appears from the contrast between the waters of purification that the Old Covenant provided for and those that are held in prospect here. There was (Num. 8:7) "water of sin," i.e., *water of purification from sin* (*B.D.B.*), called "water of expiation" (*A.R.V.*), as well as *mē niddah*, "water of impurity," i.e., to remove it (cf., Num. 19:9, 13, 20, 21, 22). It was understood also that all external cleansings of this sort— in the one case for the purifying of the Levites, in the other for the cleansing of persons who had touched a dead body—were symbolical purifications, symbolizing the purging of the soul of its guilt (cf., Ps. 51:7). In place of all symbolical sprinklings of the Old Covenant there is here promised a "spring" or "fountain" (*maqōr*). That indicates the copiousness and the effectiveness of the cleansing agency that God provides. It suggests, too, some particular work of God as a result of which the confined waters are enabled to gush forth. This work is, of course, the redemptive work of the Savior. The fountain is, therefore, a figure not only of baptism but also of the entire redemptive scheme and work whereby sinners are rendered clean and pure in the sight of God. The passage is, therefore, by no means at variance with those Scripture passages that speak of the blood of Christ as the primary and efficacious cleansing agent. In one figure this passage covers all work that God does by way of forgiving, pardoning, justifying. The New Testament is more apt to express it thus: "The blood of Jesus, His Son, cleanseth us from all sin," I John 5:7.

The expression "the house of David and the inhabitants of Jerusalem" can scarcely refer to the people. As we saw in connection with 12:10, a limited number of those who outwardly belonged to God's people actually manifested true penitence. The truly repentant group also receives this assurance of ample forgiveness and pardon.

Though the terms employed, "sin" and "uncleanness," were chosen as referring also to the evils removed by the purifying agents of the Mosaic law as we have just shown, comparing Num. 8:7 and 19:9, yet the difference between these two terms should be more closely observed. "Sin" (*chatta'th*), in the sense of missing the mark, of course involves the idea of guilt as a result of failing to reach the mark God set. The guilt of such aberrations is to be pardoned or washed away through divinely appointed means. Even *niddah* ("uncleanness")—a term that is descriptive of that which renders men unattractive in God's eyes—shall also be done away with. Both terms together could be roughly paraphrased: "all sins great and small" shall be removed.

Observe the two different uses of *le* in this verse. It first has as its object "the house of David and the inhabitants of Jerusalem." In this case it is used as a *dative of advantage.* When the next pair of objects is used, "sin and uncleanness," we have simply a *dative of reference, "for* sin," etc. There is no need of assuming the unusual meaning *against* (Sellin).

Chatta'th, with *pathach* under *teth,* requires no emendation. Though it is not a construct, the construct form is used because of the close connection in thought between the two words of this pair *(K.S.* 3375).

The cleansing that God's own children experienced will be so sincerely appropriated as to lead to the removal of all evils that are displeasing to God. By way of example only two offences are mentioned, but they are the ones that most particularly vitiated the life of Israel. If the greatest are thus done away with, all those of a smaller calibre will also have been put aside in true sanctification. So after the justification or pardon of v. 1 there comes sanctification, v. 2, even as all true repentance issues in substantial sanctification.

Even then, from one point of view, even sanctification can be called an achievement of God, for it is He "that worketh in us both to will and to do according to His good pleasure." God, therefore, says—guaranteeing this beneficent result by a solemn "oracle of the Lord of hosts"—"I will cut off the names of the idols out of the land." The "idols" are here called by a name, *'atsabbim,* which comes from a root that signifies *to fashion* or *carve;* German, *schnitzen.* That, in substance, is all that idols are—a carved something. However, if the very names shall be "cut off" so as not to be used any longer, that fact indicates how strong an aversion must have seized those who were once strongly addicted to idols. In fact, it shall come to

pass as new generations arise that the idols who were so assidu-
ously served "shall no more be remembered." That surely
marks the thoroughness of the work God will do. But such a
work cannot be merely external in character because service
of idols is a sin that is deeply rooted in men's hearts. This is,
therefore, merely another way of saying that men themselves
will under divine direction thoroughly break with these sins.
In fulfillment of this word Israel did, after the Exile, actually
abhor idolatry to such an extent that even those who were not
true Israelites at heart abandoned idols so completely that an
abhorrence of outward idolatry came to characterize Israel.
The Exile, caused by Israel's proneness to idolatry, chastened
Israel so severely that never again did this sin threaten Israel's
spiritual life.

From this reference to idolatry from which Israel was about
to be cleansed one cannot infer that this prophecy must have
grown out of pre-exilic conditions. For in situations such as
those described in Neh. 13:23–31, as this passage very plainly
indicates, lay the making of a new upsurge of idolatry.

The second major sin that had helped to hasten Israel's
corruption and her downfall was *false prophecy* although
these two sins complement each other so closely that one of
necessity practically led to the other: idol worship calls for
its prophets who teach its cults; the teaching of false prophets
may induce men to accept a heathen cult. So the second evil
must of necessity be eradicated. Though there must again be
an earnest and purposive effort on Israel's part whereby false
prophets are suppressed and banished, such activity may also
be attributed to God. God, therefore, says: "I shall also remove the prophets and the spirit of uncleanness out of the
land." The Hifil, *'a'abhir,* practically means *to remove* or *to
banish.* The fact that the word "prophets" stands as absolutely
as it here seems to do has led some interpreters to conclude
that Zechariah foretells the cessation of prophecy, which actually occurred shortly after this time, about 400 B.C. *Sellin*
advocates the extreme position that Zechariah "would rather
be regarded as anything other than an inspired man; his aim
is to be a scribe" (*Schriftgelehrter*); and also: "all prophets

are in his sight regarded as representatives of the unclean spirit."

The versions have with singular unanimity discerned the truth of the prophecy in that they followed the *Septuagint* and its good interpretative rendering, ψευδοπροφήτας, i.e., "false prophets." The intimate connection between idols and *false* prophets should suggest this thought. The term following, viz., "the spirit of uncleanness," is put on a parallel with the term prophet, and indicates very strongly that all the things listed here are sinful evils—"idols," "prophets," "spirit of uncleanness." Besides, these are evils that are removed as a result of a thorough repentance on the part of God's people. Prophecy is not to be classified under this head. Hence even *Keil's* otherwise sober judgment goes amiss, and he defines "prophets" as *good* prophets.

It may be possible that the misinterpretation of the passage was aided by the reflection that this prophecy had not come to pass. False prophets misled Israel during Christ's time and have done so ever since. Yet we are correct in saying that in the true house of David and among the true dwellers in Jerusalem false prophets are not found. On the other hand, when they do arise among those who are not the true Israel they never attain the influence that marked false prophets before this time. It must also be admitted that there are elements in this prediction which still await their complete fulfillment.

The explanatory statement, "spirit of uncleanness," is a telling characterization of false prophecy. *Ruachhattum'ah* had better be rendered thus than "the unclean spirit" (*A.V.*). The latter rendering leads one to think of some individual spirit such as those that possessed men in Christ's time whereas here rather the controlling tendency that inspired all false prophecy is referred to. We should say, less accurately: the animating principle of false prophecy. This spirit, however, deserves to be called unclean or stronger, "the spirit of uncleanness," because everything that emanates from sources other than God is *per se* unclean and results in further uncleanness as all idol worship amply testifies. In fact, uncleanness is its chief characteristic.

Though the matter is not clearly defined, it appears that two different kinds of prophets are alluded to in this passage. As will appear particularly from v. 3, such men are first of all under consideration who claim to have received a message from the Lord but lie when they say so. Yet they wish to be regarded as the Lord's prophets. But especially in v. 5 and 6 such are under consideration who are prophets of heathen cults as we shall presently see.

Verse 3. From this point forward to the end of v. 6 false prophets are under consideration. The statement is rather general so as almost to give the impression that all prophecy shall come to an end, and that, therefore, attempts to prophesy are sinful. Verse 3 is, however, in closest connection with v. 2, where false prophets were being alluded to. Moreover, the procedure followed by the parents referred to above is based on passages of the law that deal with the treatment of the false prophet only; viz., Deut. 18:20 and 13:6–10, especially v. 9, which demand that merciless extermination should be the fate of all such deceivers.

The statement begins by saying, "If a man yet prophesy." "Yet" = "still"—as *Mitchell* states it: if he "persists in posing as a prophet" in these new days when men shall abhor false prophets.

The father and the mother, the ones who begat the pretender (*yoledhaw*) would, of course, because of their close attachment to their son be regarded as the ones who would be least inclined to help to carry out the severe divine injunction given in Deuteronomy. The times that the prophet describes are, however, characterized by so pure a fervor of love for the Lord that parents who put His will first will actually take the first step in the judicial procedure against their son. This will ultimately lead to his being "pierced through" and stoned—whether the parents personally attend to the piercing through or not is immaterial. When the love of God so entirely overrules human considerations, an ideal state of obedience is achieved. *Deqaruhu* is the same verb that was in 12:10 rendered "pierced." We come nearest to its truth with the verb "stab" (*G. A. Smith*). "For his prophesying" or "when he prophesieth" (*A.V.*) literally means: "in his prophesying," but since *be* (in) has such a wide variety of meanings, it is scarcely the intention of the statement to claim that they stab him at the very time of his prophesying; they do so rather for his doing so. *Wehayah* at the beginning of the verse signifies "if and as often as" (*Mitchell*). By this one instance we are shown how strong an aversion to false prophets and how clear a perception of the harm they do shall take possession of those who sincerely repented. *Luther's* view about kindly spiritual correction cannot be reconciled with the verb "pierced."

There was a time when candidates for the office of false prophet were plentiful. In the new times (v. 4) that God will bring about men shall employ every device possible to avoid arousing the thought that they ever had any connection with such a calling. The general aversion to that office and its tremendous unpopularity will make men "ashamed" (*yebhoshu*) of having a vision (*mechezyono* from *chizzayon*). This feeling shall be general. "Everyone" (*'ish* in the general sense, whoever is called "man") shall be minded thus. Should he still conjure up visions as men were once wont to, he would be ashamed to publish them. The infinitive *hinnabe'otho* (on the form see *G.K.* 74.3.R.2) translated, "when he hath prophesied" (*A.V.*) or "when he prophesieth" (*A.R.V.*), does not imply that such prophesying is still being attempted. The whole thought rather comes under the head of that of what men will be ashamed of, namely, "visions in prophesying," as our translation suggests.

To show in a comprehensive way that everything that is reminiscent of false prophecy will be shunned, the prophet mentions the fact that the peculiar fancy of men of earlier days to attempt to appear like Elijahs by wearing hairy mantles (see II Kings 1:8, margin: "*a man* with a garment *of hair*") will also cease. This distinctive badge of prophecy shall be avoided. Their wearing it in days of old had been for the purpose of deceiving (*kachchesh*), to make themselves appear even externally as noted men of God had been known to appear.

Verse 5. Even the man who was formerly a false prophet (cf., v. 6) shall go so far as completely to disclaim the fact though he lied when he said so, and will be content to be regarded as a plain tiller of the soil. Yea, he shall claim for himself that from his youth someone sold him into such a work. To be regarded rather as a slave than as a prophet—that will be the sentiment of those days. Very emphatic is the form of the statement, "no prophet am I" (*lo' nabhi' 'anokhi*), stronger than "I am not a prophet"; for *lo'* negatives only the following noun (*K.S.* 352m). *Hiqnani* is best translated as a Kal though it is a Hifil: someone "acquired me." True, *miqneh* (cattle) comes from the same root (therefore *A.V.*: "taught me to keep cattle"), but behind the term *qanah* lies the root idea of the verb, *acquire*. *'Adham* would not in such a connection mean "everyman" (*Sellin*) but may well mean "some man" (cf. the dictionaries), and thus no textual emendation is necessary.

Verse 6. It now appears clearly that the prophet of the type last addressed obviously belongs in the class of idol prophets, for he bears marks of self-inflicted wounds such as characterized idol worship (I Kings 18:28) upon his hands. For the expression *ben yadhekha*, lit., *between thy hands,* can scarcely refer to any other part of the body than the palms of the hands and at most the inner side of the forearms, where (see *Keil*) such lacerations were wont to be inflicted. Such scars are telltale evidence; so the person charged responds briefly with an elliptical sentence, omitting: "these are the ones with," and merely saying, "which I was smitten with in the house of my lovers," (*'asher*, a kind of retained or inner object, *K.S.* 111 B). In every instance of its use in the Piel the term "lovers" (Piel participle from *'ahabh*) refers to lovers in a religious sense, "in the figure of idolatry," *Buhlen* (German). The "lovers" are the idols loved. This man admits that he was wounded in their house, that is to say, in participating in the worship of the particular divinity whom he served. The man would, no doubt, not have made this admission if he could have used evasion. Therefore his brief and surly reply. Everything in the passage is turned topsy-turvy when the words "I was wounded in the house of my friends" are construed as a reference to the Messiah (*Faussett*), or when the lovers are thought of as parents and friends who stabbed the man (v. 3) and so gave him the wounds in question. It must be remembered that two different kinds of false prophets appear in this section.

By a number of clearly portrayed scenes the prophet has made his point clear that idolatry and false prophecy will be rejected by those who are truly penitent. This, then, includes true sanctification in every department of life.

Thus the story of Judah's external and internal victory is concluded.

B. *The Lord's Victory (13:7–14:21)*

Just as the first part (chapters 9–11) of the last half of the prophet's book may be divided into two parts, a) 9, 10 and b) 11, so this second part (chapters 12–14) naturally falls into two divisions. Through the entire second half of the book there runs the note of victory, just what a small, discouraged group like God's people in Zechariah's time needed. The two halves of this last part of the book (chapters 12–14), however, differ, it appears to us, chiefly in this way: 12:1–13:6 stresses the fact that *Judah* shall have the victory; 13:7–14:21 adds the necessary supplement that the *Lord* shall gain this victory (cf., the close of 13:9; also 14:1, 3, 7, 9, 12, 16, 17, 20, 21— always the note of victory but always the emphasis on the part the Lord plays in achieving it.)

It is at the same time quite evident that this section, 13:7–14:21, is a companion piece to 12:1–13:6. In proof of this we need to point only to the common thought of victory that prevails in both. But note also how 13:7 links itself to 12:10; also 14:15 to 12:4 and 14:12 to 12:9.

We present an outline of this section, 13:7–14:21:

1. The purging of God's people occasioned by the Shepherd's death, 13:7–9
2. The deliverance of Jerusalem occasioned by the assault of her foes, 14:1–5
3. The new state of things after the Lord's day, 14:6–11
4. The confusion visited upon all enemies, 14:12–15

5. The submission of the nations, 14:16–19
6. The new state of holiness, 14:20, 21

Since criticism breaks into fragments portions of Scripture that form a perfect pattern of inner unity, it becomes doubly necessary from time to time to demonstrate that such unity is entirely possible and much more logical than are unwarranted reconstructions. So in this section it has become a well-nigh universal practice to remove 13:7–9 and append it to 11:7 because of the accidental similarity that both passages mention a "sword." Besides, it is believed, for example, that chapter 14 originally contained only verses 1–5, 12, 15–18. We shall take occasion to demonstrate the untenableness of these contentions as we advance through the section. For the present let it be suggested that a logical progression of thought runs through the whole section according to the outline.

If God achieves a victory for His own people, it is surely quite proper to have it begin with a purging, for judgment must of necessity begin at the house of God. But such a purging is often occasioned by what looks like a defeat of God or of His chosen representative—in this case the Shepherd—so this matter is mentioned first (13:7–9). A purged people is ready to be delivered; Jerusalem's deliverance is, therefore, next related after her conquest had already appeared as a settled issue, and when her foes had apparently carried the day (14:1–5). After the foes have been disposed of, the situation is ready for the bringing about of a new state of things, in this case practically a new world order; for we know that conflict between the people of God and their enemies does not surge back and forth interminably. A definite victory coupled with the restoration of all things is the ultimate issue (14:6–11). Parallel with the ultimate triumph of God's cause runs the utter confusion of all His enemies. That is, therefore, next described (14:12–15). But since not all of those who were once hostile to God's cause remain hostile but a goodly number of them will be weaned from their hostility and become humble followers of the Lord God, therefore the picture, bringing the issue to a peaceful and attractive conclusion, shows the ready submission of a goodly number of the nations (14:16–19). Finally, to cap the climax, a state of holiness is described as having been realized, a state so perfect as never to have seemed possible. So the passage rings out into a triumphant close (14:20, 21).

When efforts are made to disturb so fine a sequence of thought, which every unprejudiced judge must consider logical and natural, they deserve a rebuke.

Another thought must be stated emphatically at this point. Though the passage is cast into forms that reflect particularly the age of the prophet, it sets forth truths that apply equally to all successive ages of God's people. It is not Zechariah's time only that is under consideration, or that portion of time that lies between Zechariah's age and the advent of Christ, but all time and all situations unto the end of time are touched upon. Stripped of its purely temporal forms, the passage sets forth principles that are valid as long as the church abides.

1. *The purging of God's people occasioned by the Shepherd's death, 13:7–9*

One critic (*Sellin*) asserts that in its present place this passage is without connection with what precedes and what follows. True, it does not connect directly with what precedes because a new section begins, which aims to set the Lord's victory into the forefront. Its close connection with what follows we have just shown.

Observe also with regard to the passage as a whole that what it treats of is not so much the substance of v. 7 as of v. 8, 9. The purging of the people as it grows out of the death of the Shepherd is being considered. The most outstanding fulfillment of this situation came at the time of Christ's death. But whenever the cause of the Lord suffers a setback or divinely appointed leaders seem to be worsted, then regularly "the sheep shall be scattered." This suggests the abiding truth that underlies the passage.

✠

vs. 7–9   ⁷ Sword, awake against My shepherd and against My close associate—oracle of the Lord of hosts; smite the shepherd, and the sheep shall be scattered; and I will turn My hand to the little ones. 8 And it shall come to pass in all the land—oracle of the Lord—that two-thirds therein shall be cut off and perish, but one-third shall be left over therein. 9 And I will bring this third part into the fire, and I will smelt them as silver is smelted, and I will test them as gold is tested. These shall call upon My name, and I Myself will answer them. And I will say: It is My people; and they on their part shall say: The Lord is my God.

This passage applies to Christ in a very specific sense as His own words indicate (Matt. 26:31; Mark 14:27). In view of this authoritative interpretation all efforts to have it refer to particular outstanding personages of an earlier time are unwarranted, e.g., Menelaus whom Onias slew (*Sellin*) or the Egyptian king (*Mitchell*). The latter commentator expects to discredit opposition by remarking: "The words quoted from v. 7 by Jesus, therefore, were not in a strict sense—he does not say they were—fulfilled in His arrest and the dispersion of His disciples, but here again an incident suggests a passage of which it serves as an illustration." But Jesus said: "Ye shall be offended in Me this night, *for* it is written, I will smite," etc. That is surely the equivalent of Christ's saying: This statement is "in a strict sense" fulfilled in My case. Why, if the distinct fulfillment of the passage is plainly and authoritatively stated, brush such authoritative interpretation aside in favor of surmises on which the critics themselves cannot come to an agreement? This specific fulfillment does not, however, cancel the general application to all time that we suggested above also lies in the passage.

As to form the passage seems to be built on Jer. 47:6. The word "sword" stands first in the apostrophe. The sword does not here represent "judicial power" (*Fausset*) as it clearly does in Rom. 13:4 but is merely the most common instrument of antiquity for putting to death. It is not the authorities who are summoned to inflict death. '*Uri*, "awake," with the accent on the ultima, is the emphatic form of the imperative (*G.K.* 72.7.R.3). "My shepherd" (*ro'i*—participle *ro'eh* with suffix) is defined not only by what follows in the verse but by the passage 11:4–14 which was indubitably Messianic.

In our verse the parallel statement defines the one to be smitten as "the man that is My fellow" (*gebhor 'amithi*). *'Amith,* originally meaning "association," German, *Gemeinschaft,* is an abstract used for the concrete and comes to signify "associate." Its only other use is in Leviticus, where it is found about ten times, as in 24:19 and 6:2–7:21. In each case it is used parallel with "brother" or "neighbor" and signifies "not only similar station in life but also a communion of physical and spiritual descent" (*Keil*). So in this case "He whom God designates as His fellow cannot be a mere man, but only such a one who has part in the divine nature, yes, is of divine being." This fact alone rules out other interpretations as failing to meet the requirements of this term. For the same thought cf. also John 10:30, "I and the Father are one," and John 1:18. *Gebher,* though usually signifying "the *strong* man," is here practically the generic "man," and *'amithi* stands in apposition (*G.K.* 131.2 (a)) as *Luther* translates: *der Mann, der mir der Naechste ist.*

It seems strange that "the Lord of hosts" should command the sword to do such destructive work against one who stands so near to Him. But the mystery involved is the mystery of substitutionary atonement. Indeed, in one sense even the acts of men, wicked though they may be, are under the control of providence and so can in a sense be attributed to God. The thought is also expressed by Christ's word before Pilate, John 19:11, "Thou wouldest have no power over Me at all except it were given thee from above." Christ's citation of the word in the form, "*I* will smite," (Matt. 26:31), is, therefore, according to the sense and not literal.

The sword is first bidden "to awake," which seems beautifully rendered by *Luther: Mache dich auf—*"get busy." After it has come into play it is bidden to smite, *hakh.* (Note first a feminine imperative *'uri,* agreeing with *cherebh;* then a masculine *hakh* because of the personification of the sword as a mighty warrior.) The two successive steps in the action lend vividness to the figure. The immediate result of the smiting of the shepherd is that the sheep are scattered (*tephutsena*, plural, *constructio ad sensum* with a singular subject). If the shepherd is slain, the natural outcome is that the flock scatters. This is what the disciples did. But "the flock" (*hatstson*) is not only the disciples who were scattered at the time of Christ's capture in the garden but the flock of God's people, the Jews, who have since that time been scattered and remained in that state except when they have been brought to their true Shepherd, Jesus Christ. See 11:4ff where the same flock is referred to.

The closing statement of the verse is: "I will turn My hand upon the little ones." This un-English statement finds a good interpretation in the German version, which says: "I will turn My hand unto the little ones." The verb is *hashibhothi, cause to come back.* The hand was removed; nothing was being done. The hand is now brought back for good since the objects of God's attention are designated by a term that suggests creatures who are in need of pity, "the little ones," *tso 'arim* (cf., 11:7). This is actually the case. Though the phrase "bring back the hand upon" usually occurs in connections that connote punishment, in itself the expression is neutral. In Isa. 1:25 it is used in a good sense. The connection in which this passage is quoted in Matt. 26:31 confirms this sense, for the statement that follows, viz., v. 32, is a free paraphrase of our statement, "I will turn My hand upon the little ones," for it reads, "But after I am raised up I will go before you into Galilee." Now "going before" was the shepherd's usual mode of leading his flock; so Christ practically says: "I will again shepherd you."

This one brief touch of comfort is all that the passage offers at this point. Its dominant note is purging, yet, lest it speak too sharply, this word of comfort is inserted.

The truth which even those who trusted in the Lord needed to know was that a wholesale salvation of Israel was out of the question. Whereas Isaiah had proclaimed that "a remnant shall be saved" (cf., Isa. 6:11–13), and Ezekiel had used a division that is similar to ours (Ezek. 5), Zechariah here (v. 8) foretells that God shall have to use methods so severe as first to necessitate the destruction of two-thirds (*pi-shenáyim,* cf., II Kings 2:9). This fraction shall both "be cut off" (*yikkarethu*), segregated from the rest, let us say by captivity, and then "perish" (*yigwa'u,* pausal form) which implies actual death. So severe must this treatment be that only a third part would be left in the land.

There is no referenec here to any particular time or situation but a description of the degree of severity which God shall have to employ in purging His people that they may be made receptive for the help He has in store for them. But even this verse tells only of the first steps to be taken.

Verse 9 rounds out the picture. This "third part" (*shelishith*) which is left after the destruction of the two-thirds requires further purging. It shall be no light or trifling treatment to which it is to be exposed, for it is likened to being brought "into the fire" and to "smelting" (*tseraphtim*) as well as to "the testing of gold." The figure is not a new one. As usual, Zechariah works with the thought material of the earlier prophets; cf., Exod. 22:17ff and Jer. 9:7. Only by fiery trials can even the remnant be brought to the goal desired but here actually achieved.

The goal to be arrived at by the use of these extreme measure we are told is: "They shall call upon My name." This statement regularly implies both a true knowledge of God as He has revealed Himself (cf. "name") and a fervent and believing confession of this faith and supplication for help. No mere outward acknowledgment of formalistic use of the name is ever implied. Those who call upon the Lord thus have been brought to the point where they are truly His. God's response can, therefore, be no other than that He "answers." A blessed and natural relationship is established. This relationship finds mutual expression: God acknowledges this purged remnant as "My people"; they confess the Lord as "my God." We have here the thought expressed in Hos. 2:23–25.

The following grammatical features call for explanation. *Tseraphtim* has the plural suffix though it refers to *shelishith*—*ad sensum. Kitsroph* is active though our idiom prefers the passive rendering; likewise *kibhchon,* cf., K.S. 215a. *Yikra,* though we rendered it plural, "they shall call," is, of course, singular, conveying a thought like: everyone shall call. Note *'amarti* without a preceding conjunction; the asyndeton gives freshness to the style, cf., *K.S.* 368g.

In one other sense is this section, v. 7–9, very closely connected with the passage in which it appears. It is like unto a summary statement of chapter 14, showing both God's severity and His success in the treatment of His people. Chapter 14 unfolds these thoughts more fully.

Chapter XIV

2. The deliverance of God's people occasioned by the assault of the foes, 14:1–5

The fact that this chapter has unusual difficulties for the average Bible reader is apparent. *Luther* was ready to confess in his day: "In this chapter I [surrender], for I am not certain of what the prophet treats." He then goes on to expound it but does not refer it the *end of time* as was customary in his day but to the destruction of Jerusalem and the events that occurred at the close of Christ's ministry. Sober exegesis of the school of *Keil*, for example, has made sufficient progress to be able to interpret judiciously and correctly, in a manner that is calculated to awaken confidence. The critical school, however, devotes itself almost entirely to finding fault with the text and its message and consequently arrives at no certain conclusions.

When interpreting this section, v. 1–5, it must be kept in mind that we have just heard how God shall successfully purge His people. This thought is now to receive additional emphasis, but since Israel's situation at that time and for some time to come was and was going to be one of a nation threatened by defeat and extermination, this successful purging is described primarily as a deliverance. In other words, the defeat referred to in v. 1, 2 is mentioned merely to make room for the deliverance spoken of in v. 3–5.

✠

vs. 1–5   ¹ Lo, a day is coming for the Lord, when your spoil will be divided in the midst of you. ² For I will gather all nations against Jerusalem to battle; and the city shall be captured and the houses rifled and the women ravished; and half of the city shall go forth into captivity, and the rest of the people shall not be cut off from the city. ³ But the Lord shall go forth and fight against those nations as when He fought in the day of battle. ⁴ His feet shall stand on that day on the Mount of Olives, which is before Jerusalem on the east. And the Mount of Olives shall split through the middle toward the east and toward the west—a very great valley; and half of the mountain shall move toward the north and half of it toward the south. ⁵ And you shall flee by My mountain valley; for the mountain valley shall reach as far as Azel; yea, you shall flee just as you fled from before the earthquake in the days of Uzziah, king of Judah; and the Lord My God shall come, and all the holy ones with Him.

To disregard the style of Hebrew rhetoric leads to such difficulties as those of *Fausset* who sees the city infested by one foe (v. 1) and this foe besieged by another outside the city, "Antichrist outside would be made to besiege Antichrist within the city." In fact, to limit the things portrayed in this chapter to any one particular time is contrary to the very purpose of the whole. We have a passage that applies to "the entire Messianic time from beginning to end" (*Hengstenberg*). Our verses do not, therefore, apply to any one situation. They do not describe a siege, capture, and captivity which actually occurred. By means of a figure they describe a situation which obtains continually through New Testament times: God's people shall continually be antagonized and suffer bitter adversity at the hands of their foes and shall in consequence be brought low; but there shall always be an imperishable remnant, and that not so extremely small.

The peculiarity of Hebrew narrative style is in evidence here. In v. 1 the outcome is at once stated in headline fashion; then follow the details in v. 2. Strictly speaking, this is the sequence of events: a) nations gathered against Jerusalem, v. 2; b) the city taken and plundered, etc., v. 2; c) the spoil divided in its midst, v. 1. The emphasis sought by the author is that which the first verse conveys by mentioning the plundering: God's people are, indeed, ever like a group whose spoil is being continually divided, even as in mockery the soldiers cast lots for Christ's garments to indicate that His pretensions, as they thought, were at an end. It is to this abiding situation, which is, indeed, a remarkable occurrence, that the introductory "behold" draws attention.

Besides, this situation is one that, in God's wise providence, developes with the Lord's concurrence; for He knows that such experiences can work toward the most satisfactory development of His people. Furthermore, this "day" (*yôm*) is not the one that in Old Testament prophecy goes under the name of "the day of the Lord" (*A.V.*). For the original reads *yôm-ba' leyahweh*, "a day comes for the Lord." *Luther* has a more appropriate rendering: *Es kommt dem Herrn die Zeit* ("a *time* cometh"). The time, as suggested above, is the whole New Testament era. The conjunction "and" (*we*) in *wechullaq* is very correctly translated *when* (*G.K.* 164.1 (a)). The suffix on *your spoil* is like an objective genitive, referring to the plundered Jerusalem; otherwise no suffix would be necessary (*Sellin*).

The steps that preceded v. 1 were those that this verse (2) mentions. "All nations" (*kol-haggôyîm, the hostile peoples*) are first gathered together by the Lord. He does not incite these nations to hostility; but the author aims to express very strongly the thought that God's rule is so absolute that, unless He allowed it, none could ever venture to oppose Jerusalem. The strongest statement of that case is: *He* gathers them. The next steps are merely factors that make the scene complete. (The *Keri* suggest a verb for *tish-shagalnah* which was deemed less obscene.) That a rather generous measure of success seems to attend such hostile efforts is expressed by the idea that half the city goes forth into captivity. It is pedantic literalness when *Mitchell* computes that "if this passage were by the same author as 13:8f., the remnant would now be only a sixth of the original population." 13:7–14:5 does not relate a series of consecutive events! Nor is this a strictly literal historic account. The fact that "the rest of the people shall not be cut off from the city" allows for a substantial remnant to remain in the city of God in spite of the most bitter ravages on the part of the foe. That is always the situation in the church.

This has been recorded chiefly for the purpose of preparing

for the marvelous story of the Lord's deliverance, v. 3–5. The Lord now "goes forth" (*yatsa'*). The parallel statement in Mic. 1:3 suggests that this going forth is from heaven itself. The reference is again not to any particular instance when an individual deliverance was wrought for His own. One scene pictures the eternal truth that the Lord is continually going forth to deliver His own when their plight seems desperate. Yet this does not exclude the thought that there will ultimately be a day of final victory at the end of time. The clause, "as when He fought in the day of battle," suggests that, though no outstanding proof of His activity in behalf of His people had been noted for some time, that does not give warrant to the conclusion that He no longer works as He did in the days of old. It means rather "as he fought in the day of battle" of old, so He will still fight, though the mode of His operation may vary from age to age. This is then an allusion to all those outstanding instances of old where God engaged in battle in behalf of His people.

This (v. 4) is not a description of the day of ascension (*Luther*), nor of the inauguration of the millennium, nor of the day of final judgment. Its depicts a very general truth in very specific terms. The *specific* terms deal with a certain mountain which is after a very definite pattern cleft into a valley to be used for a very specific purpose (v. 5). The *general* truth portrayed is God's continual coming to provide a way of escape for His own from the assaults of the ungodly world, culminating, it is true, in the judgment when Christ's own shall "be caught up into the air to be ever with the Lord," I Thess. 4:17.

After He has come forth from heaven (v. 3), His feet shall on that day stand on the Mount of Olives. *Bayyom hahû'*, "on that day," may again very cٍ rectly and appropriately be rendered as *Luther* translates: *"zu der Zeit,"* "at that time," the most general possible designation of time. He takes His stand on the Mount of Olives, the site that was in Ezek. 11:23 marked by His taking His stand there when in Ezekiel's vision the glory of the Lord departed from the Temple. The scene of His departure becomes very appropriately the scene of His return. In reference to this Mount it is said: "which is before Jerusalem on the east," not as though the dwellers in Jerusalem and Judah were ignorant of this fact, or as though this were an indication of the fact that the writer was far removed from Palestine and his readers comparative strangers to Jerusalem, but because at a very early date the view seemed to prevail that from the east salvation would come even as does the sun, giving her blessed light.

So great is the Lord that at His appearing this poor old earth suffers grievously. Mountains and hills are said to tremble, to cleave, and even to melt when He deigns to set His foot on them—a majestic thought! cf., Judg. 5:5; Mic. 1:4; Nah. 1:5. Here, with vivid details, it is first depicted how "His feet stand upon the Mount." The mountain is then cleft in twain into "a very great valley," *ge' gedhôlah* (an accusative). The phrases, "toward the east and toward the west," describe the directions in which the valley runs. To make the mountain fall asunder into four parts contradicts the end of the verse, which distinctly states that "*half* of the mountain shall move toward the north and *half* of it toward the south."

What is thus pictured as a remarkable cleaving of the mountain is not only a marvelous sign that is indicative of God's power but also a mode of deliverance of the people who are in the captured city as v. 5 states.

Those commentators raise unnecessary difficulties who argue that the new valley cannot be intended as a means of flight but rather as a place of refuge, which, they further argue, was formed by a cleaving of the mountain into four parts. They also raise the objection that the enemy was not only in the city but also round about it as besiegers. Flight is, therefore, regarded as running into the hands of those without. But surely, whatever enemies were without, they were not in this new valley that was running from east to west and was provided for the escape of the people of God. Furthermore, before this scene is fully terminated, the consummation of all things has come. The Lord is come to judgment, and further dangers for the afflicted ones need no longer be dreaded.

Strange constructions, by means of farfetched conclusions

and ungrounded assumptions, in a crude, literal yet inexact interpretation, are put into this passage by the Premillennialists, who run a valley clear through the land to Askalon on the Mediterranean and bring the waters of the sea into this channel and down to the Dead Sea and arrive at startling results (*Fausset*).

This new valley which is formed is called "My mountain valley (*ge' haray*), for the Hebrew expression is inaccurately, though literally, translated "the valley of My mountains." This is the valley God has just formed by taking His stand upon the mountain. As the second clause of the verse indicates that this valley shall reach clear up to Jerusalem, the first clause must mean that men shall flee *by way of* the new valley, not *to* it (*A.R.V.* m.) nor *from* it (*Luther*). They can flee *by way of* it, for it reaches *to Azel, 'atsal,* pausal form for *'atsel.* According to the consonants this word might be a preposition, *by side* or *by the side of.* In this connection one is, however, led to expect a definite place name, at the foot of the Mount of Olives. Mic. 1:18 mentions a Beth Azel, which may be identical with this location because in compounds with *Beth* the *Beth* is at times dropped. Even if such a place cannot now be located on the strength of Scriptural evidence, it seems that the name conforms to the location if *'atzel* means *proximity.* The sense is evidently that the new-formed valley runs so near to Jerusalem that it may be used for purposes of flight.

The inhabitants of the city shall in the meantime be in such great distress—so the figurative representation pictures them —that, when the means of flight are offered, they shall flee as precipitately as men did in the days of Uzziah when the earthquake occurred. The memory of this calamity seems to have impressed men very deeply, for it alone seems to have lingered in the memories of men as being particularly distressing. Amos also mentions it, 1:1.

At this point God's appearing on the scene is described, but in terms that allow for any single deliverance that He may work for the good of His own as well as for His final coming. In fact, the latter is particularly under consideration, for the **next section describes** conditions in the final consummation.

But it cannot be that only this is thought of, for every deliverance is due to the fact that the Lord comes (*ba'*). This
verb—to *come* or *come in*—does not here stand in contrast with
yatsa', go forth (v. 3), referring to an entering into Jerusalem
(*Sellin*), because nowhere in prophetic literature is that entry
pictured as being done in the company of the "holy ones."
According to the fixed conception of the Scriptures (cf., Job.
5:1; Deut. 33:2; Matt. 16:27; 25:31) "all the holy ones" (*kol-
qedhoshîm*), are God's angels. According to the prophet's conception of the matter they do not assist Him in delivering His
own but are apparently only witnesses who delight to see what
the Lord does in the interest of His people. The prophet's interest in what he portrays is so vivid that it moves him, on the
one hand, to refer to the Lord by the appositional term "my
God," and, on the other hand, to go into direct address ("with
Thee") in prayer.

Criticism makes its usual emendations also in this passage.
On the strength of doubtful textual evidence *Mitchell* inserts
Gihon into the text; *Sellin* refers to the valley of Hinnom
because it is thought to be a fixed part of eschatological dis-
courses.

3. *The new state of things after the Lord's Day, 14:6–11*

There follows a picture of a radically new state of things
such as this world has never seen. By a comparison with the
statements of Christ we discover that the time of His last coming and that which follows are under consideration. Yet on
the whole the picture is painted in colors that are taken from
purely local conditions. All the details combine to form a
composite scene of symbolic import. Purely literalistic interpretations would result in a tragic misreading of prophecy.

✠

vs. 6–11   ⁶ And it shall come to pass in that day that there shall
not be light, the luminaries shall dwindle. ⁷ But it shall
be a unique day—it will be known to the Lord—not day
and not night; and it shall come to pass that also at
evening time it shall be light. ⁸ And it shall come to pass

in that day that living waters shall go forth from Jerusalem, half of them toward the eastern sea and half of them toward the western sea; in summer and in winter it shall be so. **9** And the Lord shall count as King over all the land: in that day shall the Lord be one and His name one. **10** All the land shall become level like the Arabah, from Geba to Rimmon, south of Jerusalem; she, however, shall be lifted up and occupy her wonted site, from the gate of Benjamin to the place of the first gate, unto the corner gate; and from the tower of Hananel unto the royal wine presses. **11** And men shall dwell therein, and there shall be no more curse; for Jerusalem shall dwell safely.

This new state of affairs is first of all described as being different in regard to the very first element that God's creative work brought into being. *Light* shall be no more *at that* time (*bayyôm hahû'* as in v. 4). The next clause shows why light shall fail: "the bright ones shall withdraw themselves." The bright ones are the heavenly bodies. *Yeqarôth* is feminine plural from *yaqar,* which word is in Job 31:26 used to describe the moon. Hence our translation—"luminaries." The verb is *yiqqaphe'u.* The form found in the text has the vowel points for the marginal *Keri;* it is derived from the root *qapha',* meaning *thicken, condense, congeal,* therefore here: *shall contract* (dwindle) (*B.D.B.*) or *sich zusammenziehen = einhuellen* (*Koenig*). The verb describes the process of a progressive shrinking of these light bearers as they dwindle away into nothing.

Since the first clause states the complete result and the second the process by which the result is arrived at, the verse is quite clear. All attempts at unnecessary reconstruction are, therefore, unnecessary. Since these attempts fail to see that the change in God's first work, "light," is mentioned merely by way of example of all changes that shall occur when the new heavens and the new earth are brought into being, they alter the text until heat and cold and frost are disposed of (a peculiar combination!) and fail to see that the fine harmony with v. 7 is thereby lost. Besides, not sensing the purpose of the different parts of the prophecy, they had expected after v. 5

the story of the downfall and the slaughter of the enemies, which is mentioned in v. 12. So they regard this passage as an insertion and say that it has little authority.

When the luminaries shrivel and fail (cf., Joel 4:15; Isa. 13:10; Matt. 24:29; Rev. 6:12) day and night, which are determined by them, also fail. The day on which this happens is, therefore, described as being "not day" (*lo'-yôm*) and "not night" (*lo'-layelah*) but as being "one," meaning a definite and distinctive type of day "known [only] to the Lord." Our translation, "unique day," captures this thought. The fact that all former arrangements have ceased to be is clear from the statement that at evening time there does not come night but light. To puzzle our mind as to how that could transpire is quite useless as the *scopus* of the passage is to indicate that "old things have passed away, behold, all things are become new." Quite in line with this one typical instance would be the conclusion that all the other works of the six days of creation will in like fashion undergo radical transformation for the better.

Instead, speaking in terms of the Holy Land, the prophet selects this manner of presentation to illustrate the new state of things more graphically. Yet here (v. 8) caution must be exercised not to interpret literally in a gross Judaizing fashion.

Because of their pureness and their freshness "living waters" (*mayim chayyîm*), waters issuing from a well or fountain and not taken from a cistern, can well represent salvation. Earlier prophets have employed this figure by letting the waters emanate from Jerusalem, cf., Joel 3:18; Ezek. 47:1ff. New features are added to the picture by Zechariah. *Sellin* presents an untenable view when he remarks on this verse that the concept of "the river of paradise" appears here "in a superficial way as a purposeless (*zweckloser*) portion of the fixed eschatological hope."

Instead of repeating the rich imagery employed by Ezekiel, Zechariah stresses two features about these waters of salvation: first, they are available for the whole land; second, they never fail. For when half of them flow to the eastern sea, i.e., the

Dead Sea, this new source of water is made available to that portion and half of the land. Again, when half flowed toward the western sea, i.e., the Mediterranean, they become available for that portion of the country. The same thought lies in the Ezekiel passage though it is differently expressed. As to the second item, it is well known that almost all the streams of Palestine are winter torrents. They abound in water during a few winter months, for the rest of the year they are dry. Not so the salvation rivers. In summer and in winter (*baqqáyitz ubhachchóreph*) they furnish an adequate supply.

Since all these features of the picture supply only the *background,* in the very midst of our passage there is now a statement of the most important feature of all in this new state of things, v. 9.

Also this picture is painted in terms of the Holy Land. Therefore *'al-kol-ha'arets,* which could be translated "over all the earth," must here be rendered as it was in v. 10. It is, however, understood that what is true in regard to one part of the earth, viz., the Holy Land, is equally true in regard to all the rest. The fact that He is King over all has always been true. He shall now really be regarded as what He actually is, for men will have come to a true knowledge of Him. This thought the prophet conveys by a slightly different turn of expression: The Lord shall be *lemelekh, for King.* We believe our translation does justice to this phrase. What Deut. 6:4ff had long ago taught Israel shall now become common knowledge throughout the land and, of course, throughout the world. "The Lord is one"—monotheism—"and His name one" —a unified revelation (*shem*) of Himself.

With the chief fact, the saving knowledge of the Lord, made plain, and His kingship established, the prophet, in symbolic language, portrays the exaltation of the King's city. Note how beautiful coherence marks every part of the chapter.

Verses 10 and 11. This is a passage like Isa. 2:1–3 and Mic. 4:1–5. In a vision Zechariah sees the land levelled and hills made low and Jerusalem alone exalted; Jerusalem is also quite the same strong city that she had been in her palmiest days. This, however, portrays spiritual realities and indicates the ultimate exaltation and strength of the church of the living God.

The picture includes the following features. First the whole land becomes level. This is the meaning of the term "like the Arabah" (*ka'arabhah, A.V.* "plain"). The Arabah is the deep cut in which the Jordan flows, and in which the Dead Sea lies. The eminent geographer of the land of Palestine, *G. A. Smith*, asserts correctly that this figure is "employed, not because of its [the Arabah's] fertility, but because of its level character." Therefore the rendering of the *A.V.* is very appropriate: "plain"; *Luther, Gefilde.* This level extends from "Geba to Rimmon." Geba was on the northern boundary of Judah, Rimmon on the southern; cf., II Kings 23:8, "from Geba to Beersheba." Geba was in reality in Benjamin, cf., Josh. 18:24. For Rimmon as being near Edom cf., Josh. 15:32. In other words, the whole extent of Judah is referred to. Mountains had, however, previously overtopped Jerusalem. The levelling down to a plain of the rest of the land would already make Jerusalem stand out. But in addition she herself "shall be lifted up" (*ra'amah*) and so be doubly exalted. Her outward position is made to correspond with her inner glory. The expression "dwell in her place," *yashebhah tachteha*, signifies "to occupy her wonted site," literally, *to sit under her.*

For his contemporaries, who had not seen the old walls of Jerusalem restored, Zechariah pictures the future in terms of a city that was rebuilt as she was in the days of her strength. Though there is some difficulty of interpretation, it appears that the places mentioned as being in the old city wall were located as follows: The Benjamin gate in the middle of the north wall. The "first" or former (*ri'shôn*) gate was apparently at the northeast corner. The "corner gate" was apparently at the northwest corner. Starting in the middle of the north wall, therefore, the building shall go to the full extent of the former limits east and west. The "tower of Hananel" was, it would seem, also located at the northeast corner. From it to "the king's wine presses," which must have been located at the southeast corner of the city, would, therefore, mark the entire length of the wall north and south. These measurements indicate that Jerusalem is thought of as becoming as glorious and as large as she ever was. For the depressed times of Zechariah even such a promise is great comfort.

To the thought of a restored city there is added the thought of a restored population—"men shall dwell therein"—again a comforting thought in view of the paucity of inhabitants. But since the whole picture presents ultimate perfection, the prophet adds: "and there shall be no more curse." *Cherem* = devoting to utter destruction and describes the evil condition rather than the outcome as does *A.V.*, "utter destruction." If there is no "devoting to utter destruction" (*A.R.V.*m) or the people are no longer guilty of the misconduct that can serve utterly to destroy the covenant relationship with God, then a new measure of holiness has come about. The city's safety is consequently insured—"Jerusalem shall dwell safely." All the terms used in this verse are of such a kind as to appeal most forcibly to Zechariah's contemporaries, for these terms present the blessings they so eagerly desired.

It should yet be pointed out that criticism draws Biblical conceptions down to the level of the crude mythological material of the heathen when *Sellin* sees in the waters flowing east and west (v. 8) a thought that is patterned after the old-Babylonian idol figures from whom two streams of water flow forth. But the leaders in Israel's thought did not borrow their religious concepts from pagan sources.

4. *The confusion visited upon all enemies, v. 12–15*

Though v. 1–5 came to a conclusion that implied that the enemies of Jerusalem would be confounded, to complete the picture adequately a separate and detailed statement of this confusion is added. Though some of the details of this sketch are somewhat gruesome, wrong sentiments are imputed to the author when it is claimed: "the writer seems to dwell with satisfaction on the horrible particulars" (*Mitchell*). Not a word indicates that he is stating more than God gives him to state, or that he gloats over the enemies' discomfiture.

Those who are critically-minded regard verses 13, 14 of this

section as an insertion of a later date but at times seem at a
loss to account for the insertion as though even the so-called
interpolations were sometimes inserted without rhyme or reason. That a good sequence of thought runs through the passage is obvious. A "blow" that God shall inflict upon the
enemies is under consideration. This "blow" is brought about
through several agencies: a) the rotting away of the living
bodies (v. 12); civil, internecine strife, one slaying the other
(v. 13); Judah's heroic warfare (v. 14). All of this shall bring
about the result that great spoil shall fall to Jerusalem's lot.
An afterthought about the severity of this "blow" on the part
of God leads the author to mention that it will strike even all
manner of beasts. Who is to decree what order of thought an
author must use? Is an order that is different from one we
should have employed proof of the fact that interpolations
were made? So criticism argues and on the strength of its
reasoning removes the offensive portions. Since when may
an author not have an afterthought? Criticism's reasoning assumes that the rules of rhetoric are rather wooden and artificial.

✠

vs. 12-15 ¹² And this shall be the plague with which the Lord
will plague all the peoples that have gone to battle
against Jerusalem: the rotting of each man's flesh while
he still stands upon his feet, and his eyes shall rot away in
their sockets, and his tongue shall rot away in his mouth.
¹³ And it shall come to pass in that day that there shall be
a great confusion from the Lord among them; so that each
man shall lay hold on the hand of his neighbor, and his
hand shall be lifted up against his neighbor's hand. ¹⁴ And
Judah also shall fight at Jerusalem. And the wealth of all
the nations round about shall be gathered together, gold
and silver and apparel in abundance. ¹⁵ And the same
plague shall be on the horse, on the mule, on the camel,
and on the ass, and on all the beasts that shall be in those
camps—the selfsame plague.

A very horrible picture, but its justification lies in this:
those that have singled out God's people as the object of their

hatred and attack have committed a singularly atrocious crime and as a result deserve a form of punishment that serves to make of them an example of divine justice. A good parallel is found in the heavy visitation that came upon Egypt because the Egyptians had shown such cruel opposition to God's people at the time of the Egyptian bondage.

A "blow" or "stroke" (*maggephah*—practically always a divine visitation) shall come upon these foes. To translate the word "stroke" makes it appear as what it grammatically is: cognate object of the verb "strike" (*nagaph*). From what follows it appears that this "stroke" was a "plague" (*A.V.*) or *pestilence*. We retain the word "plague" in our translation. The verb for "warred" (*A.R.V.*) is *tsabha'*, from the kindred noun which means the "host" that goes out into the field. "Waging war" is a broader term than "fighting" (*A.V.*), for it includes all the activities that hostility prompted them to undertake. *Hameq* means literally "a causing (his flesh) to rot" and is in apposition with the initial *maggephah* (*G.K.* 113.1 (a)). In vivid and emphatic narrative the infinitive absolute sometimes stands for the finite verb. The singular suffix on *besarō*, "*his flesh*," has the force of *each single man's*. The singular is thus used throughout the verse.

Man has hardly ever experienced a plague which was so horrible that the flesh rotted upon living bodies. But such is the case in this instance of the infliction of divine justice. The eyes and the tongue are mentioned because "the *tongue* had with bold arrogance calumniated God and His people; the *eye* had sought to discover the weaknesses of the city" (*Hengstenberg*).

As little as v. 12 depicted a particular event which was to come to pass on a particular date, but by its specific picture rather portrayed a general principle, so also v. 13 shows by a particular picture how the enemies of God's people, yea, all ungodly forces, serve to destroy one another.

Instances of how God confounded Israel's foes were not wanting in the records of the past, cf., Judg. 7:22; I Sam. 14:20; especially II Chron. 20:23; also Deut. 7:23. Here the *mehumath Yahweh*, literally, *confusion of the Lord*, "Lord" being, of course, subjective genitive, is described as including these two features: each shall first seize the other's hand with one hand in order to hold him powerless; he shall then raise up his other hand against his neighbor's hand, which is also thought of as being raised in like manner. Surely, where soldiers of one and the same army thus destroy one another, the wildest "confusion" has seized them. The parallel is 12:4.

The third part of the "stroke" of God: Judah comes to Jerusalem's assistance (v. 14). Those that are God's mutually aid one another. Judah does not fight *against* Jerusalem (on the construction with *be* see 12:2) but for her in Jerusalem. In a brief picture the enrichment of Jerusalem is then portrayed. The nations had amassed much wealth. They had hoped to enjoy it. By the irony of fate the ones whom they hated became the owners of it all. The general principle of all history is: the nations strive but have not the ultimate profit of their endeavors; the church comes into the acquired inheritance.

This verse (15) describes how thorough a work of destruction God's justice does after it becomes active. The case is parallel to that which transpired on a smaller scale when Achan and all his possessions were ordered to be destroyed (Josh. 7:24) in order to impress upon men the thought as to how thoroughly the sinner and all he has fall under the severity of God's judgment.

5. The submission of the nations to the Lord, v. 16–19

It would surely have been an extremely negative note if the matter last treated (v. 12–15) had been the conclusion of the subject "The Lord's Victory" as well as the conclusion of the entire book. What is now discussed (v. 16–19) is an obvious outgrowth of what preceded and offers as a very positive result the story of how the nations that are left after God's judgment has been carried out shall cheerfully submit themselves to the Lord.

✣

vs. 16–19   16 And it shall come to pass that all that are left of all the nations that went against Jerusalem—these shall go up from year to year to worship the King, the Lord of hosts, and to celebrate the Feast of Tabernacles. ¹⁷ Also it shall come to pass that whosoever of the various races of the earth shall not go up to Jerusalem to worship the King, the Lord of hosts, upon such shall no rain fall. ¹⁸ And if the race of the Egyptians do not go up and do not appear, then no rain shall fall on them; but the plague shall befall them with which the Lord will plague the nations who fail to go up to celebrate the Feast of Tabernacles. ¹⁹ This shall be Egypt's sin and the sin of all the nations who do not go up to celebrate the Feast of Tabernacles.

This section is of the same stamp as is the whole chapter—eschatological matters are discussed in Old Testament terms. The book of Revelation would use radically different terminology. The Old Testament terms are for the most part not used in their limited literal significance but in their broadest typical import.

Verse 16 might be paraphrased thus: all who are left at the time of the Lord's glorious victory will not do as they were wont to do in days of old, that is, continue to display hostility toward Jerusalem and take part in assaults against her, but shall deem it a privilege to celebrate, for example, festivals like Tabernacles, which served as an occasion for thanking God for His manifest care of His people in days of great danger. For the Feast of Tabernacles did commemorate God's protective guidance of Israel in the days when the nation passed through the wilderness and the desert toward the land of promise. These nations shall now acknowledge Him as "King" and as the "Lord of hosts" and shall recognize that they share His sovereign protection and shall praise Him for it. They have been converted from foes to worshipers.

It is better to view the Feast of Tabernacles as we have done above than to concentrate upon what must always have been a secondary feature of this festival, namely, the idea that it marked the conclusion of all harvesting in the land. It should be observed that by a kind of anacoluthon the subject is placed first with emphasis, to be followed by its modifiers; the verb is then separately introduced by a *waw consecutive*—an effect that we have sought to catch by resuming the subject thus:

"these shall go up." The expression "from year to year" at the same time signifies regular and faithful worship of the Lord. Verse 17. This verse attempts only to round out the picture. We may go so far as to claim that it presents a merely hypothetical case. We venture to claim that it should be paraphrased somewhat as follows: Should any of the various races of the earth be found to be so obdurate as not to join in cheerful acknowledgment of the Lord and His kingship they would be dealt with in such a way that they would be exterminated. The situation is regarded as being practically unthinkable.

Since the final outcome of things is being depicted, and since in the consummation all evil and ungodliness will have been entirely overcome, it would be quite out of keeping with the spirit of the passage to conclude that after the judgment has been carried out wicked men and sinners will still be met with in the new heavens and the new earth. The account is to be regarded as being highly idealized. In other words, *v. Orelli's* summary statement of v. 16 may be cited here. He says: "The fruit of the judgment, as was already announced in v. 9, will be *universal* acclaim before the Ruler of all, Yahweh."

An example (v. 18) of the point just made is given: should the Egyptians fail to join the worship of the Lord and fail to acknowledge Him they would be punished in the same way as were all others, that is to say, rain would be withheld, and a sharp corrective plague would befall them.

It seems that it was thought to be altogether too bold a conception for Old Testament prophets to utter that a world might exist where none would fail to accept the Lord, the King. So they claimed at least this: if a few ungodly ones were left, the Lord would set them right.

The Egyptians seem to be mentioned separately because they were the nation "that in days of old opposed Yahweh and His people with the utmost of hostility" (*Keil*) and to indicate that "even this people was to arrive at the point where it shared in the full possession of Israel's spiritual treasures."

Some commentators construe the sentence differently than we have done above by offering the rendering: "also if the clan of Egypt does not go up or enter, then upon them there shall fall the plague . . . " (*J.M.P. Smith*). This, however, necessitates striking the term *welo*—always a rather violent procedure. The words *welo 'alehem* may well be regarded as resuming the previous subject *geshem*, and so we have the meaning "then no rain shall fall on them," after the pattern established by v. 17. It strikes us that those interpreters who refuse to accept this solution are unduly apprehensive lest a statement be made that is out of harmony with the physical geography of Egypt, where no rain (at least practically no rain) falls, and water is supplied by the overflow of the Nile. We take it that the expression "no rain shall fall on them" means in the case of the Egyptians that punishment or its equivalent would befall them.

Verse 19. When it is now said, "This shall be Egypt's sin," the word "sin" (*chatta'th*) retains its primary meaning and only indirectly includes "*punishment* for sin," a meaning of the term found in Num. 32:23.

We must reassert that the prophet is not putting an undue emphasis on things ceremonial when he keeps referring to the Feast of Tabernacles. We might well indicate his point of view by saying: His concern is for the spiritual import of that festival, which is true gratitude to God for His paternal care of His people. Or we might say: The people of God will in that day celebrate the Feast of Tabernacles or any adequate New Testament equivalent.

6. *The new state of holiness, v. 20, 21*

This is the note upon which the book closes, and we may well expect a constructive utterance. In fact, these words assert that God does arrive at some definite results for good in reference to His people.

✠

*vs.*20,21   20 At that time there shall be an inscription on the bells of the horses, "Holy unto the Lord"; and the pots in the Lord's house shall be like sacrificial vessels used at the altar. 21 And it shall come to pass that every pot in

> Jerusalem and in Judah shall be holy to the Lord of hosts; and the people that sacrifice shall come and take any of them and boil meat in them. And there shall not be any Canaanite any more in the house of the Lord of hosts in that day.

One might call this one of the passages that operates on the principle of the proverb, *Ex ungue leonem,* "you recognize the lion from the mere claw." One seemingly trifling incident is recorded in order to indicate what the whole situation must be at this blessed future time. When it is said that even such trivial things as bells on the harness of horses shall be holy to the Lord and shall bear an inscription to that effect even as the high priest wore a gold band on his official cap with these very words inscribed on it (see Exod. 28:36–38), that is the equivalent of saying that such a complete state of sanctification or consecration shall mark the life of God's people that nothing shall be exempt from its all-pervading influence. Since the language is rich in Old Testament imagery it may be regarded as purely figurative and the statement completely symbolic in character, which does not even require literal fulfillment in order that its truth be realized.

A second comparison that is very similar as to its general scope is added. Whereas in days of old there were sacred vessels in the sanctuary which, as their name indicates, were used for pouring sacrificial blood upon the altar (*mizraq,* from the root *zaraq,* "to sprinkle" or "to pour") cf., Exod. 27:3; 38:3, etc., even the very ordinary pots and pans in the Lord's house that were used for boiling and serving meat shall now be regarded as equally sacred. This is another way of saying, "Nothing shall be found in the lives of God's people that is not dedicated to Him." Total consecration of life unto the Lord shall mark those days.

Verse 21. To give this thought more comprehensive expression the prophet indicates that not only Temple pots but all pots in Jerusalem and in Judah shall have similar sanctity. The prophet would obviously by this statement not for a moment imply that, as soon as you get beyond the limits of Judah, pots that are in general use shall be unholy, but rather the opposite: in the Lord's kingdom everything shall partake of the holiness which was in Old Testament days reserved for certain select areas of life. Restated, his thought would run thus: partial and imperfect sanctification shall give place to total sanctification. The time referred to is, of course, after the second coming. Though the language used would imply that Zechariah means that the sacrificial meat of, let us say, a peace offering (cf., Lev. 7:12–18) is thought of, this feature of the statement is the Old Testament dress in which the thought is clothed. He is certainly not trying to say that sacrifices after the pattern of the Old Testament shall be found in the days of the New.

The last statement must be evaluated in the same way when it is said: "There shall not be any Canaanite any more in the house of the Lord of hosts in that day." The scope of the thought is unduly limited if *Kena'ani* is taken in the meaning of "tradesman," which it sometimes has, as in Prov. 31:24; Job 40:30; or if the translation is phrased thus: "And there shall be no more any pedlar . . ." (*G.A. Smith*). Canaanites are thought of from that rather common Old Testament point of view in which they are the nation that was to be regarded as accursed because of its deep-dyed iniquity, cf. Gen. 9:25; Lev. 18:24ff; Deut. 7:2; 9:4, etc. The term is not to be taken in the strictly nationalistic sense as referring to persons who were by blood descended from Canaanite stock but rather as a designation of unworthy members of the people of God who are no better morally than were the depraved Canaanites. In the same manner of speaking Isaiah calls Israel's princes "rulers of Sodom" and the nation "people of Gomorrha" (Isa. 1:10). Such misbegotten, disappointing members of God's people just simply shall no longer be found in the days when God shall have achieved His sovereign purpose upon His own.

Index

INDEX OF SUBJECTS

INDEX OF AUTHORS